Contact and Conflict in English Studies

AUSTRIAN STUDIES IN ENGLISH

Edited by Sabine Coelsch-Foisner/
Gabriella Mazzon/Herbert Schendl

VOLUME 104

PETER LANG
EDITION

Sabine Coelsch-Foisner / Herbert Schendl (eds.)

Contact and Conflict in English Studies

Assistant editors:
Christian Grösslinger / Christopher Herzog

PETER LANG
EDITION

Bibliographic Information published by the Deutsche Nationalbibliothek
The Deutsche Nationalbibliothek lists this publication in the Deutsche Nationalbibliografie; detailed bibliographic data is available in the internet at http://dnb.d-nb.de.

Die Herausgeber danken den Förderern dieses Bandes für ihre Unterstützung:

Universität Innsbruck, Philologisch-Kulturwissenschaftliche Fakultät
Universität Salzburg, Department of English and American Studies
Universität Wien, Philologisch-Kulturwissenschaftliche Fakultät

Library of Congress Cataloging-in-Publication Data
Contact and conflict in English studies / Sabine Coelsch-Foisner ; Herbert Schendl (eds.) ; Assistant editors: Christian Grösslinger ; Christopher Herzog.
  pages cm – (Austrian Studies in English; Volume 104)
  Includes bibliographical references.
  ISBN 978-3-631-66044-7 (Print) – ISBN 978-3-653-05338-8 (E-Book) 1. Languages in contact–Austria. 2. English language–Study and teaching–Austria. 3. Code switching (Linguistics)–Austria. 4. Sociolinguistics–Austria. 5. Bilingualism–Austria. 6. Language and culture–Austria. I. Coelsch-Foisner, Sabine, editor. II. Schendl, Herbert, editor.
  P130.52.A9C66 2015
  420–dc23
                    2015024686

                ISSN 1810-4517
          ISBN 978-3-631-66044-7 (Print)
         E-ISBN 978-3-653-05338-8 (E-Book)
         DOI 10.3726/978-3-653-05338-8

              © Peter Lang GmbH
     Internationaler Verlag der Wissenschaften
            Frankfurt am Main 2015
               All rights reserved.
  Peter Lang Edition is an Imprint of Peter Lang GmbH.

  Peter Lang – Frankfurt am Main · Bern · Bruxelles · New York ·
            Oxford · Warszawa · Wien

This publication has been peer reviewed.
www.peterlang.com

Contents

Sabine Coelsch-Foisner and Herbert Schendl

Introduction: Contact and Conflict in English Studies

Contact and Conflict contains contributions to the 2012 conference of the Austrian Association of University Teachers of English as well as some invited papers reflecting current research in this subject area. The aim of the ASE conferences is to bring together scholars from various fields of English Studies, such as Anglophone literatures, critical theory, cultural studies, interdisciplinary and comparative English studies, linguistics and didactics, all taught at Austria's English departments. Most of the contributions show that these classifications are no longer as rigid as they used to be and that interdisciplinary research is thriving in all these fields. In so doing, English Studies has become rife with contact and conflict.

In linguistics, research into language contact has greatly increased in the past few decades and has found its way into different sub-fields of linguistics, particularly sociolinguistics, language change, studies on multilingualism and code-switching, as well as pidgins and creoles, see the excellent *Handbook of Language Contact* edited by Raymond Hickey in 2010. The present papers present original research projects in some of these areas, starting with a discussion of the problematic modelling of variation in language (Mazzon) and continuing with issues which seem to be quite diverse at first sight, but which are connected in various ways: issues of contact between different languages in a post-colonial setting (Onysko), the different forms and functions of English as a Lingua Franca (Seidlhofer, Dorn, Schekulin, Santner-Wolfartsberger), intergenerational contacts of, and conflicts between, bilingual refugees from the Holocaust (Duran Eppler), and hip hop discourse among Tirolian adolescents (Averill).

Gabriella Mazzon's contribution "The Expression of Societal and Cultural Conflict in Language" deals with a central issue of modern linguistics, namely how to model and explain linguistic variation, in particular in regard to conflicting cultural and linguistic norms and 'anti-norms'. Her critical discussion of this problem, which is best exemplified in the conflict between standard and non-standard varieties, spans from earlier stages of English to modern sociolinguistic theories and analyses this conflict 'within a cultural model of opposition and resistance'. Mazzon proposes that these issues might be best approached from a cognitive perspective within the model of *Figuration Kontra* developed with her participation at Innsbruck University. Many of the issues addressed in her paper are explicitly or implicitly taken up in the other linguistic contributions of this volume.

In the course of its world-wide expansion and adoption in many countries of the British empire, English has had close contacts with indigenous languages and has developed a number of varieties showing clear traces of these manifold linguistic contacts. Among these, the description of Māori English is still widely neglected, but is the object of an ongoing research project involving bilingual Māori-English speakers. In his paper, Alexander Onysko first discusses the historical linguistic setting of Aotearoa/New Zealand and the early cultural and linguistic contacts and conflicts between Māori and English. The renaissance of Māori culture and language since the late 1970s has led to a revitalisation of the Māori language and to diverse mutual contact influences on Māori and English also leading to the emergence of Māori English. The description of this particular contact variety of English is one of the main aims of the project and is illustrated with examples from a variety of contact situations, particularly from the lexicon, though methodological issues are also addressed.

The rapid spread of English as a Lingua Franca (ELF) on a global scale in recent decades has brought about a wide range of contact situations and linguistic contact phenomena, but also social – and also academic – conflicts. The linguistic description of ELF has become one of the fastest growing research fields in English linguistics, which has been greatly furthered by the compilation of the electronic VOICE corpus of ELF interactions by Barbara Seidlhofer and her team in Vienna. Their paper starts with an outline of recent developments in ELF research and the VOICE corpus by Barbara Seidlhofer, followed by three case studies on particular linguistic features of ELF. Nora Dorn looks at the use and communicative functions of the progressive in ELF interactions from a quantitative and a qualitative point of view. Claudio Schekulin's study on negative contractions shows that the range of internal variation in ELF can be well captured by analytic variationist tools. In his view this study, carried out within a sociolinguistic framework, can have an impact on traditional sociolinguistic concepts. The issue of turn-taking and speaker allocation in ELF is addressed by Anita Santner-Wolfartsberger, who also discusses the applicability of relevant concepts from conversation analysis and related fields. Similar to Schekulin, she also claims that results from ELF research can be of relevance for the study of interactional pragmatics.

Eva Duran Eppler's contribution investigates intergenerational conflict resulting from language shift and acculturation from an interdisciplinary point of view. Combining sociolinguistic methods with concepts from cross-cultural and memory research, Duran Eppler analyses a recorded discussion between different generations of Holocaust refugees which centres on issues of language transmission and use as well as cultural aspects of food consumption. Her close linguistic analysis establishes the relation between language use and identity, especially in the Vienna-born mother's frequent use of code-switching as against the London-born daughter's insistence on good English as a reflection of her assimilation to the host society. This linguistic conflict is linked to a cultural conflict concerning practices of food consumption, which also involves a grandson and thus spans three generations.

Julia Averill's paper on hip hop discourse reports on a longitudinal ethnographic study of how Tirolian adolescents use hip hop as a means of identity formation. Though the study focuses on the linguistic aspects of hip hop discourse, other cultural means of expression such as rap, dance, dress and graffiti also form part of this process. Direct observation of hip hop performance as well as interviews with the boys reveal that the informants' use of hip hop language is closely linked to the adaptation of key terms learned from rap music and video. A central question of the research project is to uncover the functions and purpose of hip hop discourse among Tirolian male teenagers and their adaptation of African American hip hop culture to their local Tirolian linguistic and cultural identity, raising questions of authenticity and alternative identities.

In literary and cultural studies, the topic of this volume is addressed in terms of such conflicting zones or points of contact as the intersections between literature, science and the arts (Fuller, Coelsch-Foisner/Herzog), 'high art' and 'mass culture' (Mösch), and childhood and crime in current crime fiction (Flothow).

What the individual papers suggest is both the topicality of such contact zones and ways in which cultural issues are complicated in the light of the aesthetics, genre dynamics and artistic strategies of individual works and sites of literature.

David Fuller, speaker of honour at the 2012 conference, illustrates how the 'creative contact with other disciplines in an academic context can be fraught with difficulties', while 'thinking beyond disciplinary boundaries is natural to unfettered intelligence and inherent in criticism'. According to Fuller, method is the key issue of such conflict: whilst literature is 'situated knowledge', in other disciplines, such as the sciences, the cultural construction of knowledge plays a lesser role and method is universal. Arguing that 'the perception of any work [of art] can be deepened by placing it in a variety of human contexts – that is, by reaching out into the worlds in which it was made and the worlds in which it has had and now has meanings', he discusses some striking examples of recent multi-media art productions in which he himself collaborated. These include a ballet based on Marlowe's *Edward II*, choreographed by David Bintley and an opera about Alzheimer's disease, *The Lion's Face*, with a score by Elena Langer and libretto by Glyn Maxwell, launched at the Brighton Science Festival.

The precise nature of offstage research in the dramatic context, which Fuller describes as a crucial question in the latter production, is also a central issue in the debate about the two cultures revisited by Sabine Coelsch-Foisner and Christopher Herzog for the purpose of mapping science plays. Addressing the current interest in science, both in the theatre and in drama criticism, Coelsch-Foisner and Herzog pinpoint the epistemological flaws in attempting to define science plays as sites for knowledge transfer and to categorise them with regard to scientific content and science communication. Arguing that science plays must first and foremost be studied as plays, they concentrate on the semiotics of drama and offer a metaphorical approach to its space and figures. To this end, they apply George Lakoff and Mark Johnson's theory of metaphors and explore the relevance of the concept of 'novum' underlying Darko Suvin's approach to science fiction for science drama. Exemplary readings of Caryl Churchill's *A Number* (2002) and Elfriede Jelinek's *Kein Licht* (2011/12) serve to demonstrate how drama transforms scientific knowledge into situated knowledge.

Crime fiction furnishes another example of such cultural 'situatedness', as Dorothea Flothow's study of the changing role of childhood in crime novels shows. As distinct from the 'Golden Age Whodunit' with authors such as Agatha Christie and Dorothy Sayers, children feature prominently as victims, witnesses, conspirators and criminals in more recent novels by Reginald Hill, Kate Atkinson, Ian Rankin, Ruth Rendell and Val McDermid. Flothow examines these roles in connection with issues of child abuse, youth crime and violence. While thus placing the constructs of childhood emerging from crime fiction in the context of changes in British culture and changing discourses about children, she also stresses the prejudices revealed in many of these novels and concludes that British crime fiction constitutes 'a more thoughtful place of debate of contemporary issues than its status as a popular genre would lead one to assume'.

A similar case of contact and conflict, notably that between 'high' culture and 'mass culture', *ars* and *techné*, is discussed by Matthias Mösch, whose focus is on the creative reception of Thomas Bernhard. In his comparative reading of the latter's *Concrete* (1982) and William Gaddis' *Agapē Agape* (2002) in terms of 'dramatised crises of cultures', Mösch draws the reader's attention to an intriguing example of intertextuality, showing how both authors subversively engage with their respective cultural environments. Severely criticising state institutions, religion and commerce, Gaddis is shown to have followed Bernhard's narrative model of dismantling 'exclusivist cultural agendas' in favour of a communal model of art production and reception 'beyond this rift'.

The editors would like to thank all contributors for helping shape the profile of Austrian Studies in English, all colleagues reading individual papers, Christopher Herzog and Christian Grösslinger for helping put together the manuscript, and the Departments of English and American Studies of the Universities of Salzburg, Vienna and Innsbruck for making possible the publication of this volume.

September 2014

GABRIELLA MAZZON

The Expression of Societal and Cultural Conflict in Language

1. Language variation and cultural models

The problem of modelling and explaining language variation, which has been in the forefront of many branches of modern linguistics ever since its beginnings, continues to be discussed, especially in relation to the systematic connection of formal variation with specific extralinguistic categories.

The danger of oversimplification and reductionism in describing variation is ever-present, and various schools of thought have tried to find their own solutions, often ultimately failing to account for the multiplicity and complexity of the phenomenon. Within functional and socio-cultural perspectives, the existence and persistence of variation, and its relation to language change, have more and more often and influentially been seen as the expression of social opposition and struggle. Roughly said, this struggle is created by the juxtaposition between an elite that imposes a standard variety (that carries group-identity values, with which the elite itself identifies), and other strata of society that perpetuate their own identity-carrying language forms (Milroy and Milroy 1993). This paper attempts a systematisation and discussion of such analyses within a cultural model of opposition and resistance, with reference to various phenomena of linguistic variation as cultural manifestation, mostly in connection with English-speaking contexts.

The coexistence of cultures, and their interrelationships, have been an object of concern and analysis for a long time; before the onset of modern social sciences, the necessity to accommodate various cultural models within a pattern of (more or less peaceful) coexistence of different human groups on a territory gave rise to a discourse that was conveyed by myths and epics. In particular, sensitive manifestations of cultures, such as language, were the focus of narratives trying to conceptualise and explain language variation – usually in negative terms. The pressure to conform to one form of language was represented by such diverse manifestations as the myth of Babel and the English-Only movements (Nelde 1996: 295; Machan 2009: 83-4), passing through Early Modern standardization advocates and their prescriptive stance, the search for a 'scientific language' during the Enlightenment (Eco 1993), the Romantic ideal of a 'genius' or 'character' of a language (see e.g. Hitchings 2011: 90 ff.), and the related rhetoric of nineteenth-century nationalistic movements.[1]

Symmetrically, the stigma against language variation, depicted as disruptive for society, proceeded from the often-quoted 'shibboleth' episode in the Bible to the mid-twentieth-century BBC ban on non-RP (Received Pronunciation) speakers, passing through the discrimination (through ridiculing and stereotyping, when not through active exclusion from social benefits) of non-standard varieties since the late Middle Ages, and through the prescriptivism of education planning in imperial times (Scott and Machan 1992: 22; Gray and Mazzon 2011).

Throughout the ages, there have been attempts at describing language varieties as homogeneous and identifiable objects, based on rational choices of individuals and groups within any society. As a crucial system of identity, language does embody allegiances and in-group dynamics, but it equally importantly represents strife and opposition within society. Although mainstream sociolinguistics has (at least initially) mostly drawn from a positivist view of society, where conformism prevails and all participants tend to the same goals, alternative strands have been formulated (G. Williams 1992: 39-40). The inspiration for this already came in 1960, when J. Milton Yinger published the seminal article "Contraculture and Subculture", in which language is mentioned as one of the manifestations of "inverse or counter values (opposed to those of the surrounding society) in face of serious frustration or conflict" (Yinger 1960: 627). In that article, the concepts of 'subculture' and 'counterculture' are claimed to form a continuum, according to the extent to which the conflict with the mainstream culture is central in defining the values of the alternative culture – this paradigm lends itself to be applied to a number of sociolinguistic observations, starting from Yinger's own examples, i.e. 'adolescents' and 'delinquents', both groups that have been the object of extensive linguistic investigations. Yinger's work was accompanied by several other contributions within sociology, such as those by Roszack (1969), Goffman (2004), and Marcuse (1956, 1964), and this gave the possibility to interpret the concept with reference to various social sciences, with the idea that conflict and crisis are inherent in society. One recent development of this is the *Figuration Kontra*, developed at the University of Innsbruck.[2] Briefly said, the model attempts to

---

1 For early claims of excellence of 'national' languages in the Renaissance, see Eco (1993: 105 ff.).

2 This conception was also discussed in a workshop within the CEnT ('Cultural Encounters and Transfer') research platform of the University. I would like to thank the organisers for providing the basis for the reflections in this paper through several round tables. The results of this workshop have been published in Heimerdinger, Kistler and Hochhauser

represent countercultural phenomena through a classification that takes into account parameters such as 'intrinsic-*transformatorisch*' vs. 'extrinsic-*evolutionär*' (referring to the motivation of the phenomenon, i.e. whether it is aimed at changing an existing reality or at overthrowing it), or 'individual/artistic' vs. 'collective/ social' (e.g. a single work of literature or art vs. an ecologist movement); the most important parameter for us in the perspective of the present paper is the axis of '*Entwurf*' vs. '*Reaktion*', i.e. whether the phenomenon is an innovative attempt to change the cultural landscape or whether it represents a reaction against the imposition of a cultural pattern.

The reviewing and discussing of some ways in which societal conflict has been described in linguistics can be useful to explore the extent to which a model of counterculture can be applied to language variation.

2. Modelling variation as conflict and resistance

The first systematic integration of societal conflict within linguistic models came in the early 1970s, when Peter Trudgill, applying the quantitative method developed by William Labov to British data, explained the divergent language behaviour of informants of different social classes and genders in terms of *covert prestige* (Trudgill 1974: 89) and defined this prestige as *anti-norm*.[3] This innovative concept revealed that the persistence of non-standard varieties, far from being the unwanted side-effect of 'imperfect acquisition' or, worse, 'sloppiness and laziness' (Preston 2002: 135-45), is a marker of alternative identities and value systems within societies.[4] Slightly over ten years earlier, Labov had argued for "The Logic of Non-Standard English" (1969), claiming that non-standard forms of language are generally rule-governed as the standard, a claim that is today taken for granted

---

(2013). I would also like to thank Matthias Mösch for his suggestions on 'classic' counterculture references, and Sandra Handl for discussions on the cognitive perspective.

3   This definition has become traditional, but see Algeo (1992: 168) for an apt commentary on the term: "The prestige among its speakers of a dialect typical of the lower classes is sometimes called 'covert' because those who actually value it highly, as shown by their use of it, publicly denigrate it or give higher rank to the standard upper-class dialect, which therefore has 'overt' prestige. The prestige of lower-class language is frequently not covert, however. Instead its speakers may cheerfully, even aggressively, acknowledge their preference for it or assert its inherent superiority. They perceive its effectiveness and the inappropriateness of standard English within their community".

4   In Machan's (2009: 50) words, "[w]hether particular linguistic features are judged synchronic variants, diachronic developments, errors, or inconsequentialities depends a good deal on who is doing the judging and when".

in linguistics, but still finds resistance among the lay public (Preston 2002: 147). The innovation brought to sociolinguistics by Trudgill is the idea that the anti-norm of non-standard varieties can be a force of attraction for whole groups in a population: although the standard is overtly recognised as prestigious, this does not entail that the whole population will tend to adopt it and employ it consistently (Trudgill 1972). This explains why the normative-prescriptive tradition, especially vocal in British society, though imposing so many trends and attitudes, has never managed to fully implement its ideal of conformism and unification. The campaigns enacted at various levels, especially within the educational system, and aimed at enforcing a monolithic and elitarian view of language norms, have managed to impose that view on a large part of society, but they have also created equally important negative associations with the standard.[5] These were revealed and proved experimentally through the psychosocially oriented Matched Guise Technique (Lambert 1967; Lee 1971; Giles and Johnson 1981; Coupland and Bishop 2007), where the systematic evaluation of socio-economic and personality features of speakers through their accents became evident; however, this connection has been within society for a long time, as the 'shibboleth' episode in the Bible shows: regardless of their inherent characteristics, "differences between dialects [...] can be *made* socially and politically significant" (Chilton 1997: 176; original italics).

The prescriptive tradition, which accompanies standardisation and the establishment of a national language, is socially and politically significant, since its aim is to try and enforce one language variety throughout a territory to symbolise its political, social, ethnic, and cultural homogeneity. This homogeneity is of course largely mythical (G. Williams 1992: 128-30), and this kind of myth is instrumental to the construction of a conflict-less society, a myth itself.[6] The various strands of purism that have developed in Europe in the past centuries, for instance, by stressing the opposition against foreign influxes on a national language, have the aim of constructing an illusion of unity: "Concentrating on war *between* sovereign states can obscure violence *within* states arising from the exploitation of linguistic and cultural differences whether by established governments or by competing political groups" (Chilton 1997: 177). Language is crucial to nationalistic arguments (Hitchings 2011: 133 ff.), and can contribute to the justification of conflicts,

---

5 "If a certain pronunciation comes to be regarded as a prestige feature in a particular community, then it will tend to be exaggerated. *This kind of process can also take place in the opposite direction*" (Trudgill 1974: 23; italics added).

6 On 'illusory unification' as 'forced unity' in Marcuse, see, for instance, Kellner (1991: xxxiii).

similarly to religion;[7] as will be further illustrated below, this often takes the form of a "contrastive self-identification" (Fishman 1989 [1972]:[8] 284-7).

In a less idealistic scenario than that depicted by the pursuit of language homogeneity as 'universal brotherhood', language, as a field of knowledge, is also a field of power relations; therefore, the persistence of anti-norms, and indeed of language variation, can be explained as divergence and resistance. If standardisation is "part of the legitimisation of inequality" (G. Williams 1992: 145), this can engender reactions on the part of people representing different sets of values. The pressure to conform to a form of language that mirrors a social order enforced by the dominant culture cannot be eventually stronger than the expression of identity (G. Williams 1992: 197) – "in some situations, regional dialects, by reinforcing local cultures and local identities, may act as a counter to nationalism" (Trudgill 2002: 29). In other words,

> [t]o some speakers, such competition inspires greater dialect loyalty to a stigmatised yet historical and unique variety; to others, it suggests progressive, sociolinguistic assimilation. To all such speakers, the fact that this kind of competition has meaning reflects naturalized social responses to what is in the end [...] neutral linguistic variation (Machan 2009: 58).

Thus, the tendency of non-standard varieties to persist, and even to spread, can become a legitimised form of resistance against pressure towards standardised language behaviour (Milroy and Milroy 1991: 115; G. Williams 1992: 214). The textbook case in this sense is certainly the case of Martha's Vineyard, studied in depth by Labov (1963; for a revised analysis carried out many years later, and partly contradicting the original results, see Blake and Josey 2003), where it appeared that the local accent was diverging from the standard at an increasing pace. This classic case in sociolinguistics was only to some extent discussed within a traditional model of counterculture, since it seemed a case of language change 'from below' the level of consciousness (Trudgill 1974: 24), while counterculture was considered as stemming from conscious intention to react against the mainstream culture (in *Kontra* terms, as *Reaktion*), or as the attempt (equally conscious) to

---

7 "The ever-present link between language and religion [...] not only sanctifies 'our language' but helps raise language into the pale of sanctity even in secular culture. Under secular-nationalist auspices, language becomes part of secular religion, binding society together and mobilizing it to face whatever its challenges are taken to be" (Fishman 1989: 7).

8 The volume published by Joshua Fishman in 1989 gathers some previous articles and some new parts. The original references are not given separately here, but the dates of original publication are indicated in square brackets.

develop an alternative social model (i.e. an *Entwurf*). A more fitting example
was considered to be the Ebonics debate (see e.g. Collins 1999), in which the
legitimacy of African American Vernacular English was defended as an identity
marker, since "conscious ethnicity movements are more than likely to become or
incorporate conscious language movements as well" (Fishman 1989 [1980]: 218),
not least because of the general tendency to "use language change and variation
to advance particular social positions, neutralize challenges to these positions,
and displace discussion from social issues to linguistic ones" (Machan 2009: 82).

The variability that persists in language behaviour and, at least partly, the
direction of change, can be ultimately explained by a model of competing
cultural identities if we are prepared, for instance, to integrate a cognitive and constructionist perspective (Watts 2011: 5); according to this view, the speaker tends
to select salient variants in his/her language behaviour, whether consciously or
unconsciously, in response to several types of group pressure, which can be in
conflict.[9] The problem with this perspective, however, is that it focusses on the
individual, while the concept of culture is associated with a collective dimension.
Another problem is the tendency to conceive languages as separate and discrete
objects, itself a consequence of the dominance of standard languages: in contrast
with this static and reified view of languages as entities,

> [f]rom a variationist point of view, a language is a dynamic phenomenon. It is appropriate
> to liken languages to relatively fluid and variable physical states, and to use process models
> rather than product or static models in describing them (Milroy and Milroy 1997: 63).

Usually, the conflictive element of language differentiation follows binary models,
as in the early definitions of societal bilingualism and diglossia (Ferguson 1959;
Fishman 1967), and is viewed in association with other linguistically relevant
aspects, for instance ethnicity and religion. The latter has a well-known incidence
in distinguishing between varieties of Arabic, which led eventually to their differentiation in social status within the Arab world, or between Hindi and Urdu,
which, conversely, are very similar but are used by different religious groups in
the same communities, and are officially considered separate languages. Ethnic
differentiations can equally be decisive in establishing language differences:

> [t]he recognition of language boundaries, the interpretation of language boundaries and
> the manipulation of language boundaries are all ethnically encumbered behaviours, as are

---

9   On the way in which cultural dynamics can be better understood if the unconscious
     dimension is added, and rationality is not considered the exclusive driving force of
     social beings, see for instance Roszak (1969: 50-1).

either the acceptance or the rejection of whatever language boundaries that may "exist" at any particular time (Fishman 1989 [1977]: 35).

Advances in cognitive sociolinguistics (Geeraerts, Kristiansen, and Peirsman 2010) can help overcome this dichotomy, for instance if the cognitive perspective is integrated in the study of language and ideology (Dirven, Hawkins, and Sandikcioglu 2001), since the cognitive perspective hypothesises the universality of some concepts and metaphors that impinge on language attitudes and ideology.

A more flexible and prototype-oriented approach can help overcome the tendency to adopt binary perspectives. The next two sections explore some macro-examples of language variation and conflict.

3. Individuals and groups; conscious and unconscious identity marking

The importance of collective identification does not mean that individual choices do not play any role, as emphasised by Fishman himself (1989 [1977]: 46). Various models, especially within early sociolinguistics, have tried to explain the variability within the language output of individuals in terms of the individual him/ herself. Starting with the notion of *idiolect* (Bloch 1948), which was for a while successful, and following with Weinreich's (1953, 1954) concept of *diasystem*,[10] these models saw variation as something traceable to the individual. Most of these views were based on the generally dualistic nature of many linguistic theories, but were not ultimately tenable because variation shown at the individual level cannot be so rigorously compartmentalised, as Fishman admits (1989 [1980]: 192). Our life, especially in modern times, is made up of several identities and patterns of behaviour, which make up a complex repertoire. The individual's behaviour can vary consciously or unconsciously, not only in micro-aspects such as those exemplified in most quantitative studies, but also when different language systems are involved, i.e. in code-switching and code-mixing (Myers-Scotton 1993), which can also take place at different levels of consciousness. At the meta-level of language attitudes, as will be mentioned below, there can also be a coexistence of different norms and values.[11] It is really still unclear how this 'multiple

---

10 The cultural counterpart of diasystem, i.e. *dinomia* or *diethnia*, was invoked by Fishman when trying to transpose the notions of societal bilingualism and diglossia onto the individual plane (Fishman 1989 [1980]: 189-90).

11 The way in which Darwinism filters into language studies and contributes to create prejudice can be seen also in the 'hierarchical' classification of diglossic situations, with a 'High' and a 'Low' language, which are definitely loaded terms (J. M. Williams

competence' is stored in the mind and activated, although research subfields in sociolinguistics, such as accommodation theory and social network analysis (Giles,
Coupland, and Coupland 1991; Milroy and Milroy 1985; Scott 2000), have tried
to offer explanations.

A better way towards understanding the forces that condition language variation seems thus now to be at the level of the sub-groups within a society, rather
than at that of the individual, a perspective that also allows a more direct comparison with the models of 'subculture' and 'counterculture', as Halliday (1978:
178-9) remarked. Important applications of the ideas of conflict and resistance in
language to sub-groups came from functional linguistics in the 1970s, but were
anticipated by Bloomfield:

> [w]e believe that the differences in density of communication within a speech community
> are not only personal and individual, but that the community is divided into various sys-
> tems of sub-groups such that the persons within a sub-group speak much more to each
> other than to persons outside their sub-group. The lines of weakness and, accordingly,
> the differences of speech within a speech community are local – due to mere geographic
> separation – and non-local, or as we usually say, social (Bloomfield 1933: 476).

This 'principle of density', as Bloomfield himself defined it, paved the way for the
later network analysis, where one of the main parameters is precisely the level of
density of the network (Fox and Fox 2004: 68-70). Even before the study of social
networks was systematised, a different strand emerged, which had to do with a
more explicit, if more circumscribed, side of language as (counter)identity, when
M. A. K. Halliday wrote about 'anti-society', represented by an 'anti-language', in
terms of a "society that is set up within another society as a conscious alternative
to it. It is a mode of resistance, resistance which may take the form either of passive
symbiosis or of active hostility and even destruction" (Halliday 1978: 164). Anti-
language is not only parallel to anti-society, but generated by it, in the same way
as society generates, and then is expressed by, language. The definitions provided
by Halliday are clearly compatible with the concept of counterculture, but the rest
of his treatment of the topic clarifies that he only refers to specific elements of
language, i.e. those pertaining to specific groups' jargons. In particular, one of his
examples is the jargon or 'cant' of the underworld in Elizabethan England, where

---

1992: 96 *passim*). For the role of conceptual metaphors and their influence on language
attitudes see Watts (2011: 7 ff.). For the coexistence of different and apparently conflicting attitudes and norms, the term *schizoglossia* was coined (Kandiah 1981); this is
itself a term that is not neutral, and can also refer to the emerging of different language
behaviour above and below the level of consciousness.

the emphasis in selecting expressive means was precisely on creating a 'parallel world', which would have its own code that conveyed not only denotational values but also, and perhaps principally, alternative social values –[12] the importance of such an 'anti-language' resides more in its cohesive function than in its secrecy (Halliday 1978: 165-7). Forms of slang and jargon are therefore means of opposition, differentiation, and stigmatisation of society, but also function to regulate groups internally (Martín Rojo 2010).[13] These groups can also reproduce structures from mainstream society with a reversing and subversing aim, as in the 'king of thieves' or the 'laws of coney-catching' – 'kings' and 'laws' are institutions from the mainstream society that are then reversed, but still refer back to the original concepts of 'king' and 'law' (Barisone 1989: 94 ff.). In this sense, the anti-language is alternative to, but also contiguous with, language norms, and this may lead us to consider such manifestations as typical of a sub- rather than of a counterculture. It is a form of opposition that is partly tolerated and integrated in society; it is an anti-norm that presupposes, and is in fact based on, the norm, as are the various reversal practices of carnival (where often there is also an appointed 'king', with a parodical mimicry of official paraphernalia), or the 'Boy Bishop' of the late Middle Ages (MacKenzie 2012). In this sense, jargons and slangs (and to some extent 'field-specific' languages) are doubles and parasites of language in a similar fashion to the way in which 'subculture' is parasitic and derivative of culture, and therefore not necessarily 'against' it in general (Cohen 1955).

This dimension of 'anti-language' is however the closest to the current models of counterculture, also in the formulation of the *Figuration Kontra*, in that it signals a voluntary, rational effort (*Entwurf*) to create an alternative reality and/or mode of socialisation, which is indeed often against (*gegen*) the dominant culture, with which it is in a tension relationship, and to which it is a reaction (*Reaktion*). In this sense, the further examples given by Halliday (1978: 170-1) are the early Christian community and the feminist movements, which also created their own 'alternative' codes, through the application of general language processes (e.g. sound metathesis, or metaphor), but with alternative meaning styles and coding orientations (Halliday 1978: 175-7). A similar analysis could be applied to

---

12 The 'subculture' of the criminal world was already identified by Yinger (1960) as one of the most typical examples of the phenomenon. The perception of the Elizabethan underworld and of its 'cant' as anti-society is described for instance in Barisone (1989), where the numerous co-temporary treatises trying to unveil it, label it, and thus reduce its subversive powers, are mentioned.

13 Albeit in pre-theoretical and non-technical terms, this is acknowledged also in some of the traditional definitions of slang, such as those reported by Partridge (1970: 5-9).

the so-called 'slanguage' of youth in Britain, which employs several elements of expressive grammar (e.g. extragrammatical morphology, such as generalised -s derivation; Mattiello 2013) as well as semantic shifts, polysemy and ambiguity; the aims of this encoding, again, range from secrecy to in-group marking ('fashion'), to the signalling of opposition against adult culture (Mattiello 2008). It must be noted that adolescents and young adults are also the focus in Yinger (1960) and other studies in sub- and counterculture, and also the object of specific sociolinguistic studies (starting with Cheshire 1982; Romaine 1984), for instance in relation to sub-codes, such as hip-hop culture (Alim 2006).

Thus, various sub-groups in society tend to cluster around different forms of language (and different patterns of social behaviour), which in turn tend to be perceived as variously prestigious according to their degree of association with the network (G. Williams 1992: 108). Social networks, and similar sub-groups such as discourse communities (Swales 1990) and communities of practice (Wenger 1998) cut across dialect areas and highlight different patterns of language variation, based on sociocultural factors that do not necessarily overlap with 'regions', or with settlement patterns over an area. A 'network map' of a linguistic area appears thus quite different from 'ordinary' language maps, with the distribution of variant tokens impossible to identify with areas separated by isoglosses of any absolute validity.[14]

Language is often used as a locus of opposition and criticism between groups, be it neighbouring villages, rival youth gangs, or political factions.[15] What is more interesting for the sociolinguist, as mentioned, is that the language behaviour of groups tends to be systematic and consistent, though variable, *below* the level of consciousness. In other words, language behaviour tends to align itself with other patterns of socialisation without being necessarily a conscious decision; a speaker can adopt a range of slang items, or adhere to the conventions of a discourse community, or switch between different accents, with specific social aims; among these is the signalling of the speaker's belonging to a subculture, for reasons that we call

---

14   The awareness of this has deeply influenced new trends in dialectology, especially in the conception of linguistic atlases; similar reflections have been developed in archaeology, when it became clear that the distribution of cultural products such as manufacts or decoration patterns is not so easily mapped in self-contained 'areas' (among many examples, see e.g. Anderson and Faught 1998).

15   For instance, the famous *Proposal for Correcting, Improving and Ascertaining the English Tongue* by Swift has been interpreted as political invective against the *Spectator* circle of intellectuals (Watts 2011: 173 ff.), themselves the object of investigation as linguistic social network (e.g. in Fitzmaurice 2000).

'covert prestige' as a shorthand way to refer to a cluster of psychosocial features which express the conflictive aspects of our life as social beings. A case in point can be seen in gender linguistics; on the one hand, traditional sociolinguistics has claimed that women tend to show systematically more standard-oriented language behaviour, while men typically exhibit adherence to the 'anti-norm' as part of their male identity in many communities (Trudgill 1974: 84-8). The same kind of argument has been put forth later in historical sociolinguistics (Nevalainen and Raumolin-Brunberg 2003), with the specification that female text-producers (rather under-represented in any historical corpus anyway) often appear as early adopters rather than innovators. The general motivation for this is that women are allegedly more prone to conform to high prestige norms because they are more strongly pressurised to aspire to upward social mobility, and are therefore more sensitive to the social stigma attached to the anti-norm (Wodak and Benke 1997: 140 ff.). The association between female features of social identity and standard-oriented language behaviour can indeed become so close that men adopting this kind of language behaviour can be the object of derision in some groups, in the same way as members of a dialect community can be socially penalised for 'putting on airs' if they employ standard-like language. These are some of the manifestations of social stigma within a community that involve language. The following section explores this topic in a broader perspective.

4. Conflicting ideologies and the politics of language

As mentioned above, the closest connection that can be drawn between language variation and cultural dynamics is in the field of language attitudes and of conscious interventions on language, such as language planning measures. The discourse on language attitudes (Agheyisi and Fishman 1970), especially in relation with nationalism, ensues through the building of myths that express a social dynamics of conflict and opposition, using metaphors such as that of a language (as often of a nation) as a living being,[16] which has a 'life-cycle', can 'grow', or must be kept 'healthy' and 'pure' (Watts 2011: 11 ff.). Thus, ideas of 'progress', 'perfection' or 'degeneration' percolate into language discourse and are incorporated into ideologies that can be used to reinforce elitarian and discriminatory conceptions, which can become monolithic and exclusive of alternatives to a prescribed norm. Among these myths, as skilfully illustrated by Watts (2011), are

---

16 This long-standing metaphor is perpetuated in our age in the connections between linguistics and biology, which were influential in several models of language change as 'evolution' and in cognitive historical linguistics (Frank and Gontier 2010: 32-46).

those of the 'longevity' or 'unbroken tradition' of a language, which tend to ignore the variation that emerges in manuscripts, especially in the centuries before the standardisation of English. The history of the language is written, so to speak, from the point of view of the 'winners', i.e. only the language forms and variants that represent the social elites are considered legitimate, ancient, pure, and 'correct'. These are not conceptions that are limited to the lay public; in spite of the alleged objectivity of linguistics, the academia has not been immune from bias. It is only recently, for instance, that the first linguistic history of Northern English has been published (Wales 2006); the 'alternative histories' of English (Watts and Trudgill 2002) have only started to find visibility in the academic space, and so have the 'lesser-known varieties' of English (Schreier et al. 2010).

The promotion, and often the enforcement, of the standard have frequently occurred through the building of a rhetoric based on disparaging all other varieties. Negative comments about northern English dialects, issued by writers based in the richer and more powerful south, antedate the standardisation process, since they go back to the twelfth century and have basically never stopped since (J. M. Williams 1992: 70), while the close association between dialect (or accent) and moral qualities such as 'friendliness', 'honesty', and 'authenticity'[17] goes back to the eighteenth century (Watts 2011: 33-4). Such close association, typical of British culture in many ways, more than of other European cultures, was anticipated during Elizabethan times, when country speech started to be branded as 'rude, barbarous, boorish' as opposed to the socially more 'civil, polite, smooth' speech of the educated classes (J. M. Williams 1992: 73). From the end of the sixteenth century onwards, there is also discourse about the 'corrupt and false speech' that is, basically, everything except the forms employed in 'the king's court' (Mazzon et al. 2012); very soon afterwards, language came to be considered a key factor in social-class placement, along with dress code and other behavioural patterns (J. M. Williams 1992: 83). This is only the beginning of what will later become standard-based purism. A good example of such ideological battles, concerning Britain after the first wave of industrialization and urbanization, is in Joyce (1991), see also Hitchings (2011: 143 ff.); a contemporary example is the debate about 'Estuary English' (Mazzon 2008; Hitchings 2011: 212-13). In these cases, we can

---

17 It is in general typical of many countercultures and subcultures to support 'authenticity' in their own mythical discourse. For this myth in the USA in the 1960s see Suri (2009: 47); similar arguments are put forth by ecologist movements, and by groups that argue against the negative sides of 'progress', e.g. the Amish (Fishman 1989 [1980]: 192-3). Ideas connecting language change with biological 'degeneration' have been circulating for many centuries (see e.g. Machan 2009: 16-17; Gray and Mazzon 2011).

conceive of such conflicts as representative of conflicts between the inherently 'local' character of cultural identity and the tendency to 'global' perspective, typical of states and empires. Purism is in fact an expression of this tension between local and global (Silverstein 1998: 90-2). This is due to the fact that very often "people within local language communities actively position themselves with respect to the political orders of contemporary nation-states and more encompassing international political institutions" (Silverstein 1998: 101), which leads to language becoming a site of struggle, whether about status- or education-language planning, or about strategic code-switching as a way to convey allegiance to group identity (G. Williams 1992: 122 ff.).

This struggle builds on another myth, that of the 'homogeneity' of a language within a political unit, very often applied to the whole culture via the concept of *Kultursprache* (Watts 2011: 115 ff.), which in fact means the language of a dominant politics, education, literature. This is also connected with purism, particularly the opposition against language mixture, a discourse which also goes back several centuries. This virulent strand of purism tries to suppress not only language change related to contact (seen, in this ideology, as 'contamination'), but also phenomena such as systematic code-switching that are, in a way, a means to indicate multiple identities and to negotiate allegiance in multicultural environment (McColl Millar 2000: 172 ff.).[18] The latter ideology is particularly visible in post-colonial environments,[19] where ethnic, socioeconomic and other issues often find expression in 'language questions' or 'language battles', sometimes taken to the extreme of riots and physical confrontation. The counterpart is the discourse of language rights (Skutnabb-Kangas and Phillipson 1995) and of linguistic imperialism (Phillipson 1992), which interpret the whole range of factors in the spread of colonial languages in terms of social and intercultural struggle (Canagarajah 2005). This concerns not only the interplay between English and 'indigenous languages', but also the cline of varieties and the reference norms involved.

On the one side, there is a clear struggle for social dominance between the coloniser language and the colonised language, including the discourse of 'English as a killer language' and other constructions of imposition vs. resistance (Watts 2011: 259 ff.). Within these scenarios, however, there are dynamics that are internal to each postcolonial community (Pennycook 1994, 1998; Mair 2003), in which

---

18 Myers-Scotton (1993: 127) reports that Pakir (1989: 381) had already made this explicit when referring to 'unmarked' code-alternation to suggest "a 'we-code' which draws upon some subcultural conventions inaccessible to outsiders".

19 The controversial term 'postcolonial' is employed here in a purely chronological sense.

English varieties and norms have been incorporated into dynamics of inclusion, exclusion and/or discrimination (Schneider 2007).

The use of English as a 'High' language, in connection with high education, socioeconomic privilege, and political power has created the space for other counter-discourses, identities, and patterns of behaviour. The development of internal norms (eventually aiming at reproducing a standard vs. non-standard dynamics through appropriation, Machan 2009: 66), the conveying of divided allegiances through mixed varieties, the planning decisions connected not only to education systems and public life but also, for instance, to spelling,[20] are all manifestations of the fact that the tendency to reproduce conflict dynamics through language strifes, which are a symbolic locus of inter-group conflicts (Nelde 1996: 290-4), has been transferred to postcolonial contexts.

5. Conclusion

The extension of a value system in which language forms act as social discriminators has deeply influenced large parts of the world. More than the transplantation of English or French *per se*, it is the monolithic, prescriptive, elitarian orientation that accompanies the spread of these languages (mostly conveyed through education planning) that has given rise to phenomena that can be interpreted as cultural opposition.

One problem in integrating these phenomena is that classic definitions of subculture and counterculture start from the assumption that manifestations of these phenomena are intentional and based on rational choices; this is also at the root of the formulation of the *Figuration Kontra*, and would seem to be in conflict with language variation phenomena 'from below'. As mentioned above, this could be overcome through the adoption of a cognitive perspective, in which this coexistence of conscious and unconscious elements is applied to all cultural manifestations (Pires de Oliveira 2001: 37). The axis of the *Entwurf* vs. *Reaktion* (i.e. a counterculture as

---

20 In this connection, literature has an important role, both in relation to the choice of English as a medium for writing, and to the forms that English takes, down to the spelling decisions: "Many of the improvements of standard spellings coincide with common spelling errors, and this allows different writers to arrive independently at the same conventions. It also helps to give the system the character of an *antistandard* rather than a local standard" (MacAfee 1983: 40; original italics). These issues become even more pressing when those contexts are taken into account where pidgins and creoles have developed that are struggling to acquire legitimisation as means of expression alternative to the dominant values.

internal or external, transformational or aiming at an evolution of the dominant culture) in the model is perhaps the only one in which there are clear-cut applications to linguistic phenomena, for instance slang, or jargons, or language rights movements, as opposed to purism and prescriptivism. The other axes, i.e. collective vs. individual, and 'real' opposition (i.e. *gegen*) vs. integration, seem to offer different challenges to such applications. A further development of the model could provide useful insight for incorporation of linguistic variation in a perspective of cultural opposition.

References

Agheyisi, Rebecca and Joshua Aaron Fishman. 1970. 'Language attitude studies. A brief survey of methodological approaches'. *Anthropological Linguistics* 12:5: 137-57.

Algeo, John. 1992. 'Sociolinguistic attitudes and issues in contemporary Britain'. In: Tim William Machan and Charles Scott (eds.), *English in Its Social Contexts. Essays in Historical Sociolinguistics*. Oxford: Oxford University Press, 155-77.

Alim, H. Samy. 2006. *Roc the Mic Right: The Language of Hip Hop Culture*. London: Taylor and Francis.

Anderson, David G. and Michael K. Faught. 1998. 'The distribution of fluted Paleoindian projectile points: Update 1998'. *Archeology of Eastern North America* 26: 163-87.

Barisone, Ermanno. 1989. *Il gergo dell'underworld elisabettiano*. Genova: Il Melangolo.

Blake, Renée and Meredith Josey. 2003. 'The /ay/ diphthong in a Martha's Vineyard community. What can we say 40 years after Labov?'. *Language in Society* 32: 451-85.

Bloch, Bernard. 1948. 'A set of postulates for phonetic analysis'. *Language* 24:1: 3-46.

Bloomfield, Leonard. 1933. *Language*. New York: Henry Holt.

Canagarajah, A. Suresh. 2005. 'Dilemmas in planning English/Vernacular relations in post-colonial communities'. *Journal of Sociolinguistics* 9:3: 418-47.

Cheshire, Jenny. 1982. *Variation in an English Dialect. A Sociolinguistic Study*. Cambridge: Cambridge University Press.

Chilton, Paul A. 1997. 'The role of language in human conflict: Prolegomena to the investigation of language as a factor in conflict causation and resolution'. *Current Issues in Language and Society* 4:3: 174-89.

Cohen, Albert K. 1955. *Delinquent Boys: The Culture of the Gang*. London: Routledge and Kegan Paul.

Collins, James. 1999. 'The Ebonics controversy in context. Literacies, subjectivities, and language ideologies in the United States'. In: Jan Blommaert (ed.), *Language Ideological Debates*. Berlin: Mouton de Gruyter, 201-34.

Coupland, Nikolas and Hywel Bishop. 2007. 'Ideologised values for British accents'. *Journal of Sociolinguistics* 11:1: 74-93.

Dirven, René, Bruce Hawkins, and Esra Sandikcioglu (eds.). 2001. *Language and Ideology. Volume I: Theoretical Cognitive Approaches*. Amsterdam: John Benjamins.

Eco, Umberto. 1993. *La ricerca della lingua perfetta nella cultura europea*. Rome/Bari: Laterza.

Ferguson, Charles Albert. 1959. 'Diglossia'. *Word* 15: 325-40.

Fishman, Joshua Aaron. 1967. 'Bilingualism with and without diglossia; diglossia with and without bilingualism'. *Journal of Social Issues* 29:2: 29-38.

Fishman, Joshua Aaron. 1989. *Language and Ethnicity in Minority Sociolinguistic Perspective*. Clevedon/Philadelphia: Multilingual Matters.

Fitzmaurice, Susan. 2000. 'The Spectator, the politics of social networks, and language standardisation in eighteenth century England'. In: Laura Wright (ed.), *The Development of Standard English 1300-1800. Theories, Descriptions, Conflicts*. Cambridge: Cambridge University Press, 195-218.

Fox, Renata and John Fox. 2004. *Organizational Discourse. A Language-Ideology-Power Perspective*. Westport, CT: Greenwood Publishing.

Frank, Roslyn M. and Nathalie Gontier. 2010. 'On constructing a research model of historical cognitive linguistics (HCL): Some theoretical considerations'. In: Margaret E. Winters, Heli Tissari, and Kathryn Allan (eds.), *Historical Cognitive Linguistics*. Berlin: De Gruyter Mouton, 31-69.

Geeraerts, Dirk, Gillie Kristiansen, and Yves Peirsman (eds.). 2010. *Advances in Cognitive Sociolinguistics*. Berlin: Mouton de Gruyter.

Giles, Howard and Patricia Johnson. 1981. 'The role of language in ethnic group relations'. In: John C. Turner and Howard Giles (eds.), *Intergroup Behaviour*. Oxford: Blackwell, 199-243.

Giles, Howard, Justine Coupland, and Nikolas Coupland. 1991. *Contexts of Accommodation: Developments in Applied Sociolinguistics*. Cambridge: Cambridge University Press.

Goffman, Ken. 2004. *Counterculture Through the Ages: From Abraham to Acid House*. New York: Villard.

Gray, Geoffrey and Gabriella Mazzon. 2011. 'Persuasive discourse and language planning in Ireland'. *Linguistica e Filologia* 31: 37-64.

Halliday, Michael Alexander Kirkwood. 1978 [1976]. *Language as a Social Semiotic: The Social Interpretation of Language and Meaning*. London: Edward Arnold.

Heimerdinger, Timo, Erich Kistler, and Eva-Maria Hochhauser (eds.). 2013. *Gegenkultur*. Würzburg: Königshausen and Neumann.

Hitchings, Henry. 2011. *The Language Wars. A History of Proper English*. London: John Murray.

Joyce, Patrick. 1991. 'The people's English: Language and class in England c. 1840-1920'. In: Peter Burke and Roy Porter (eds.), *Language, Self, and Society. A Social History of Language*. Cambridge: Polity Press, 154-90.

Kandiah, Thiru. 1981. 'Lankan English schizoglossia'. *English World-Wide* 2:1: 63-81.

Kellner, Douglas. 1991 [2002]. 'Introduction to the second edition'. In: Herbert Marcuse, *One-Dimensional Man: Studies in the Ideology of Advanced Industrial Society*. Boston, MA: Beacon Press, xi-xxxix [London: Routledge, xi-xlviii].

Labov, William. 1963. 'The social motivation of a sound change'. *Word* 19: 273-309.

Labov, William. 1969. 'The logic of non-standard English'. In: James Alatis (ed.), *Georgetown Monograph Series on Languages and Linguistics* 22. Washington, DC: Georgetown University Press, 1-44.

Lambert, Wallace E. 1967. 'A social psychology of bilingualism'. *Journal of Social Issues* 23: 91-108.

Lee, Richard R. 1971. 'Dialect perception: A critical review and re-evaluation'. *Quarterly Journal of Speech* 57: 410-17.

MacAfee, Caroline. 1983. *Glasgow*. Amsterdam: John Benjamins.

Machan, Tim William. 2009. *Language Anxiety. Conflict and Change in the History of English*. Oxford: Oxford University Press.

MacKenzie, Neil. 2012. *The Medieval Boy Bishops*. Kibworth Beauchamp: Matador.

Mair, Christian (ed.). 2003. *The Politics of English as a World Language. New Horizons in Postcolonial Cultural Studies*. Amsterdam/New York: Rodopi.

Marcuse, Herbert. 1956 [1998]. *Eros and Civilization. A Philosophical Inquiry into Freud*. London: Routledge.

Marcuse, Herbert. 1964 [2002]. *One-Dimensional Man: Studies in the Ideology of Advanced Industrial Society*. London: Routledge and Kegan Paul.

Martín Rojo, Luisa. 2010. 'Jargon'. In: Mirjam Fried, Jan-Ola Östman, and Jef Verschueren (eds.), *Variation and Change: Pragmatic Perspectives*. Amsterdam: John Benjamins, 155-70.

Mattiello, Elisa. 2008. 'Lexical innovation in the language of young English people'. In: Susan Kermas and Maurizio Gotti (eds.), *Socially-Conditioned Language Change: Diachronic and Synchronic Insights*. Lecce: Edizioni del Grifo, 471-93.

Mattiello, Elisa. 2013. *Extra-Grammatical Morphology in English. Abbreviations, Blends, Reduplicatives and Related Phenomena*. Berlin: Mouton de Gruyter.

Mazzon, Gabriella. 2008. 'Gone with the river: Estuary English as the new norm replacing RP?'. In: Susan Kermas and Maurizio Gotti (eds.), *Socially-Conditioned Language Change: Diachronic and Synchronic Insights*. Lecce: Edizioni del Grifo, 205-27.

Mazzon, Gabriella, Angelo Deidda, Maria Grazia Dongu, and Geoffrey Gray. 2012. 'Nation-building through language and literatures in the history of the British Isles'. In: Ignazio Putzu and Gabriella Mazzon (eds.), *Lingue, letterature, nazioni. Centri e periferie tra Europa e Mediterraneo*. Milan: Franco Angeli, 77-179.

McColl Millar, Robert. 2000. 'Covert and overt language attitudes to the Scots tongue expressed in the *Statistical Accounts of Scotland*'. In: Dieter Kastovsky and Arthur Mettinger (eds.), *The History of English in a Social Context. A Contribution to Historical Sociolinguistics*. Berlin: Mouton de Gruyter, 169-98.

Milroy, James and Lesley Milroy. 1985. 'Linguistic change, social network and speaker innovation'. *Journal of Linguistics* 21:2: 339-84.

Milroy, James and Lesley Milroy. 1991. *Authority in Language. Investigating Language Prescription and Standardization* (2nd edn.). London: Routledge.

Milroy, James and Lesley Milroy. 1993. 'Mechanisms of change in urban dialects: The role of class, social network and gender'. *International Journal of Applied Linguistics* 3:1: 57-77.

Milroy, James and Lesley Milroy. 1997. 'Varieties and variation'. In: Florian Coulmas (ed.), *The Handbook of Sociolinguistics*. Oxford: Blackwell, 47-64.

Myers-Scotton, Carol. 1993. *Social Motivations for Code-Switching. Evidence from Africa*. Oxford: Clarendon Press.

Nelde, Peter Hans. 1996. 'Language conflict'. In: Florian Coulmas (ed.), *The Handbook of Sociolinguistics*. Oxford: Blackwell, 285-300.

Nevalainen, Terttu and Helena Raumolin-Brunberg. 2003. *Historical Sociolinguistics: Language Change in Tudor and Stuart England*. London: Longman.

Pakir, Anne. 1989. 'Linguistic alternates and code selection in Baba Malay'. *World Englishes* 8: 379-88.

Partridge, Eric. 1970. *Slang To-Day and Yesterday* (4th edn.). London: Routledge and Kegan Paul.

Pennycook, Alastair. 1994. *The Cultural Politics of English as an International Language*. London: Longman.

Pennycook, Alastair. 1998. *English and the Discourses of Colonialism (The Politics of Language)*. London: Routledge.

Phillipson, Robert. 1992. *Linguistic Imperialism*. Oxford: Oxford University Press.

Pires de Oliveira, Roberta. 2001. 'Language and ideology. An interview with George Lakoff'. In: René Dirven, Bruce Hawkins, and Esra Sandikcioglu (eds.), *Language and Ideology. Volume I: Theoretical Cognitive Approaches*. Amsterdam: John Benjamins, 23-47.

Preston, Dennis R. 2002. 'The story of good and bad English in the United States'. In: Richard James Watts and Peter Trudgill (eds.), *Alternative Histories of the English Language*. London/New York: Routledge, 134-51.

Romaine, Suzanne. 1984. *The Language of Children and Adolescents: The Acquisition of Communicative Competence*. Oxford: Blackwell.

Roszak, Theodore. 1969. *The Making of a Counter Culture: Reflections on the Technocratic Society and its Youthful Opposition*. New York: Anchor Books.

Schneider, Edgar W. 2007. *Postcolonial English. Varieties Around the World*. Cambridge: Cambridge University Press.

Schreier, Daniel, Peter Trudgill, Edgar W. Schneider, and Jeffrey P. Williams (eds.). 2010. *The Lesser-Known Varieties of English. An Introduction*. Cambridge: Cambridge University Press.

Scott, Charles and Tim William Machan. 1992. 'Introduction: Sociolinguistics, language change, and the history of English'. In: Tim William Machan and Charles Scott (eds.), *English in Its Social Contexts. Essays in Historical Sociolinguistics*. Oxford: Oxford University Press, 3-27.

Scott, John P. 2000. *Social Network Analysis. A Handbook* (2nd edn.). London: Sage.

Silverstein, Michael. 1998. 'Contemporary transformation of local linguistic communities'. *Annual Review of Anthropology* 27: 401-26.

Skutnabb-Kangas, Tove and Robert Phillipson. 1995. 'Linguistic human rights, past and present'. In: Tove Skutnabb-Kangas and Robert Phillipson (eds.), *Linguistic Human Rights: Overcoming Linguistic Discrimination*. Berlin: Mouton de Gruyter, 71-110.

Suri, Jeremi. 2009. 'The rise and fall of an international counterculture, 1960-1975'. *The American Historical Review* 114:1: 45-68.

Swales, John M. 1990. *Genre Analysis: English in Academic and Research Settings*. Cambridge: Cambridge University Press.

32Gabriella Mazzon

Trudgill, Peter. 1972. 'Sex, covert prestige and linguistic change in the urban British English of Norwich'. *Language in Society* 1: 179-95.

Trudgill, Peter. 1974. *Sociolinguistics*. Harmondsworth: Penguin.

Trudgill, Peter. 2002. *Sociolinguistic Variation and Change*. Washington, DC: Georgetown University Press.

Wales, Katie. 2006. *Northern English: A Social and Cultural History*. Cambridge: Cambridge University Press.

Watts, Richard James. 2011. *Language Myths and the History of English*. Oxford: Oxford University Press.

Watts, Richard James and Peter Trudgill (eds.). 2002. *Alternative Histories of English*. London: Routledge.

Weinreich, Uriel. 1953. *Languages in Contact*. New York: Linguistic Circle of New York.

Weinreich, Uriel. 1954. 'Is a structural dialectology possible?'. *Word* 10: 388-400.

Wenger, Etienne. 1998. *Communities of Practice: Learning, Meaning, and Identity*. Cambridge: Cambridge University Press.

Williams, Glyn. 1992. *Sociolinguistics. A Sociological Critique*. London/New York: Routledge.

Williams, Joseph M. 1992. ''O! When Degree is Shak'd': Sixteenth-century anticipations of some modern attitudes toward usage'. In: Tim William Machan and Charles Scott (eds.), *English in Its Social Contexts. Essays in Historical Sociolinguistics*. Oxford: Oxford University Press, 69-101.

Wodak, Ruth and Gertraud Benke. 1997. 'Gender as a sociolinguistic variable: New perspectives on variation studies'. In: Florian Coulmas (ed.), *The Handbook of Sociolinguistics*. Oxford: Blackwell, 127-50.

Yinger, John Milton. 1960. 'Contraculture and subculture'. *American Sociological Review* 25:5: 625-35.

Alexander Onysko

Māori English on the Background of Cultural and Linguistic Contact in Aotearoa – New Zealand

1. Introduction

New Zealand or Aotearoa ('the long white cloud') has been home to a particular situation of contact between two peoples ever since James Cook discovered the islands in the South Pacific and encountered the indigenous Māori population. Contact between the Polynesian people and the mainly British settlers has generated a history of conflict moulding the socio-cultural and linguistic landscape of what has become the nation of New Zealand. In literature, indigenous writers such as Witi Ihimaera and Patricia Grace have created acclaimed portrayals of Māori life in postcolonial New Zealand. Their stories reflect a relation between the indigenous language Te Reo Māori and English, which exemplifies Hans Peter Nelde's observation (1997) that language contact is tantamount to language conflict. Thus, in sociolinguistic terms, the evolving relation of linguistic contact and conflict has given rise to diverse instantiations of influence between the Māori language and English up until today. It is the intention of this paper to describe the different major scenarios of language contact and focus on the notion of Māori English, which plays a controversial role in this discussion. In particular, the article aims to reframe the understanding of the term from a purely descriptive label for a socio- and ethnolect to a variety of English spoken in New Zealand that reverberates a diverse and unique experience and world view representative of the bicultural and bilingual reality of parts of the Māori people today. As such, Māori English turns into a variety that bears a trace of Maoriness, enriching the use and expressivity of English in New Zealand.

2. A brief history of contact and conflict in the land of the long white cloud (Aotearoa)

Frequently, language contact is the result of contact between people and their ways in negotiating meaning in conversation when they do not know or only partially know each other's languages. Such a situation characterizes the first contacts between the European explorers and the Māori people in New Zealand. Before the arrival of the Europeans, the Māori tribes had already lived on the island for centuries developing their culture and language.[1] On his first voyage to New Zealand in 1769, James Cook claimed the land for the British Empire, and, from the beginning of the nineteenth century, English settlers started to arrive, at first in small numbers from Australia. From the second half of the nineteenth century, however, large numbers of English speaking settlers headed to New Zealand from Great Britain.

The early contact between speakers of English and Māori people was facilitated by the work of missionaries, who set out to document the Māori language and to establish a written form (e.g. Kendall 1815, 1820). This time of early contact was also characterized by mostly peaceful co-existence as English speakers were few and far between. However, without jurisdiction in place, some settlers took advantage of the situation and land speculations and other lawless activities started to threaten the relations between the indigenous people and the newcomers. In 1840, the British crown felt the need to take control of the situation and sent a representative, Captain Hobson, to New Zealand to negotiate a treaty with the Māori people in order to establish British sovereignty over the territory (Hay, Maclagan, and Gordon 1988). The result of these negotiations was the Treaty of Waitangi between representatives of the British Crown and a fair number of Māori chiefs in 1840.

The Treaty of Waitangi turned out to be a highly controversial document which has continued to influence the relations between Māori and Pākehā (a Māori term for people of non-Māori descent) up until today. Initial controversy over the treaty arose as Māori felt cheated by the English when parts of their land fell into the possession of English settlers and government institutions after the signing of the treaty. As Fenton and Moon (2002) point out, serious misunderstandings and grievances over the treaty arose because its Māori translation was prepared in a hasty manner. Furthermore, the translator in charge, the Reverend Henry Williams, strongly believed in the importance of convincing the Māori chiefs to sign the document. In the English original, the Treaty of Waitangi basically asked the indigenous people to cede their sovereignty to the Queen of England, who in return granted them the rights of citizens of the British Empire. However, among other omissions and shortcomings, the concept of 'sovereignty' was mistranslated by Williams, who chose the term *kawanatanga* (a loan of English 'government')

---

1   The arrival of the first Polynesian settlers in New Zealand is loosely dated around 1000 AD (cf. contributions in Sutton 1994). According to Māori wisdom, the original settlers arrived on separate *waka* ('canoes') making landfall on different parts of New Zealand.

instead of *rangatiratanga* and *mana* as proper translation equivalents (Fenton and Moon 2002: 34-5). Thus, Māori leaders at the time could not have been aware of the full consequences when signing the treaty and were led to believe

> that they were agreeing to and signing a concession of limited power only, a viewpoint clearly expressed by the comment on events by the Kaitaia chief Napera Panakareao: "the shadow of the land goes to Queen Victoria but the substance remains with us" (quoted in Adams 1977: 235). (Fenton and Moon 2002: 34)

After the treaty was in place, numbers of immigrants to New Zealand increased drastically, which aggravated the strife of Māori people for self-determination and land rights, culminating in a series of military campaigns and battles in the 1860s known as the New Zealand Wars (cf. Belich 1987). At that time, military defeat was not the only threat to the Māori people as the rising number of immigrants also introduced sicknesses that caused the demise of many Māori. As a consequence, the Māori population had shrunk to about half of its size at the end of the nineteenth century, reaching its lowest number of 42,113 in the census held in 1896 (M. King 1981: 280). Throughout the twentieth century, the concerns of Māori people remained largely unheard, and they became marginalized in mainstream English speaking New Zealand despite some representation in the New Zealand parliament and the work of inspiring leaders such as Sir Apirana Ngata (1874-1950). The Māori language had no status in the young nation of New Zealand, and education was carried out in English only. Nevertheless, Māori people remained adamant to claim back land that was confiscated or unlawfully taken from them in the aftermath of the signing of the Treaty of Waitangi. Successful involvement of Māori as part of New Zealand troops in World War I and World War II won official recognition in New Zealand's public and political spheres. In addition, the Māori King movement (*kingitanga Māori*), most notably under the leadership of the late Māori Queen, Dame Te Atairangikaahu (1937-2006) provided strong support for the revival of Māori arts and culture. In 1975, Māori activism eventually proved successful on a national level when a land march attracting several thousand supporters ended at the New Zealand Parliament in Wellington with the engaged participants calling for recognition of the Treaty of Waitangi and investigation into their land rights. As a result, the Waitangi Tribunal was set up in the same year, providing a legal base for Māori to claim back unlawfully taken possessions. This event marked the beginning of a cultural renaissance for Māori people in New Zealand which continues up to the present (cf. Belich 2001). Milestones of this renaissance are the founding of immersion pre-schools (*kōhanga reo*) as well as immersion and bilingual schools to revitalize the Māori language. Legal support for the Māori language was granted in the

Māori Language Act of 1987, which made Māori an official language of New Zealand.[2] As a consequence, the New Zealand government has assumed responsibility in fostering the Māori language including such measures as setting up a Māori Language Commission, providing public funding for Māori educational institutions, and granting airspace for Māori radio and TV. Furthermore, some land claims have been settled since the inception of the Waitangi Tribunal and several others are currently investigated.

Even though this brief depiction of some important events in the history of Māori and Pākehā relations provides a simplified account of a complex picture, it outlines a general frame of contact and conflict between the indigenous population and the mainly English speaking settlers. In fact, this socio-historical situation forms a baseline for understanding the effects of contact on language change and development in both Māori and English as outlined in the next section.

3. Scenarios of contact between Te Reo Māori and English

The historical events of contact between Māori and Pākehā left their marks on both the Māori language and English. As well-documented in a number of studies on language contact (cf. Thomason 2001: 21-5), social factors are the most relevant for determining the extent to which one language can become influenced by another one. In situations where speakers of one language are in a dominant position over speakers of another language, with dominance being manifested as socio-economic, military, and political supremacy, this social dominance frequently leads to a strong impact on the language of the oppressed group. Even though the actual reasons for such dominance can be manifold and the attitude of speakers to their own language use remains as the most decisive factor for the extent of language contact, such a situation of unequal power between speakers and languages in contact characterizes a great number of contexts where a regional or heritage language struggles for survival in the face of a majority language and culture.

In his work, Van Coetsem has incorporated the notion of dominance to describe two types of asymmetrical scenarios of transmission in language contact: SL (source language) agentivity or imposition and RL (recipient language) agentivity or borrowing (2000: 35). A scenario of imposition occurs when the source language is dominant over the recipient language. These cases of contact are

---

2   Today, Māori and New Zealand Sign Language are, *de jure*, the only official languages of New Zealand while the majority language English remains as a *de facto* official language in New Zealand (Ray Harlow, p.c.).

characterized by strong influences of the SL on the RL including not only heavy lexical borrowing (Thomason 2001: 71) but also contact-induced changes in the grammar or phonology of a language, which are usually more resistant to contact influences. On the other hand, RL agentivity describes a situation in which the recipient language is dominant over the source language of transmission. This is labeled as borrowing in Van Coetsem's model. While not all scholars working in the field of language contact would unanimously agree with Van Coetsem's use of the term borrowing, which is in fact often applied as a general cover term for a range of contact-induced phenomena on all levels of language (cf. Sakel 2007 and Matras and Sakel's 2008 use of matter and pattern loans), one can, in line with Thomason's borrowing scale from "casual contact" to "intense contact" (2001: 70-1), safely interpret RL agentivity as an example of peripheral lexical borrowing (i.e. loanwords that do not enter the core vocabulary of a language). This role is played, for example, by English as a global language and the lexical influence it exerts on many stable languages today (cf. Görlach 2002 for an overview of English lexical influence on different European languages).

In the context of contact between English and Māori, Van Coetsem's model fits well to describe the different effects that English and Māori have brought to bear on each other. In the early phase of contact, Māori did not undergo large changes as contact with the first settlers only happened on a small scale and Māori remained the dominant culture in Aotearoa. This is also supported by the fact that no pidgin Māori/English developed during that time of contact (Clark 1990). The role of the missionaries in devising a written form of Māori and in creating the first translations of parts of the Bible into Māori (first published in 1827) could have potentially led to some incursion of English influence into the newly coined written standard of Māori. Some evidence for English loans in Māori clerical texts can be found in Duval's thesis (1995), which includes about 2500 distinct loans and was compiled as a preliminary version of a Māori loanword dictionary based on written documents, mostly word lists and clerical texts in Māori between 1815 and 1899 (cf. Duval and Kuiper 2001). Loanwords in this compendium exemplify not only Christian terminology, such as *bihopa* (E. 'bishop'), *apotoro* (E. 'apostle'), *ahere* (E. 'angel'), *Kerito* (E. 'Christ'), but also prove that the Māori language expanded its lexicon with various types of terms referring to new concepts imported from English culture as in *koti* (E. 'coat'), *pereti* (E. 'plate'), *kau* (E. 'cow'), and *tepu* (E. 'table') to name just a few. Despite that, as Duval and Kuiper (2001: 254) point out, the question remains of how widespread such borrowings were in the Māori community as printing was almost exclusively under the authority of Pākehā immigrants, who acquired Māori as a second language and might have shown bilingual transfer effects in their use of Māori. This discussion thus highlights that the early contact between the *Tangata Whenua* ('the people of the land') and the English speaking settlers up until the second half of the nineteenth century was characterized by a language contact scenario of RL agentivity from the perspective of the recipient language Māori.

A similar situation of contact also characterizes the effects that Māori, in turn, had on the English language during that period. Thus, already Captain Cook's writings contained some Māori words that became borrowings in English such as *pa* ('fortification'), *kumara* ('sweet potato'), and *haka* ('ritual posture chant') (Deverson 1991). Throughout the nineteenth century, further borrowings from Māori were adopted in English, mostly place names and designations of native flora and fauna (e.g. *kauri, totara, kowhai,* and *pohutukawa* as types of trees and *kiwi, tui, weka,* and *kakapo* as types of birds). Many of these borrowings bear specific local references, and they have led to an extension of the New Zealand English lexicon without any more profound contact-induced changes. Thus, English, just like Māori, functioned as a dominant recipient language as described in the case of RL agentivity.

In fact, right from the beginning of colonization, the influence of Māori on New Zealand English has remained at the same level of lexical borrowing with some differences in the amount of intake from Māori. Thus, for the most part of the twentieth century, the rate of borrowing slowed down due to the general marginalization of Māori people and culture in New Zealand society. Only with the advent of the Māori Renaissance at the end of the 1970s, did Māori gain a stronger foothold in the dominant culture and more loans relating to specific Māori cultural concepts started being used again in English. The Māori Renaissance also coincides with the development of New Zealand English into an endonormative variety (cf. Schneider 2007: 131), i.e. as a variety of English that is developing according to its own norms. Indeed, the Māori element in English has assumed the role of a unique lexical marker of New Zealand English and, as such, also as a part of mainstream New Zealand identity as highlighted for the first time by Deverson (1991: 18-19) and repeatedly emphasized in more recent studies on Māori loanwords (e.g. Kennedy 2001; Macalister 2007; Degani 2010).

In general, the lexical influence of Māori on New Zealand English has triggered a substantial amount of research. In *A Dictionary of Maori Words in New Zealand English*, Macalister (2005) gathers 981 Māori terms that occur as loanwords in New Zealand English. However, when investigating the knowledge of Māori loans, Macalister (2008: 75) estimates that the average New Zealander knows the meaning of about 70-80 common noun loans. This is a further indication of the peripheral lexical impact of Māori on English and that the nature of the contact scenario is one of RL agentivity. As far as the frequency of occurrence of Māori loans in New Zealand English is concerned, there is currently no unanimous trend, but results depend on the type of register and genre. The majority of research on Māori loans is based on written language such as newspapers (Davies and Maclagan 2006; Calude and James 2011), school journals and parliamentary debates (Macalister 2006), and children's picture books (Daly 2007). As an exception, De Bres (2006) investigates TV newscasts, and a few researchers work with a mixture of spoken and written data in the Wellington Corpora (Kennedy 2001; Kennedy and Yamazaki 2000) as well as in the Wellington Spoken Corpus and in a recent newspaper corpus (Onysko and Calude 2013). Among these studies, Macalister (2006: 11) notes a slight increase in the use of Māori borrowings from 3.29 loans per 1000 words in 1850 to 8.8 in 2000. However, the short term diachronic comparison of spoken language in De Bres (2006) and of a selection of major New Zealand newspapers in Davies and Maclagan (2006) do not show a significant increase over the last few decades. A close analysis of the three well-known Māori loans of *Maori*, *Kiwi*, and *Pakeha* does not yield a common trend either; instead, it highlights the fact that the frequency of use for these individual loans developed unevenly from 1995 to 2011 (Onysko and Calude 2013). On the other hand, the most frequent Māori loans function as productive agents of word formation in New Zealand English as noticeable in a fair number of hybrid compounds in recent issues of a popular New Zealand newspaper (Degani and Onysko 2010). Tying together these results from different studies on the impact of Māori loans on New Zealand English, it seems safe to assume that contact influence from Māori to English will remain an example of stable RL agentivity in the foreseeable future if no remarkable socio-political and attitudinal change will occur in New Zealand (such as efforts to achieve bilingualism in Māori and English in New Zealand society at large).

Turning the attention back to Māori as a recipient language, a clear change of the contact scenario has occurred from RL agentivity until mid-nineteenth century to SL agentivity or imposition. The military conflicts over land between Māori and Pākehā which culminated in the 1860s increased Pākehā resentment against the indigenous people in the latter half of the nineteenth century and measures of assimilation became more strongly favoured by the colonial government. An important decision in this regard was the Native Schools Act of 1867 (lasting until 1969, cf. Calman 2012), which led to the establishment of English medium schools in rural areas where most of the Māori still lived at that time. The schools had a strict policy of only allowing English and with the beginning of compulsory education in 1894, Māori children were exclusively educated in English in this type of schools. In order to make a living in Pākehā dominated New Zealand, a good mastery of the English language and ability to adapt to Pākehā culture became a necessity for Māori people. Due to that, many parents stopped passing the language on to their children creating a gap in the intergenerational transmission of Māori (cf. Chrisp 2005; Harlow 2007: 2). This was a major reason why Te Reo Māori became a severely endangered language in the twentieth century.

The assimilatory attitude of the dominant Pākehā culture towards a Māori minority from the end of the nineteenth century onwards translates into a scenario of imposition (SL agentivity) in sociolinguistic terms. As predicted by Van Coetsem's model of language contact, dominance of English not only led to language shift among large parts of the Māori people, but it also caused more profound contact-induced changes in the language.[3] On the level of phonology, Harlow et al. (2009) show that the front vowels in Māori have raised in parallel to New Zealand English front vowels and that there is an increase in the aspiration of plosives in Māori following the English model (2009: 148-9). Changes in the grammar of the language have been mentioned in Harlow (2001: 185, 212). In young speakers of Māori, certain changes from pronominal coordination to the use of conjunctions (following the English model) have been noted as well as structural calques leading to a direct transfer of English sentence structure, word order, and use of prepositions in Māori. King and Syddall (2011) observe that Māori phraseology has undergone change due to contact with English, especially by a process of calquing English phrases in Māori. Furthermore, a study by Degani (2012) investigates the impact of lexical borrowing from English into the core vocabulary of Māori. If a language shows lexical influence from another language among its most frequently used terms, this can be considered as an indication of strong contact influence (cf. Thomason 2001: 70-1). Looking at the 1000 most frequent words in the Māori Broadcasting Corpus (Boyce 2006), Degani finds about 10% of English loanwords in the data (2012: 18).

Despite the imposition of English on Māori, the most recent history of contact has experienced a strengthening of the indigenous language. As mentioned at the end of the previous section, the Māori language has gained official recognition in New Zealand and measures of language revitalization have been up and running since the early eighties, most notably Māori immersion kindergartens, Māori medium schools, bilingual schools, and Māori academic institutions. It is a major aim of Māori education to promote skills in the Māori language, culture, arts and traditional knowledge. As a result, there are now new generations of children growing up with Māori as a first language and achieving a high degree

---

3   Eliasson (1990) shows that codeswitching can also occur among bilingual speakers of Māori and English.

of bilingualism from an early age on. These young people represent a generation of hope for the well-being of *Māoritanga* ('Māori culture, practices, and beliefs') including the successful maintenance of the language. At this point, it is still difficult to assess whether these measures will have the necessary knock-on effect so that the Māori language will turn into a fully functional everyday community language that, ideally, would be widely heard across New Zealand. Thus far, there are indications that measures of language revitalization have been able to slow down the overall loss of speakers as survey data by Te Puni Kokiri for 2001 and 2006 and New Zealand Census data for the same years show (cf. W. Bauer 2008 for a critical assessment of survey methodologies and census results). Among various estimates given in the literature, the result from the New Zealand census in 2006 (as reported in W. Bauer 2008) is generally taken as a benchmark for the current spread of the Māori language.[4] According to that, about 23% of the Māori population is able to hold a conversation in Māori with reasonable fluency when averaging across all age bands and regional differences (W. Bauer 2008: 56). This underlines the still critical state of the language.

On the background of these scenarios of language contact which show more profound changes of Māori on the one hand, and some lexical influence in general New Zealand English on the other hand, the interplay of Māori and English is also discernible in the variety called Māori English in New Zealand today. As described in the original definition by Benton (1966; see section 4 below), Māori English or the English spoken by Māori people has a particular significance in the landscape of language contact in New Zealand. It can serve as an instrument of expressing Māori cultural conceptualizations in English, and, thus, it could form a bridge between the two cultures promoting mutual understanding of Pākehā and Māori world views.

4. Māori English: ethnolect, sociolect, and contact variety?

During his research into the performance of Māori school children in English medium schools, Benton described a separate variety of Māori English as "a set of subdialects, originating in the acquisition of English by earlier generations of Maori speakers and involving semantic, lexical and grammatical features 'transferred' from Maori and standardized in adult speech" (1966: 79). This definition emphasizes the fact that the origin of Māori English lies in a contact scenario of second language acquisition during which transfer features of a learner's first

---

4   The results of the latest New Zealand census are expected at the end of the year 2013. These results will provide further insights into the state of the Māori language.

language can show up in the second language. However, as stated in Benton's definition, it is the process of standardization that is important for the creation of Māori English, i.e. the process by which certain transfer features become fixed as they get replicated across a community of speakers without the original transfer effect being remotivated for each individual speaker. In this way, Māori English turned into the code of a speaker community, and debates over the status of the variety have brought arguments in favour of considering Māori English a sociolect on the one hand, and an ethnolect on the other. L. Bauer describes Māori English as a "social dialect of New Zealand English, one of whose functions is to indicate solidarity with Maoris and/or their aspirations" (1994: 413). His description is motivated by the observations that, first of all, Māori English is not exclusively used by Māori people and that, secondly, not all Māori people use this variety (1994: 413). In contrast to Bauer's implicit stance that an ethnolect would have to be spoken uniformly by all members of an ethnicity and not by any outsiders, research on the variety of Māori English concedes to the flexible nature of lan-guage use in that speakers can shift their ways of speaking according to speech context, leading to a continuum of Māori English which is more or less close to general New Zealand English. Thus, already Richards (1970) observed that Māori English can be employed with a high degree of variability, distinguishing two types of the variety in terms of their closeness to Standard New Zealand English, and a similar distinction has been put forward in more recent work by Holmes (2005).[5]

The definition of a variety called Māori English has also been complicated by the fact that, as Bell notes, "differences between varieties tend to be relative rather than absolute. Few if any features are likely to be unique to Maori English" (2000: 222). In fact, many of the phonological, morphosyntactic and discourse features identified as characterizing to some extent the use of English by Māori people are relative markers, which can acquire a degree of indexicality by their interplay and their overall rate of occurrence in discourse. On the phonological level, several studies have described the devoicing of final /z/ (Holmes 1996; Maclagan, King, and Jones 2003), the use of unaspirated /t/ (Holmes 1997; Bell 2000), a less cen-tralized kit vowel (Bell 2000; Warren and Bauer 2004), the fronting of back vowels (Bell 2000), and a more syllable-timed rhythm (Holmes and Ainsworth 1996; Warren 1998; Szakay 2008). Among these characteristics, some traces of contact origin from Māori can be found for unaspirated /t/, mirroring the way the dental

---

5   In the larger context of World Englishes, it is frequently the case that varieties can show internal variation between forms more removed from a standard variety, i.e. basilectal forms, to instantiations that are closer to a standard variety, i.e. acrolectal forms, (cf., e.g., Kortmann et al. 2004).

plosive is articulated in Māori, for the lack of centralization in line with vowel quality in Māori, and, most notably, for a syllable-timed rhythm which is a characteristic prosodic feature of Māori in contrast to the nature of English as a more stress-timed language. As a mixture of phonological and lexical traits, pragmatic characteristics of the variety include high rising terminals (Allan 1990; Britain 1992; Szakay 2008), the tag *eh* (Meyerhoff 1994; Stubbe 1999), addressee-oriented expressions (e.g. *you know*; Stubbe 1999; Bell 2000), minimal feedback (Stubbe 1998), and the varied use of quotatives (e.g. *like, say, go*; D'Arcy 2010), while differences in narrative structure (Holmes 1998) and the use of humour (Holmes 2005; De Bres et al. 2010) have also been mentioned. From these pragmatic features, only the use of minimal feedback in conversation can be straightforwardly related to Māori discourse conventions of listening silently and without giving much verbal and non-verbal back-channelling cues in formal conversational contexts whereas the opposite is generally the case in English. To complete the picture of linguistic characteristics attributed to Māori English in the literature thus far, J. King (1995), among others, notes that the English used by Māori people can show a higher incidence of Māori terms than present in general New Zealand English. This is probably also a result of the fact that Māori people tend to speak more often about their own concerns relating to Māori culture, which is expressed in Māori concepts and terms.

Despite L. Bauer's assertion that the use of features characteristic of Māori English is rather dependent on social factors than ethnicity, studies by J. King (1999) and D'Arcy (2010) highlight the important function of the variety as a marker of ethnic and cultural group identity. In an insightful study based on interviews with Māori students, J. King (1999: 26-30) shows that the key motivation for using the variety is the expression of Māori cultural identity through the conversational enactment of common values such as building relations and sharing concerns (*whakawhanaungatanga*), supporting each other (*awhi*), and generous care for each other (*manaakitanga*). To this, D'Arcy (2010) adds empirical evidence on differences in the use of quotatives (e.g. *be like, go, say*) between Pākehā and Māori New Zealanders. For her, these differences signal the use of a diverse ethnolinguistic repertoire, which, according to Benor (2010: 160) is defined as a "fluid set of resources that members of an ethnic group may use variably to index their ethnic identities". As applied in D'Arcy's study (2010), Benor's notion of an ethnolinguistic repertoire is particularly adequate for capturing the essential function of Māori English since it focuses on individual and contextually based acts of identity construction thus allowing for individual and intra-group variation as well as out-group use of the variety. Furthermore, the notion of ethnolinguistic repertoire avoids the pitfall of trying to delineate ethnicities and ethnolects as discrete categories.

Summing up findings in research on Māori English thus far, it can be said that some of its features have originated from language contact in the context of bilingual language acquisition while there is also some overlap with characteristics of New Zealand English in general. A major advance in the discussions on whether Māori English is a sociolect or an ethnolect has been made by characterizing the variety as an ethnolinguistic repertoire. This emphasizes that the major function of Māori English is signalling in-group identity and empathy. As a consequence, any social descriptors are merely symptomatic for the historical development of New Zealand society and are not constitutive to the use of the variety.

From a current perspective, research on Māori English has not yet explored the conceptual level of how Maoriness in terms of cultural values and beliefs can be expressed through the medium of English. However, the expression of concepts pertaining to a Māori view of the world could add important insights into the nature of Māori English as an ethnolinguistic repertoire. In addition, there is another aspect that has so far largely escaped the attention of research. This is the fact that, due to language revitalization, young generations of bilingual and bicultural speakers of Māori and English grow up in New Zealand today. Their bilingual experience might be a source of new contact features resulting in a dynamic construction of the variety and potentially inspiring change in Māori English. The last section of the paper will offer a first approach to addressing these issues and expand the understanding of Māori English as an ethnolinguistic repertoire.

5. Focusing on the expression of Maoriness in Māori English

In order to capture whether Māori English can serve as a vehicle for communicating culturally specific concepts, a conceptual-semantic analysis of the variety is necessary. The importance of such an investigation has already been mentioned by Benton:

> Thus, although a lot of searching has been done for Maori English, no consistent pattern has been found [...]. It may be however, that the trees have escaped notice – let alone the forest – because the woodsmen have been too preoccupied with examining the leaves. The metaphorical and analogical mode of thought and expression characteristic of the skilled speaker of Maori may well survive where the language itself has disappeared. It is this approach to language, together with a partly autonomous metaphorical system at the level of everyday speech, rather than any detail of grammar or vocabulary, which may underlie [...] 'Maori English'. (1985: 117-18)

Despite Benton's call for exploring how concepts are expressed in Māori English, virtually no research until today has addressed this issue. In his description, Benton puts special emphasis on the fact that Māori ways of conceptualizing frequently entail the use of metaphoric language. This observation can be taken as a hypothesis for an analysis of Māori English in that the variety would be strongly characterized by the culturally-specific use of metaphors when compared to general New Zealand English. Furthermore, the assumption can be made that parts of the metaphorical language will be specifically connected with the expression of Māori cultural concepts and the Māori world view, i.e. they will contribute to the expression of Maoriness through the use of English.

In research on World Englishes, the analysis of cultural conceptualizations and metaphors is a fairly recent development. Thus far, Wolf and Polzenhagen's (2009) analysis of selected English varieties in Africa offers an application of conceptual metaphor theory and cultural models. In a series of studies, Sharifian (2006, 2010, 2011) promotes the notion of cultural conceptualization as "an integral aspect of a cultural group's collective cognition, and language acts as a memory bank for storing and communicating this group-level cognition" (2010: 3368). Taking the example of Australia, Sharifian (2006, 2010) shows that Aboriginal cultural concepts can surface in the English used by Aborigines leading to serious misunderstandings by Anglophone speakers of Australian English due to their unfamiliarity with Aboriginal culture and ways of thinking.

In the context of New Zealand, Sharifian's notion of cultural conceptualization appears as similarly relevant since traditional Māori values and their world view are very different from New Zealand European culture. Thus, it is reasonable to expect that the use of English by Māori, particularly by those that have grown up as bicultural and bilingual speakers, can show instances of Māori cultural conceptualizations. If that is the case, it will be necessary to partially reframe the understanding of Māori English as an ethnolinguistic repertoire, including the unique function of this variety of English to express Maoriness in the sense of specific cultural concepts pertaining to the Māori world. Thus, the following working definition of the variety of Māori English can be postulated:

Māori English is an ethnolinguistic repertoire which signals a speaker's identification or sympathy with Māori people and Te Ao Māori ('the Māori world') and which can serve as a vehicle to express Maoriness through the medium of the English language.

Based on this premise, a colleague of mine, Marta Degani from the University of Verona, and I initiated an investigation of Māori English during a one-year research stay as visiting scholars at the *Te Pua Wānanga ki te Ao (The School of Māori and Pacific Development)* at the University of Waikato, New Zealand.[6]

---

6   We are greatly indebted and thankful to the following people at the School of Māori and Pacific Development (SMPD) as well as in the Linguistics Programme at the University

While a detailed description of the research project can be found in Onysko and Degani (2012), a quick overview of the empirical data collection is provided below before an analysis of three excerpts from the data illustrates the occurrence of cultural conceptualizations in Māori English as spoken by Māori bilingual people.

In order to investigate the expression of cultural conceptualizations and the use of figurative language dependent on the factors of Māori ethnicity and bilingualism, Māori bilingual speakers of Māori and English made up the main target group of participants in the study. As control groups, we also recruited ethnically Māori monolingual speakers of English, Pākehā monolingual speakers of English, and non-Māori bilingual speakers of English and another language. Following approval of the project by the ethics commission of the School of Māori and Pacific Development, we were able to invite participants that would fit in these groups to contribute to our collection of data. All volunteer participants were studying at the University of Waikato at the time of data collection, which lasted from January 2011 to August 2011. In total 142 people participated; their mean age is 26 within a range from 17 to 69 (19 participants are 40 years and older). University students are not a representative sample for society at large, but, for the purposes of this study, focusing on this group facilitates comparisons between Māori and Pākehā New Zealanders (cf. Onysko and Degani 2012 for more details on methodology and participant groups). For testing the occurrence of cultural conceptualizations and the use of figurative language, we settled on a narrative task which was designed to have the same set of stimuli while allowing individually different narrations. In line with a tradition of research using photographs as narrative stimuli (cf. Harper 2002; Harrison 2002; Ketelle 2010), we gave our participants a set of three images showing typical New Zealand landscapes devoid of any people or other animate beings. The participants were told to select one of the landscape shots featuring a beach, a gravel road, and a lake and then take their selected picture as a starting point to recount a story. The notion of story was applied loosely to any type of event or association that came to mind in this particular situation. The stories were audio recorded and had an average length between ten and twenty minutes. First transcriptions of the data indicate a possible average of about 2500 to 3000 words per recording. The recorded narrations are of a hybrid type: usually, a monologic opening

---

of Waikato: Ray Harlow, Linda Smith, Tom Roa, Keely Smith, Haupai Puke, Sophie Nock, Hineitimoana Greensill, Raukura Roa, and Donna Campbell (all at SMPD), as well as Julie Barbour, James McLellan, and Daryl MacDonald (in the Linguistics Programme) and all participants in the study.

sequence of the participant is followed by a co-constructed narration between the interviewers and the participant. This comes close to the notion of 'small stories' in narrative research, which can help to create an authentic narrative context in a research environment (cf. Bamberg and Georgakopoulou 2008; Georgakopoulou 2007).

The transcription of the data and the analysis is still ongoing. This is why the three excerpts shown below have been selected to provide positive evidence that the English used by Māori people can express culturally specific concepts. While these examples thus support the observation that the expression of Maoriness is an essential feature of Māori English, the bigger picture about the differences in the use of English between Māori and non-Māori interlocutors in the narrative task and about the possible influence of bi- or monolingualism is still awaiting more extensive comparative analysis, also in terms of figurative language use. The first excerpt is taken from the speech of a Māori bilingual participant (female, age 23) prompted by the beach picture:

Excerpt 1
[…] like and it's still *tapu* – so you are not allowed to go there, and they've got a few of these spots along their beaches and then they have *rahui* as well so that you don't, ahm, take all the fish or like take all the seafood, so you can't go into certain areas, so that like all the fish and seafood kind of grows back or, whatever yeah and apparently when her father was younger they just didn't go to the beach 'cause of things like that
[transcription mark-up removed, emphasis by author]

In this passage, Ahurewa (pseudonym) talks about the concept of *tapu* and *rahui*, which are of central relevance to Māori culture. She explains both of these notions that, in this case, apply to a beach. The meaning of *tapu* is rendered as a prohibition, i.e. a person is not allowed to go to a specific place or to perform a certain action. Closely related to that is the notion of *rahui*, which Ahurewa describes in this passage as a restriction on fishing in order to preserve the natural balance and allow the regeneration of seafood and fish. In Māori culture this type of *rahui* is frequently employed for purposes of conserving the environment and its natural resources, mostly in the form of food supplies (Mead 2003: 197). In this sense, a conservation *rahui* shows the close relation of the Māori people to their environment and to their awareness about the importance of sustainable co-existence of people and natural resources. In her association to the picture of a beach, these Māori concepts play an important role for Ahurewa, and they are inextricably encoded in their Māori forms. As such, the Māori terms emerge as culturally bound insertions in the English narration. In terms of the storyline, *tapu* and *rahui* are mentioned as the main reason that some members of the older generation did not go to the beach very often.

The next excerpt from the speech of a different Māori bilingual participant (female, age 30) is an example of Māori ancestral knowledge. The narration was stimulated by the picture of the gravel road:

Excerpt 2

[…] 'cause around here we've got *Maungatautari* and she's a female according to our legends and then we've got *Maunga Pirongia* who is a male, ahm, and *Maungatautari* was known as, ahm, a mountain that looks after her people, so that was – it was a bountiful place, heaps of food, the tracks, the landscape was friendly whereas *Maunga Pirongia* and I'm –'cause I'm from both these *maungas*, ahm, he's a male not a good, ahm, provider, ahm, and people have died on that mountain 'cause it's it's quite treacherous terrain, so we we don't have *maraes* on the mou- on that mountain 'cause it's not it's not safe, so that – my my dad is from *Pirongia* and my mum is from *Maungatautari*, yeah and they yeah they are not – well it's central King Country, mmh…

[transcription mark-up removed, emphasis by author]

The mountains in the background of the gravel road provided a stimulus for Marata (pseudonym) to talk about her homestead on the mountains (*maunga*) referred to as *Maungatautari* and *Maunga Pirongia*. Drawing on Māori wisdom, Marata describes the female and male characters of the mountains and their related attributes as, on the one hand, a safe place and a provider for the people (*Maungatautari*) and, on the other hand, a dangerous and treacherous terrain (*Maunga Pirongia*). The female and male characteristics are reflected in her parents who come from the respective places. Marata also mentions a further central concept of Māori culture, the *marae*, which is the center of Māori cultural life for every subtribe (*hapu*) who owns and runs the *marae* (loosely translated as 'ceremonial meeting grounds'). Importantly, the *marae* offers a place for Māori people to connect to their ancestors, to feel at home, and to have the right to participate in discussions as well as the obligation to help with work on the *marae*. As described in Mead (2003: 96), these aspects of the *marae* contribute to a sense of identity. Marata's mention of the *marae* is thus resonating with her associations about her ancestral land.

Going beyond what Marata says in her narration, her words are a testimony of the Māori world view, which bestows its natural surroundings with a *mauri* (loosely and incompletely translated as 'life force'). In this way, the natural surroundings can become metaphorically animated as it is also expressed in Māori wisdom on the creation of life on earth, which only became possible by the physical separation of earth mother (*Papa-tū-ā-nuku*) and sky father (*Rangi-nui*). The animated view of nature and all life on earth stands in strong contrast to a Western hierarchical perspective of humans dominating life on earth as encapsulated in a Great Chain of Being Metaphor (cf. Lakoff and Turner 1989: 166-213). In light of this, it is the Māori perspective which gives way to a sustainable and respectful relation to nature.

Finally, the third excerpt connects to the concept of the *marae* mentioned before and touches upon a specific event traditionally held there. The narration is given by yet another Māori bilingual participant (female, age 26), who talks about the picture of the gravel road:

Excerpt 3
Yeah, yeah ah, it's it's it's probably my main *marae* there and that's where all the *tangihanga*, oh you know like when we go back home if it's immediate family, so I've lost quite a few people – you know immediate first cousins and aunties and uncles and stuff, quite a few and so that's our main our main *marae* that we go to and yeah that really just brings it all back and, ahm, reminds me of *tikanga*, ahm although I didn't get the *reo* growing up as much as I wanted to…
[transcription mark-up removed, emphasis by author]

In her narration, Airini (pseudonym) recollects going back home to her *marae* for participating in a *tangihanga*, which is a traditional Māori funeral ceremony. Mourning the people who have passed on is a significant activity, and a *tangihanga* can last for several days depending on the status of the deceased and in order to accommodate people who have to travel from far away to the home grounds of the deceased. Airini remembers participating in such events for members of her own extended family. Moreover, thinking of being at the *marae* also brings back memories to traditional Māori *tikanga* (Māori 'protocols and ways of doing things') held there and to the fact that these are inextricably related to the Māori language (*reo*), which she would have liked to get exposed to more as she was growing up.

As in the previous passages taken from the narrations of Māori bilingual speakers of Māori and English, Airini connects experiences from Māori cultural life with the picture prompts. Being very different from New Zealand European ways of life, the Māori cultural key concepts (e.g. *marae, tangihanga, tikanga, rahui,* and *tapu,* as well as proper names) are expressed in their Māori form, and they function as central notions around which the English narration is built. This indicates that the selected speakers associate to the pictures from a Māori cultural frame, which is textually marked by Māori cultural designations and which, for the narration at large, can bear implications to underlying values of a Māori world view such as the special relation to the land in terms of ancestry and sustainable living. These examples are thus a clear indication that the expression of Maoriness can be an important factor of the use of English by Māori bilingual and bicultural people and further research on the variety of Māori English will have to make a more comprehensive and comparative account of that.

6. Conclusion

This article has been written with the aim in mind to provide a succinct description of the major language contact scenarios that have accompanied the historical relations between the indigenous people of Aotearoa and the English settlers from first contact to the present day. Among the different instantiations of mutual influence, a particular focus was laid on the variety of Māori English since it has remained a controversial and evolving notion in linguistic research. As a background to language contact between Te Reo Māori and English, Van Coetsem's model of imposition (SL agentivity) vs. borrowing (RL agentivity) provides a fitting frame for mapping the peripheral influence of lexical borrowing that Māori had on the English tongue throughout their history of contact. On the other hand, a situation of initial borrowing of English into Māori has changed into a scenario of imposition in line with the historical events in the aftermath of the signing of the Treaty of Waitangi. Oppression of the Māori people and assimilation to Pākehā dominated cultural and political life in New Zealand have led to a rapid loss of the Māori language, to the point of threatening its survival. Only since the 1970s and 1980s when obligations towards the Māori people formalized in the Treaty of Waitangi were given legal power, has the Māori language received official government support and measures of language revitalization have been implemented. Despite these positive developments for the language which have supposedly stabilized its numbers of speakers, the future of the Māori language is still uncertain, and the language would have to be more strongly empowered on a socio-economic level in New Zealand as a whole.

In the wake of language shift from Māori to English, a third scenario of language contact emerged as a consequence of second language acquisition. Described in Benton (1966) as the variety of Māori English, the standardization of certain contact-induced features from Māori mixed with other features of New Zealand English soon met the curiosity of a number of linguists working on language variation in New Zealand. Māori English became described on the levels of phonology and pragmatics and researchers were uncertain about the status of the variety as an ethnolect or a more general sociolect. Recent research based on a constructivist approach to ethnicity and identity has advanced the description of Māori English as an ethnolinguistic repertoire. Building on this crucial characterization of the variety, the current article extends the understanding of Māori English by observing that the expression of Maoriness, i.e. the verbalization of Māori cultural concepts and world view, is an essential element of the variety. Based on ongoing research that explores the role of Maoriness in a narrative task, the final section of the article provides first evidence of how Māori cultural conceptualizations can become expressed in the use of English by Māori bilingual and bicultural people. Further data analysis of the recorded narrations will allow a comparison between Māori and non-Māori narrators and between monolingual and bilingual participants. This is not only important for getting a better idea about how the expression of Māori cultural knowledge can characterize the English used by Māori people, but it is also a crucial step towards fostering intercultural understanding in Aotearoa – New Zealand.

References

Adams, Peter. 1977. *Fatal Necessity: British Intervention in New Zealand 1830-1847*. Auckland: Auckland University Press.

Allan, Scott. 1990. 'The rise of New Zealand intonation'. In: Allan Bell and Janet Holmes (eds.), *New Zealand Ways of Speaking English*. Wellington: Victoria University Press, 115-28.

Bamberg, Michael and Alexandra Georgakopoulou. 2008. 'Small stories as a new perspective in narrative and identity analysis'. *Text & Talk* 28:3: 377-96.

Bauer, Laurie. 1994. 'English in New Zealand'. In: Robert Burchfield (ed.), *The Cambridge History of the English Language. Vol. V: English in Britain and Overseas: Origins and Development*. Cambridge: Cambridge University Press, 382-429.

Bauer, Winifred. 2008. 'Is the health of Te Reo Maori improving?'. *Te Reo* 51: 33-73.

Belich, James. 1987. *The New Zealand Wars and the Victorian Interpretation of Racial Conflict*. Auckland: Auckland University Press.

Belich, James. 2001. *Paradise Reforged: A History of the New Zealanders from the 1880s to the Year 2000*. Honolulu: University of Hawai'i Press.

Bell, Allan. 2000. 'Maori and Pakeha English: A case study'. In: Allan Bell and Koenraad Kuiper (eds.), *New Zealand English*. Amsterdam: John Benjamins, 221-48.

Benor, Sarah Bunin. 2010. 'Ethnolinguistic repertoire: Shifting the analytic focus in language and ethnicity'. *Journal of Sociolinguistics* 14:2: 159-83.

Benton, Richard A. 1966. *Research into the English Language Difficulties of Maori School Children 1963-1964*. Wellington: Maori Education Foundation.

Benton, Richard A. 1985. 'Maori, English, and Maori English'. In: John B. Pride (ed.), *Cross-Cultural Encounters: Communication and Miscommunication*. Melbourne: River Seine Publications, 110-20.

Boyce, Mary. 2006. A corpus of modern spoken Māori [Ph.D. thesis]. Wellington: Victoria University of Wellington.

Britain, David. 1992. 'Linguistic change in intonation: The use of high rising terminals in New Zealand English'. *Language Variation and Change* 4:1: 77-104.

Calman, Ross. 2012. 'Mātauranga – Māori education – The native schools system, 1867 to 1969'. In: *Te Ara – The Encyclopedia of New Zealand*. http://www.TeAra.govt.nz/en/matauranga-maori-education (last accessed on March 28, 2013).

Calude, Andreea S. and Paul James. 2011. 'A diachronic corpus of New Zealand newspapers'. *New Zealand English Journal* 25: 1-14.

Chrisp, Steven. 2005. 'Maori intergenerational language transmission'. *International Journal of the Sociology of Language* 172: 149-81.

Clark, Ross. 1990. 'Pidgin English and pidgin Maori in New Zealand'. In: Allan Bell and Janet Holmes (eds.), *New Zealand Ways of Speaking English*. Clevedon: Multilingual Matters, 97-114.

Daly, Nicola. 2007. 'Kūkupa, koro, and kai: The use of Māori vocabulary items in New Zealand English children's picture books'. *New Zealand English Journal* 21: 20-33.

D'Arcy, Alexandra. 2010. 'Quoting ethnicity: Constructing dialogue in Aotearoa/New Zealand'. *Journal of Sociolinguistics* 14:1: 60-88.

Davies, Carolyn and Margaret Maclagan. 2006. 'Māori words – read all about it. Testing the presence of 13 Māori words in four New Zealand newspapers from 1997-2004'. *Te Reo* 49: 73-99.

De Bres, Julia. 2006. 'Maori lexical items in the mainstream television news in New Zealand'. *New Zealand English Journal* 20: 17-34.

De Bres, Julia, Janet Holmes, Meredith Marra, and Bernadette Vine. 2010. 'Kia ora matua: Humour and the Māori language in the workplace'. *Journal of Asian Pacific Communication* 20:1: 46-68.

Degani, Marta. 2010. 'The Pakeha myth of one New Zealand/Aotearoa: An exploration in the use of Maori loanwords in New Zealand English'. In: Roberta Facchinetti, David Crystal, and Barbara Seidlhofer (eds.), *From International to Local English – and Back Again*. Frankfurt am Main: Peter Lang, 165-96.

Degani, Marta. 2012. 'Language contact in New Zealand: A focus on English lexical borrowings in Māori'. *Academic Journal of Modern Philology* 1: 13-24.

Degani, Marta and Alexander Onysko. 2010. 'Hybrid compounding in New Zealand English'. *World Englishes* 29:2: 209-33.

Deverson, Tony. 1991. 'New Zealand English lexis: The Maori dimension'. *English Today* 26: 18-25.

Duval, Terry. 1995. A preliminary dictionary of Māori gainwords compiled on historical principles [Ph.D. thesis]. Christchurch: University of Canterbury.

Duval, Terry and Koenraad Kuiper. 2001. 'Maori dictionaries and Maori loan-words'. *International Journal of Lexicography* 14:4: 243-60.

Eliasson, Stig. 1990. 'English–Maori language contact: Code-switching and the free morpheme constraint'. In: Rudolf Filipović and Maja Bratanić (eds.), *Languages in Contact: Proceedings of the Symposium 16.1 of the 12th International Congress of Anthropological and Ethnological Sciences*. Zagreb: University of Zagreb, 33-49.

Fenton, Sabine and Paul Moon. 2002. 'The translation of the Treaty of Waitangi: A case of disempowerment'. In: Maria Tymoczko and Edwin Gentzler (eds.), *Translation and Power*. Amherst/MA: University of Massachusetts Press, 25-44.

Georgakopoulou, Alexandra. 2007. *Small Stories, Interaction, and Identities*. Amsterdam: John Benjamins.

Görlach, Manfred (ed.). 2002. *English in Europe*. Oxford: Oxford University Press.

Harlow, Ray. 2001. *A Māori Reference Grammar*. Rosedale/New Zealand: Pearson Education.

Harlow, Ray. 2007. *Māori: A Linguistic Introduction*. Cambridge: Cambridge University Press.

Harlow, Ray, Peter Keegan, Jeanette King, Margaret Maclagan, and Catherine Watson. 2009. 'The changing sound of the Māori language'. In: James Stanford and Dennis Preston (eds.), *Variation in Indigenous Minority Languages*. Amsterdam: John Benjamins, 129-52.

Harper, Douglas. 2002. 'Talking about pictures: A case for photo elicitation'. *Visual Studies* 17:1: 13-26.

Harrison, Barbara. 2002. 'Photographic visions and narrative inquiry'. *Narrative Inquiry* 12:1: 87-111.

Hay, Jennifer, Margaret Maclagan, and Elizabeth Gordon. 1988. *New Zealand English*. Edinburgh: Edinburgh University Press.

Holmes, Janet. 1996. 'Losing voice: Is final /z/ devoicing a feature of Maori English?'. *World Englishes* 15:2: 193-205.

Holmes, Janet. 1997. 'Maori and Pakeha English: Some New Zealand social dialect data'. *Language in Society* 26:1: 65-101.

Holmes, Janet. 1998. 'Narrative structure: Some contrasts between Maori and Pakeha story-telling'. *Multilingua* 17:1: 25-57.

Holmes, Janet. 2005. 'Using Māori English in New Zealand'. *International Journal of the Sociology of Language* 172: 91-115.

Holmes, Janet and Helen Ainsworth. 1996. 'Syllable-timing and Maori English'. *Te Reo* 39: 75-84.

Kendall, Thomas. 1815. *A korao no New Zealand*. Sydney: G. Howe.

Kendall, Thomas. 1820. *A Grammar and Vocabulary of the Language of New Zealand*. London: Church Missionary Society.

Kennedy, Graeme. 2001. 'Lexical borrowing from Maori in New Zealand English'. In: Bruce Moore (ed.), *Who's Centric Now? The Present State of Post-Colonial Englishes*. Oxford: Oxford University Press, 59-81.

Kennedy, Graeme and Shunji Yamazaki. 2000. 'The influence of Maori on the New Zealand English lexicon'. In: John M. Kirk (ed.), *Corpora Galore: Analyses and Techniques in Describing English*. Amsterdam: Rodopi, 33-44.

Ketelle, Diane. 2010. 'The ground they walk on: Photography and narrative inquiry'. *The Qualitative Report* 15:3: 547-68.

King, Jeanette. 1995. 'Māori English as a solidarity marker for te reo Māori'. *New Zealand Studies in Applied Linguistics* 1: 51-9.

King, Jeanette. 1999. 'Talking bro: Māori English in the university setting'. *Te Reo* 42: 19-38.

King, Jeanette and Caroline Syddall. 2011. 'Changes in the phrasal lexicon of Māori: *Mauri* and *moe*'. *Yearbook of Phraseology 2011*: 45-69.

King, Michael. 1981. 'Between two worlds'. In: William Hosking Oliver and Bridget R. Williams (eds.), *The Oxford History of New Zealand*. Wellington: Oxford University Press, 279-301.

Kortmann, Bernd, Kate Burridge, Rajend Mesthrie, Edgar W. Schneider, and Clive Upton. 2004. *A Handbook of Varieties of English*. 2 Vols. Berlin/ New York: De Gruyter.

Lakoff, George and Mark Turner. 1989. *More than Cool Reason: A Field Guide to Poetic Metaphor*. Chicago: Chicago University Press.

Macalister, John. 2005. *A Dictionary of Maori Words in New Zealand English*. Oxford/New York: Oxford University Press.

Macalister, John. 2006. 'The Maori presence in the New Zealand English lexicon, 1850-2000: Evidence from a corpus-based study'. *English World-Wide* 27:1: 1-24.

Macalister, John. 2007. 'Weka or woodhen? Nativization through lexical choice in New Zealand English'. *World Englishes* 26: 492-506.

Macalister, John. 2008. 'Tracking changes in familiarity with borrowings from te reo Māori'. *Te Reo* 51: 75-97.

Maclagan, Margaret, Jeanette King, and Irfon Jones. 2003. 'Devoiced final /z/ in Māori English'. *New Zealand English Journal* 17: 17-27.

Matras, Yaron and Jeanette Sakel. 2008. 'Modelling contact-induced change in grammar'. In: Thomas Stolz, Dik Bakker, and Rosa Salas Palomo (eds.), *Aspects of Language Contact*. Berlin/New York: De Gruyter, 63-88.

Mead, Hirini Moko. 2003. *Tikanga Māori: Living by Māori Values*. Wellington: Huia Publishers.

Meyerhoff, Miriam. 1994. 'Sounds pretty ethnic, eh: A pragmatic particle in New Zealand English'. *Language in Society* 23: 367-88.

Nelde, Hans Peter. 1997. 'Language conflict'. In: Florian Coulmas (ed.), *The Handbook of Sociolinguistics*. Malden/MA: Blackwell, 285-300.

Onysko, Alexander and Andreea S. Calude. 2013. 'Comparing the usage of Māori loans in spoken and written New Zealand English: A case study of *Maori, Pakeha*, and *Kiwi*'. In: Eline Zenner and Gitte Kristiansen (eds.), *New Perspectives on Lexical Borrowing: Onomasiological, Methodological, and Phraseological Innovations*. Berlin/New York: De Gruyter, 143-70.

Onysko, Alexander and Marta Degani. 2012. 'Introducing a project on the role of bilingualism in English and Te Reo Māori for New Zealand English'. *LAUD: General and Theoretical Papers*, No. 78: 1-18. (http://www.linse.uni-due.de/online-shop/details/679.html)

Richards, Jack C. 1970. 'The language factor in Maori schooling'. In: John Ewing and Jack Shallcrass (eds.), *Introduction to Maori Education*. Wellington: New Zealand Universities Press, 122-32.

Sakel, Jeanette. 2007. 'Types of loan: Matter and pattern'. In: Yaron Matras and Jeanette Sakel (eds.), *Grammatical Borrowing in Cross-Linguistic Perspective*. Berlin/New York: De Gruyter, 15-30.

Schneider, Edgar W. 2007. *Postcolonial English. Varieties around the World*. Cambridge: Cambridge University Press.

Sharifian, Farzad. 2006. 'A cultural-conceptual approach and World Englishes: The case of Aboriginal English'. *World Englishes* 25:1: 11-22.

Sharifian, Farzad. 2010. 'Cultural conceptualisations in intercultural communication: A study of Aboriginal and non-Aboriginal Australians'. *Journal of Pragmatics* 42: 3367-76.

Sharifian, Farzad. 2011. *Cultural Conceptualisations and Language: Theoretical Framework and Applications*. Amsterdam: John Benjamins.

Stubbe, Maria. 1998. 'Are you listening? Cultural influences on the use of supportive verbal feedback in conversation'. *Journal of Pragmatics* 29: 257-89.

Stubbe, Maria. 1999. 'Research report: Maori and Pakeha use of selected pragmatic devices in a sample of New Zealand English'. *Te Reo* 42: 39-53.

Sutton, Douglas (ed.). 1994. *The Origin of the First New Zealanders*. Auckland: Auckland University Press.

Szakay, Anita. 2008. *Ethnic Dialect Identification in New Zealand: The Role of Prosodic Cues*. Saarbrücken: VDM Verlag Dr. Müller.

Thomason, Sarah. 2001. *Language Contact: An Introduction*. Edinburgh: Edinburgh University Press.

Van Coetsem, Frans. 2000. *A General and Unified Theory of the Transmission Process in Language Contact*. Heidelberg: Winter.

Warren, Paul. 1998. 'Timing patterns in New Zealand English rhythm'. *Te Reo* 41: 80-93.

Warren, Paul and Laurie Bauer. 2004. 'Maori English: Phonology'. In: Bernd Kortmann and Edgar W. Schneider (eds.), *A Handbook of Varieties of English*. Berlin/New York: De Gruyter, 614-24.

Wolf, Hans-Georg and Frank Polzenhagen. 2009. *World Englishes: A Cognitive Sociolinguistic Approach*. Berlin/New York: De Gruyter.

Acknowledgements

The author would like to thank Marta Degani for inspiring discussions that led to the writing of this paper. Furthermore, the author would like to thank Herbert Schendl and an anonymous reviewer for insightful comments and suggestions on an earlier version of this paper.

Barbara Seidlhofer/Nora Dorn/Claudio Schekulin
and Anita Santner-Wolfartsberger

Research Perspectives on English as a Lingua Franca

1. Introduction

The linguistic branch of English studies has traditionally focused on the diachronic and synchronic description of English as the language of its native speaking communities. This is still the primary object of description in most dictionaries and grammars and these sustain the privileged status of native-speaker English. The primacy of this English has, of course, not gone unchallenged. Apart from this Inner Circle English, as Kachru calls it, there are the Englishes of the Outer Circle, which also have legitimate claims for recognition (Kachru 1985, 1992). In Outer Circle communities, as in those of the Inner Circle, there are varieties of English which serve as a means of communication and social identity. These so-called World Englishes, essentially those varieties of the language that have developed in post-colonial countries where English was originally imported from the Inner Circle, have now been extensively described and discussed and lay claim to represent a distinctive paradigm of enquiry.

But English in the world is by no means confined within these two circles but as both a consequence and a driving force of globalization has spread well beyond them. English has expanded and continues to expand, but not only in what Kachru calls the Expanding Circle, countries not colonised by the Inner Circle, where English is a foreign language with no majority or official role to play. English is expanding everywhere on a global scale. As David Crystal puts it, "There has never been a language so widely spread or spoken by so many people as English." (Crystal 2003: 189) And these people come from all three circles, drawing on the language as a resource to communicate with one another in networks of interaction far more diverse and complex than those that make connections in conventional speech communities.

These networks operate across the whole range of domains of international use: from those related to leisure like tourism and youth culture, to those of business and economic development, to those, like diplomacy, immigration control and conflict resolution, which often have to do, quite literally, with matters of life and death. These international uses of English and the obvious significance they have for human well-being in the present globalized world cannot simply be ignored, or dismissed as peripheral because they do not conform to normal conventions of Inner or Outer Circle usage. There is clearly a need, not to say a responsibility, to recognise these uses of English as having a reality and a legitimacy in their own right, and to understand how these users draw on the resources of the language to achieve their communicative purposes. It is this recognition that has led to a broadening of the scope of English studies to include a field of research that is concerned with English as a Lingua Franca (ELF), defined as "*any use of English among speakers of different first languages for whom English is the communicative medium of choice, and often the only option.*" (Seidlhofer 2011: 7, original italics). Over the last decade or more, ELF research has developed from a novel minority concern to a flourishing field of study. This is also reflected in the fact that the *Journal of English as a Lingua Franca* (JELF) was founded/launched in 2012[1] and that the first chapter of the *Year's Work in English Studies*, entitled "English Language", has had a section on "English as a Lingua Franca" since 2012 (Seidlhofer and Dorn 2012).

This paper presents three examples of ELF research. The first two investigate features of the use of English as a Lingua Franca recorded in VOICE, the Vienna-Oxford International Corpus of English, a computer corpus of audio recordings and transcriptions of spoken ELF interactions. Compiling a corpus of genuinely interactive spoken data is incomparably more difficult and time-consuming than one of written data, but as it is in speech that variability in language is most readily discernable, the decision to focus on spoken interactions seemed imperative. Relieved of the self-monitoring, standardizing pressure of writing, the interactants' negotiation of meaning in real-time, spontaneous talk allows us to observe the use of what Labov refers to as the vernacular, where attention is paid to communicative content rather than to linguistic forms themselves (Labov 1984: 29). In addition, when the speech events are highly interactive, this also allows some measure of insight into how mutual understanding among the interlocutors is co-constructed.

VOICE comprises over one million words (some 111 hours) of naturally occurring, non-scripted face-to-face interactions via ELF, covering a range of domains: professional (business, institutions, research), educational, and leisure. The 151 interactions recorded in the corpus are complete speech events of various types such as conversation, service encounter, meeting, press conference, question–answer session, interview, or workshop discussion. The speakers come from some

---

1   JELF is published by De Gruyter Mouton, see http://www.degruyter.com/view/j/jelf.

50 different (mainly but not exclusively European) lingua-cultural backgrounds, including a minority (seven per cent) of native speakers of English. The transcripts are supplemented by detailed event descriptions giving information about the nature of the speech event and the interaction taking place, as well as about the participants in these ELF interactions. The corpus is freely accessible for research purposes, also in a part-of-speech tagged version (http://www.univie.ac.at/voice/). In addition, 23 recordings of transcribed speech events can be listened to online.

Although VOICE contains data from a range of different domains, it is, like any other corpus, only a selective sampling of actual language usage. There is, therefore, no claim in the studies reported on in this chapter that their observations have any general validity across all uses of ELF. The aim of their enquiry is not to identify distinctive features which would typify ELF as a 'variety' but to consider the possible conceptual and communicative significance of variation as such. The first study focuses attention on how the grammatical features in its data function in ways that do not conform to standard convention and looks for explanations as to why this should be so. The second study investigates how ELF in itself is variable, but in ways that are characteristic of all language use. In both cases, comparison is the means not the end of their enquiries.

One issue that arises in the process of empirical studies of this kind is the extent to which it actually makes sense to think of English or any language, according to tradition, as a bounded entity and stable frame of reference. It is indeed generally the case that explorations into ELF and its range of use have prompted a reconsideration of concepts of language that have been taken for granted over centuries – though the currently thriving field of research into code-switching and multilingualism during the earlier history of English reminds us that the nineteenth-century nation state ideology has not always been with us (see Schendl 2004, Schendl and Wright 2011). In the twenty-first century, just as globalization necessarily calls for some rethinking of the concept of community, so the globalized, and globalizing, use of ELF naturally calls for a rethinking of the concept of English. The third study in this paper is centrally concerned with how the use of ELF calls into question authorized ways of thinking. Here it is shown how the dynamics of ELF interaction cannot be satisfactorily accounted for by the generally accepted tenets of Conversation Analysis.

The two key terms in the title of this volume, 'Contact and Conflict', apply with particular aptness to the studies in this article, and indeed to the entire ELF enterprise. The study of ELF is essentially the study of contact, and Ehrenreich (2011) in an insightful paper has argued that contact linguistics provides it with a particularly appropriate theoretical framework, as with its conceptual tools, as well as its overall perception of language, [it] is particularly apt for the analysis of English as an international contact language because it acknowledges language contact effects as "testaments to the creativity of humans faced with the need to break down language barriers and create a common medium of communication" (Winford 2003, 1f.). (Ehrenreich 2011: 13)

ELF research over the last few years has yielded a wide range of contact phenomena of particular significance for sociolinguistics. It should be emphasised that although one talks about languages in contact, it is of course not languages as such that come into contact (or conflict) but people. Languages have no intrinsic agency. What comes across so clearly in studying ELF is that individual users make language contact happen in the very process of online interaction, re-aligning, combining or meshing elements from whatever linguistic resources they have at their disposal – mainly, of course, from English, but from other sources as well. It is not so much that ELF is a contact language, but that ELF is a variable linguistic means for individuals to make contact with one another. And of course by the very fact that these individuals cannot initially rely on a shared set of preconceived linguistic or cultural conventions, conflicts may arise. And then there is a need for speakers to negotiate by exploring alternative linguistic forms in their repertoire to find out which will best serve their purposes. How far conflicts get resolved will of course vary, depending on the willingness of interactants to accommodate to each other.

Obviously enough, research on a previously unrecognized linguistic phenomenon may also give rise to conflicts of an intellectual nature, such as when this research leads us to challenge established concepts in linguistics, such as '(speech) community', 'language/variety', 'native speaker' and 'competence' (cf. Hülmbauer and Seidlhofer 2013). Both as a phenomenon and as an area of study, ELF has aroused a good deal of animated debate and even animosity. For instance, it has been said that the study of ELF is ideologically motivated; if this means that ELF researchers have particular views of the role and development of global English in the world, then of course it is. But so is every other way of thinking about 'English'. Ideologies can either seek to bring about change in society, or to support conformity. Obviously, continuity of what is familiar is less noticeable than change, and this is precisely what defenders of the general validity of Standard English tend to overlook. Whether one believes in the need for change in established ways of thinking, or for preserving the status quo, there is some obligation, one would suppose, to provide explicit grounds for belief through argument and empirical evidence.

So the studies in this article are all, in different ways, studies of contact and conflict in that they are concerned with how people make use of English as a means, often the only means, of making contact with each other across the lingua-cultural divides that are potentially conflictual and would otherwise keep them apart. Globalization makes it both possible and necessary for people to make contact with one another on an unprecedented scale. And the use of English as a Lingua Franca is currently really the only effective way they can do so.

2. Mission –ing possible? Exploring the progressive in English as a Lingua Franca

The first case study focuses on the use of the progressive in English as a Lingua Franca and is based on a more extensive study (Dorn 2011).[2] As Comrie (1976: 33) has pointed out, "the English Progressive has, in comparison with progressive forms in many other languages, an unusually wide range" of uses. This is why the progressive is considered an area of difficulty in studies concerned with learner English (see for instance Swan and Smith 2001),[3] but also what makes it of particular interest in the study of English as a Lingua Franca.

The aim of this study is to investigate how this form is used (or being used?)[4] in ELF interactions, in which the ability to communicate is of primary importance. The data used come from VOICE, more precisely from the speech event type *conversation*, which is defined as "a speech event at which people interact without a predefined purpose" (VOICE 2009: Corpus header).[5] This makes conversations in VOICE highly varied, covering a wide range of topics. The data are, moreover, highly interactive and the speakers come from a range of lingua-cultural backgrounds.

What makes the mission of investigating the progressive a seemingly impossible one, as alluded to in the section heading, is the fact that the corpus was not tagged for parts of speech (POS) at the time the study was carried out.[6] Consequently,

---

2   Although a variety of different terms are used to refer to the combination of *be* and an *–ing* participle, only the term *progressive* will be used in this paper. To my knowledge there is only one other study concerned with the progressive in ELF, namely Ranta (2006).

3   Studies dealing with this structure in learner English include Axelsson and Hahn (2001) and Eriksson (2008). For studies on the progressive in native speaker English see for instance Scheffer (1975), Joos (1964) and Römer (2005), for the New Englishes see Baskaran (2004), Schmied (2006) and Collins (2008).

4   The humouristic touch – (being?) – is Mair and Hundt's (1995).

5   While the official corpus header is quoted here as the source for the sake of accuracy, the very same descriptors are also easily accessible on the VOICE project's website, at: http://www.univie.ac.at/voice/page/corpus_information.

6   A POS-tagged version of VOICE was published in 2013. (VOICE-Homepage 2013a)

analyzing the progressive meant having to perform the time-consuming task of going through a lot of data manually.

This very process, however, had the effect of making features of the progressive in ELF usage particularly apparent. It became clear that it is not always used in the expected form of *be* followed by an *–ing* participle. Thus, some instances can be considered 'incomplete' from a formal point of view. A range of such cases could, however, on co-textual and contextual evidence, still be regarded as progressives. The following extract contains an instance of an 'incomplete' progressive, marked in bold.[7]

519   S3: = you <@> don't <2> see </2></@> him @@@ (.)
520   S1: <2>hm </2>
521   S1: not **wearing** my glasses now

(Extract 1: VOICE 2009, LEcon8: 519-21)

Here the situational context, namely S1 not being able to see a certain person, makes it very likely that the underlying structure is *I am not wearing my glasses now*. As in spoken and highly interactive language use incompleteness of structures is common, and completeness is not a decisive factor for communicative effectiveness, it seemed appropriate to include such cases in the analysis, while recognising that there is necessarily some degree of subjectivity in doing so.

In order to investigate the use of progressives in the data as thoroughly as possible, they are analyzed from both a quantitative and a qualitative point of view. The quantitative analysis aims at establishing how frequently and in which forms the progressive features in these interactions. Since ELF use is frequently compared to English as a Native Language (ENL) and often considered a 'simplified' version of it (Prodromou 2007: 48), data from VOICE is compared to British native speaker data from the British component of the International Corpus of English (ICE-GB). The data from ICE-GB are the *direct conversations* which share many characteristics with the ELF data from VOICE, thus making a comparison possible.[8]

As concerns the overall frequency of the progressives, 1,037 progressives were identified in the texts of the speech event type *conversation* in VOICE (i.e. in a total of 158,047 words), while in the *direct conversations* from ICE-GB, 1,594 progressives were identified (in a total of 185,208 words). This corresponds to about 66 progressives per 10,000 words in VOICE and about 86 per 10,000 words in ICE-GB. As these figures show, progressives are less frequently used in the data

---

7   The VOICE transcription conventions can be accessed at the project's website (see VOICE Project 2007).

8   Although only parts of the two corpora form the basis of the analysis, these subcorpora will nevertheless be referred to as VOICE and ICE-GB respectively.

from VOICE, but they are not infrequent in the ELF data either. This means that progressives are certainly a relevant structure in the use of ELF.

Table 1 shows the distribution of the forms in which the progressives occur in VOICE and in ICE-GB.[9]

Table 1: Forms of the progressives in VOICE and ICE-GB

Form	VOICE %	VOICE N	ICE-GB %	ICE-GB N
PRESENT	74.95	742	65.38	1035
PAST	19.19	190	26.78	424
PRESENT PASSIVE	0.81	8	1.33	21
PAST PASSIVE	0.10	1	0.38	6
PRESENT PERFECT	2.63	26	1.77	28
PAST PERFECT	0.20	2	0.25	4
MODAL	1.11	11	1.33	21
FUTURE	1.01	10	2.15	34
INFINITIVE	–	–	0.63	10
Total	100	990	100	1583

The progressive can occur in many different forms and in combination with different tenses, in different modalities and in both active and passive voice, but as can be seen in Table 1, only a smaller range of possible combinations is found in the data. That is, in both sets of data there is a clear preference for present and past progressive active, although the percentages differ. This finding is in line with what other corpus studies have shown (see for instance Collins 2008: 232; Smith 2002: 319). For all other forms the numbers of occurrences and the percentages are rather low. Moreover, there is only one form that is exclusively found in the data of ICE-GB and not in the VOICE data, i.e. the infinitive. However, this form is rather infrequent in the ICE-GB data. Thus, practically the same level of complexity is found in the two sets of data, which indicates that the progressive in ELF is not used in a simplified way.

---

9   Due to the chosen approach not all progressives could be considered in the analysis. As mentioned above, formally 'incomplete' instances where co- and contextual evidence indicates that a progressive was intended were considered as such. Cases where it was clearly possible to reconstruct which form of be was intended were accordingly counted in Table 1. For details see Dorn (2011: 39-46).

Table 2 shows the twenty verbs most frequently used as participles in VOICE and ICE-GB.[10]

Table 2: Verbs most frequently used in the progressive in VOICE and ICE-GB

VOICE			ICE-GB		
	%	N		%	N
1. *going*	11.09	115	1. *doing*	11.50	179
2. *doing*	4.82	50	2. *going*	9.77	152
3. *saying*	4.63	48	3. *saying*	5.98	93
4. *looking*	4.34	45	4. *coming*	4.24	66
5. *coming*	4.24	44	5. *talking*	4.11	64
6. *talking*	3.76	39	6. *getting*	3.28	51
7. *taking*	3.28	34	7. *trying*	3.02	47
8. *trying*	3.09	32	8. *looking*	2.96	46
9. *working*	2.89	30	9. *having*	2.83	44
10. *speaking*	2.31	24	10. *working*	2.70	42
11. *studying*	1.93	20	11. *being*	2.57	40
12. *getting*	1.83	19	12. *thinking*	2.31	36
13. *thinking*	1.74	18	13. *taking*	1.67	26
14. *living*	1.54	16	14. *sitting*	1.16	18
15. *playing*	1.35	14	15. *telling*	1.03	16
16. *standing*	1.35	14	16. *using*	1.03	16
17. *walking*	1.35	14	17. *wondering*	0.96	15
18. *staying*	1.25	13	18. *reading*	0.90	14
19. *being*	1.06	11	19. *wearing*	0.90	14
20. *happening*	0.96	10	20. *asking*	0.84	13

(*50% cut-off points* noted between rows 10 and 14 in VOICE, and after row 10 in ICE-GB)

---

10 However, it should be noted that this refers only to the basic verb form itself and is thus very general; phrasal verbs such as *look for*, which were also found in the data, were not counted separately.

As the table shows, in VOICE more verbs make up 50% of all occurrences, namely thirteen compared to ten in ICE-GB. This indicates that the progressive is distributed more evenly among different verbs compared to the data from ICE-GB. Interestingly, *doing*, a rather general verb, is also much more frequent in ICE-GB, which supports this assumption.

The quantitative analysis shows that the progressive is a relevant structure and not used in a simplified way in ELF. The findings based on Table 2 furthermore raise the question whether the progressive is used with more or different meanings in ELF. This is investigated next, in a qualitative analysis of what the progressives may express when used in ELF, or more precisely, which underlying functions the progressives can have.

A qualitative analysis of the progressive shows that it can express a range of different functions, but there is considerable disagreement about these functions or meanings (cf. Eriksson 2008: 32). However, some meanings are frequently found in accounts of the progressive in ENL grammars, and seem to be widely accepted in ENL (see for instance Quirk et al. 1985: 197-8; Huddleston and Pullum 2002: 162-72). They can therefore be considered *canonical*. Thus, 'expressing a situation as in progress', '(limited) duration' and 'future reference' are identified as canonical functions. *Non-canonical* functions are then those which are not found in ENL grammars.

As regards the functions of the progressive in the ELF data, it should be noted that there is considerable overlap and one instance of the progressive usually expresses more than one function, be it a canonical or non-canonical one. Thus, it is simply an impossible mission to assign a progressive to a single function or category.

The above-mentioned canonical functions frequently feature in the progressives in the ELF data. However, also some non-canonical functions could be identified. For reasons of space, only one example of a non-canonical function, which I call the *historic progressive* can be discussed here (for further functions see Dorn 2011: 88-107). When used to express this function, the progressive makes what is being said more lively and more immediate, even though what is being described is not happening at the moment of speaking. Thus, the progressive creates a mental picture of immediacy and of an action as being 'in progress'.

The following extract illustrates this function of the progressive in a contact situation between people from different lingua-cultural backgrounds: a group of people who do not know each other are discussing differences of their university systems during the lunch break of a seminar. S5, a Turkish exchange student, is pointing out the lack of what he calls 'social environment' at his university by using progressives to describe what the students do regularly.

159   S5: = because (.) er in MY university i don't know: what's about yours? (.) there is
       no place to sit and (.) talk to (.) other persons in my <12> university </12>
160   S2: <12>oh:</12> there's no social =
161   S5: = there's no there's <13> no so- social </13> environment yeah (.)
162   S2: <13>hm:</13>
163   S5: everybody's **coming** to school university (1) **taking** courses and after (.) that
       going to (.) er: their home. (.)
164   S2: mhm. (.)
165   S5: there is no social environment no (1) c- but the er city is very good. (.) er the
       transportation and the (.) everywhere is green (1) i like it (.)

(Extract 2: VOICE 2009, EDcon250: 159-65)

Here, I would argue, the progressive creates a mental picture in the head of the listener, who can somehow see what is happening, i.e. the progressive has the function of making the situation described more lively.

To conclude, the study on the progressive in ELF data from VOICE suggests that it is an important structure that can realize different communicative needs. Moreover, in none of the progressives investigated could it be identified as the trigger of a non-understanding,[11] which suggests that it is a communicatively highly effective structure for ELF speakers.

3. Negative contractions in VOICE: a variationist approach

What the previous case study has demonstrated is how a particular linguistic structure can be functionally exploited as a communicative resource – e.g. for expressing *immediacy* in the case of the progressive. The analysis furthermore investigated how co-textual, highly localized conditions might lead to the choice of one form over the other. This motivated variation between forms, as a universal and fundamental feature of all language use, can not only be analyzed at the micro-level of individual choices, but also at the macro-level of variation across locales, speaker groups, or domains of use. The second case study takes this macro-level perspective, using as an example contractions in ELF talk.[12]

---

11 The analysis of communicative effectiveness follows Pitzl (2010).
12 The kind of analysis put forward in the following is usually referred to as (variationist) sociolinguistics. Whether or not variation between the simple and the progressive could also be viewed as sociolinguistic in nature is, of course, a matter of debate. Since the variation arguably has the potential to change the denotative meaning of an expression, it would not meet the strict definition of a sociolinguistic variable. However, the analysis of frequencies in different types of data, but also the qualitative analysis (which pointed to a strong attitudinal component in some uses of the progressive) demonstrate that the

There are two major types of contractions in the English language: negative (or *not-*) contractions and verb (or auxiliary) contractions (Biber 1999: 1128). The frequencies of both of these *vis-à-vis* full forms have been found to exhibit clear stylistic stratification in traditional native-speaker data, in addition to a shift towards contracted forms over recent decades (cf. Biber 1999: 1128; Millar 2009: 210ff; Yaeger-Dror 1997). However, since most contexts to which they apply allow for either negative (NEG) or auxiliary (AUX) contraction (cf. Table 3), another question that arises is which factors influence speakers in their choice of one over the other.

Table 3: Full and contracted forms (from Yaeger-Dror, Hall-Lew, and Deckert 2002: 8)

Full Form	*not*-Contracted	Aux-Contracted
He *cannot*	He *can't*	—
He *has not* done that	He *hasn't* done it	He*'s not* done that
We *will not* do it	We *won't* do it	We*'ll not* do it
We *have not* done it	We *haven't* done it	We*'ve not* done it
He *is not* here	He *isn't* here	He*'s not* here
We *are not* here	We *aren't* here	We*'re not* here

Tagliamonte and Smith (2002) demonstrate that the array of regional British dialects they investigated exhibit different preferences in this regard. Though Yaeger-Dror (2001: 181) focuses primarily on what could be termed the pragmatic or stylistic dimension, she also concedes that "[i]n English, *not*-negation is both a dialect and pragmatic variable, and pragmatic/ideational and dialectal issues are not always simple to tease apart."[13] Given the nature of the data at hand and the

---

variable certainly has a sociolinguistic element. That is to say, while in the case of traditional sociolinguistic variables, such as contractions, the informational content of the variation (the *signifié*) is assumed to be strictly pragmatic, stylistic, or social in nature, the data on the progressive demonstrates that there is constant 'contact and conflict' between *informational* and *interactional* meanings of linguistic structures, and that the two cannot always be neatly separated, something which will also become apparent in this case study.

13 Indeed, several other articles in the same volume (Eckert and Rickford 2001) deal with this vexing issue of the interrelationship between stylistic and social variation – another point of 'contact and conflict' in sociolinguistic theory.

overarching concerns of research into ELF, the pragmatic/ideational dimension seems to be the more rewarding site of research in this context.

However, the three competing realizations of the variable, and the dialectal preferences just discussed, add a considerable amount of complexity in this regard (cf. Yaeger-Dror 1997: 10). For this case study, therefore, the modal auxiliary *can* was selected. Since this modal does not have a contracted form (cf. Table 3), only NEG contraction is possible when it is negated. This removes the additional complexity of competing types of contractions, presenting a more straightforward choice for speakers between one full, and one contracted form respectively. It can thus be expected that this case will more clearly present the pragmatic dichotomy between full and contracted forms, and it is this variable which will be analyzed in the now familiar VOICE corpus, with some comparative data extracted from a contemporary corpus of spoken American English.[14]

On the face of it, the issue might seem quite straightforward: the number that is of interest is the proportion of contracted forms in relation to all negated instance of the modal *can*. However, in variationist research, it is necessary to define very clearly the "variable context" (Tagliamonte 2012: 113) also sometimes referred to as "the envelope of variation" (Meyerhoff 2011: 23). That is to say, it is paramount to exclude – as far as possible – those cases that do not allow, syntactically, for both variants to occur. Usually excluded from the variable context in the study of negative vs. auxiliary contractions are contexts in which the modal/auxiliary under investigation occurs as part of the predicate of a question, as (Standard) English does not allow verb contraction in these instances because of inversion (cf. Tagliamonte and Smith 2002: 264ff.), such as in example (1).

(1) *Why cannot we teach language?* (*StE)
(2) *Why can we not teach language?*

Along similar lines, there can be expected to be a pull in the direction of the contracted form *can't* in such cases, since the inversion necessary in well-formed Standard English questions would require the (intuitively speaking) rather formal *Can* SUBJECT *not* construction for the full negative to occur, such as in example (2).

However, ELF research presents a special challenge in this regard, as there might be conflict between a priori assumptions imported from previous research and the data at hand. This was brought home in full force, when – not in the corpus data analyzed here, but in a naturally occurring ELF conversation observed – a rather proficient speaker of ELF, an academic speaking as a panelist at

---

14 Viz. MICASE (2002); discussed in more detail below.

an international conference, asked (verbatim) the question used as example (1) above, viz. *Why cannot we teach language?*[15] It seems, therefore, that in contrast to ENL, questions are not necessarily and categorically outside the variable context in ELF data, allowing *can't* and *cannot* to occupy the same position even in questions, at least for some speakers and on some occasions. This would obviously speak against removing these instances from the variable context.

While these considerations are undoubtedly relevant from a theoretical point of view, and serve to illustrate some fundamental methodological challenges of variationist research – and how the contact with ELF data can serve to throw these conflicts into sharper relief – in the present study they were negligible from a purely practical point of view, as the number of these contexts was exceedingly low. So while the tables below give the numbers including interrogative contexts of the kind discussed above, the figures would change only marginally if one followed a more 'traditional' definition of the variable context and excluded the respective tokens.

Following the methodology just outlined, Table 4 gives the proportion of contracted forms of negated *can* for the different domains of VOICE. What becomes immediately apparent is that one can observe a rather neat sociolinguistic cline in the percentages of contracted forms within the given variable context, starting at 94.5 % in the *leisure* domain and dipping as low as 27.8 % in the domain *professional business*.

Table 4: Proportion of NEG contractions for negated can *in VOICE (2009), overall and by domains.*

	contracted forms (%)	N
VOICE overall	63.6	937
Domains		
Leisure	94.5	128
Education	74.8	310
Professional Organizational	59.5	306
Professional Research	40.0	60
Professional Business	27.8	133

---

15 What the speaker meant was that – even in a second or foreign language context – language is *acquired* rather than *learned*, and consequently cannot be *taught*.

A similar picture emerges if the same dependent variable is plotted against the second major socio-contextual variable available in the VOICE corpus: the speech event type (Table 5). Although there is some degree of correlation between these two sociolinguistic categories, since not all speech event types occur in all of the domains, the two are sufficiently independent to merit separate analysis.

Table 5: Proportion of NEG contractions for negated can *in VOICE (2009), overall and by* speech event types

	contracted forms (%)	N
VOICE overall	63.6	937
Speech event types		
CONVERSATIONS	88.8	197
INTERVIEW	81.5	27
SERVICE ENCOUNTER	80.0	10
SEMINAR DISCUSSION	76.9	52
WORKING GROUP DISCUSSION	74.4	223
WORKSHOP DISCUSSION	52.3	174
MEETING	40.7	189
PANEL DISCUSSION	30.8	39
Q&A SESSION	20.0	20
PRESS CONFERENCE	16.7	6

As in the case of the breakdown by domains above, the ranking arrived at in this fashion, i.e. by ordering speech event types according to the internal linguistic criterion of NEG contractions, is arguably exactly the same one would arrive at if one were to embark on the same task relying on the external, sociolinguistic descriptors that formed the basis of the sampling frame used in the compilation of the corpus. While it is not possible at this point to demonstrate this in detail, one example shall serve here as an illustration, viz. the drop in the dependent variable between the speech event type *working group discussion* and the speech event type *workshop discussion*. While the labels might sound deceptively similar, their descriptions mirror the rise in formality between the two, since the former is essentially a more intimate and hands-on version of the latter:

wgd (working group discussion)
A working group discussion is defined as a speech event at which a (temporarily formed) subgroup of a larger group discusses a particular problem or question in order to suggest ways of dealing with it.
wsd (workshop discussion)
A workshop discussion is defined as a speech event at which a specific group of people exchanges views, ideas or information on a particular topic.

VOICE (2009: corpus header)[16]

While it had been implicitly hypothesized that such patterns of structured variation would be found in the data, this is by no means trivial given the fundamentally different nature of ELF talk. In other words, while a site of contact and potential conflict between different lingua-cultural backgrounds and norms, ELF is by no means haphazard and devoid of sociolinguistic regularity. Labov's (1994: 158) assessment that "the ordered heterogeneity of styles is a normal and functional aspect of sociolinguistic structure" thus also holds for ELF, underlining its natural linguistic character. In fact, as far as this may be judged from the limited evidence presented here, ELF speakers seem to make use of the stylistic variable of contractions just as much as traditional sociolinguistic communities composed predominantly of native speakers, if not more so. The latter is suggested by the assessment that "*Not*-contraction [...] has become the norm in most varieties of spoken British and American English" (Yaeger-Dror, Hall-Lew, and Deckert 2002: 79). To further test this assumption of different sociolinguistic patterns in ELF and native-speaker data, some comparative data was extracted from the Michigan Corpus of Academic Spoken English (MICASE 2002).[17]

As the name suggests, this is a corpus of North American English. Remarkably, however, as in the VOICE corpus, this descriptor is to be viewed as a strictly external one. Just as the VOICE corpus, MICASE contains data from any speakers who were present at speech events selected as appropriate for the sampling frame along clearly defined external criteria. This means that the corpus contains speech samples from native speakers and non-native speakers

---

16 As above (cf. note 5), while the official corpus header is quoted here as the source for the sake of accuracy, the very same descriptors are also easily accessible on the VOICE project's website, at: http://www.univie.ac.at/voice/page/corpus_information.

17 This was deemed preferable to comparisons with analyses from other studies, as these mostly relied on rather specialized types of data (e.g. political speeches, journalistic writing), or excluded full forms from their analysis entirely, focusing only on the contrast between NEG and AUX contractions.

of English. Native speakers of (mostly) North American English naturally represent the majority in this population, but no speakers are excluded based on linguistic criteria. These parallel methodologies (of using external criteria only) in the compilation of the two corpora interestingly lead to roughly inverse speaker proportions as a natural result of the two different social settings surveyed: 7.07 % of words are uttered by native speakers of English in VOICE (*VOICE Website* 2013b), whereas 12 % of words are uttered by non-native speakers in MICASE (*MICASE Website* 2013).

The strictly external sampling criteria for both VOICE and MICASE can thus be considered exemplary of a trend in corpus research which takes account of the natural diversity present in any linguistic community, which methodologically speaking also represents a more consistent inductive approach, but which – needless to say – is in conflict with the traditional dialectological preference for the NORM (non-mobile, older, rural, male) speaker (cf. Milroy and Gordon 2003: 52), or even a 'lower-case norm speaker' defined along less stringent criteria.

A second aspect that calls for comment as regards the choice of MICASE is the label *academic*. It must be stressed in this relation that MICASE employs a rather inclusive definition of this term, and the compilers took "pains to record a wide variety of academic speech events" (Simpson et al. 2007: 4), including ones of a rather informal nature (e.g. campus tours, etc.), and thus the corpus lends itself to an analysis of stylistic variation.

Two corpora will, in practice, always vary along several dimensions, not only the one which is the independent variable under investigation (e.g. ELF vs. North American English in the current study). Suffice it to say that the speech events in VOICE and MICASE were judged to be in large part similar in their external sociolinguistic settings and thus provide some basis for a comparative analysis. If anything, MICASE could be argued to contain a somewhat larger proportion of speech events of a more formal nature, as it also contains a relatively large number of lectures. The results reported in Table 6 could be considered all the more surprising, therefore, since they indicate that NEG contractions are considerably more frequent in the North American data.

Table 6: Proportion of NEG contractions for negated can *in VOICE (2009) and MICASE (2002), including by* interactivity rating *for the latter*

	contracted forms (%)	N
VOICE overall	63.6	937
MICASE overall	88.0	1665
MICASE by *interactivity rating*		
HIGHLY INTERACTIVE	91.5	720
MOSTLY INTERACTIVE	88.7	362
MIXED	87.2	250
*HIGHLY MONOLOGIC	85.5	76
MOSTLY MONOLOGIC	78.6	257

In addition to the overall figures for VOICE and MICASE, Table 6 presents a breakdown by interactivity rating for the MICASE data, the major socio-stylistic factor available in that corpus. The results demonstrate how the North American data likewise exhibits stylistic stratification, albeit inside a much narrower band.[18]

Even more intriguing is a breakdown of the MICASE numbers by (native) speaker status. As illustrated in Table 7, the proportion of NEG contractions for non-native speakers in MICASE is remarkably similar to the one found in VOICE.

Table 7: Proportion of NEG contractions for negated can *in VOICE (2009) and MICASE (2002), including by* (native) speaker status *for the latter*

	contracted forms (%)	N
MICASE overall	88.0	1665
MICASE by *speaker status*		
NATIVE SPEAKERS	90.7	1491
NON-NATIVE SPEAKERS	64.9	174
VOICE overall	63.6	937

18 The category *highly monological* is marked with an asterisk, as it does not follow the predicted pattern; however, it must be noted that the frequency in this category is based on a much smaller sample and is therefore bound to be less representative.

What might be the explanation for the clear difference in the overall frequency of contractions in the two sets of data – ELF on the one hand, and North American English on the other? One line of argument might be that the patterns are indicative of something akin to a "colonial lag" (cf. Trudgill 2010: 130ff.), "the phenomenon that transplanted societies are linguistically more conservative than the motherland variety" (Dollinger 2008: 132). However, this reasoning would fail to reflect the radically different external sociolinguistic situation of ELF; neither would it account for the range of the sociolinguistic cline in the ELF data, or the remarkable parallels between non-native speakers in VOICE and MICASE.

A more promising route of argumentation therefore starts out from a consideration of the functional processes underlying the variation in other contexts studied. Yaeger-Dror (1997: 23) argues that in the case of NEG contraction, there is an underlying conflict between two fundamental principles of verbal interaction: the "Cognitive Prominence Principle (of informational content)", on the one hand, and the "Social Agreement Principle (of interactional intent)", on the other. While the former would require the negative to be prominent, the latter would favor its reduction.

If this is combined with the frequent observation that ELF speakers strive for heightened explicitness in their messages (Seidlhofer 2011: 99), this goes some way towards an explanation of the patterns observed in the data. It is interesting to note in this regard that rather than obviating the role of the Social Agreement Principle, the fundamentals of the ELF interactions studied here merely seem to shift 'the goalposts'. They move the range of the variation, extending it considerably, but do not remove meaningful variability or 'ordered heterogeneity' as a linguistic fact per se. This underlines Tagliamonte's (2012: xv) assertion that "variationist sociolinguistic principles and practices, the identification and study of patterns, [...] can be applied in virtually any study of language", and likewise the natural sociolinguistic character of ELF.

So while ELF data might highlight the inherent conflicts of traditional sociolinguistic constructs such as the clearly circumscribed speech community or neatly defined varieties (cf. Seidlhofer 2011: 64ff. for a much broader discussion of these issues), there are also many points of contact and continuity between traditional (socio-)linguistic research and research on ELF. The two most prominent which can be identified on the basis of the present case study would be the power of functional explanations to account for formal patterns, and the centrality of ordered heterogeneity in (socio-)linguistic structure.

4. Turn-taking in ELF business interactions

The central topic of the third case study is an investigation of turn-taking in ELF talk, i.e. "the process through which the party doing the talk at the moment is changed" (Goodwin 1981: 2). As such, turn-taking is "the essential characteristic that distinguishes conversations from monologic speech" (Meierkord 2000: 3.1.1) and is of particular interest for branches of linguistics studying spoken interactions (as opposed to written texts). Since much of what we know about English as a Lingua Franca today comes from research on spoken rather than written language use (*VOICE Website* 2013c), turn-taking is consequently also of high importance for ELF research.

The present-day interpretation of turn-taking was initiated by the sociologist Erving Goffman already in the 1950s (Goffman 1955; see also Gramkow Andersen 2001: 48). Nevertheless turn-taking in spoken interaction only became a prime focus of linguistic research after the publication of Sacks, Schegloff, and Jefferson's (1974) seminal article "A simplest systematics for the organization of turn-taking for conversation". Although having its roots in sociology, Sacks et al.'s turn-taking model had a tremendous and long-lasting influence on linguistics and is still considered canonical reading.

To simplify somewhat, the framework assumes a space of interaction accessible to all participants in the conversation. This interactional space is called the *floor*. Participants in the interaction then alternate in occupying this floor by making their contributions to the conversation, which are called *turns*. As soon as the current speaker has moved from speaker to hearer, the now vacant position of speaker is taken up by the former listener and a new turn begins. Hence, the default allocation of speakership of talk-in-interaction assumed by the model is that "at least, and no more than, one party speaks at a time in a single conversation" (Schegloff and Sacks 1973: 293). Any distribution of speakership that does not correspond to this default status, either no speaker, i.e. silence, or two or more speakers talking at the same time, i.e. simultaneous speech, is marked as a 'noticed event' by the interactants and interpreted as a violation of turn taking rules requiring repair (Schegloff and Sacks 1973: 293f.). Even though this strict interpretation of any overlap constituting a violation of the system was modified later on by Schegloff (2000: 42), simultaneous speech is still often viewed as a "problem" that needs to be "resolved" as quickly as possible (e.g. Sidnell 2001: 1275).

Despite its enduring influence, Sacks et al.'s framework has also been severely criticized. This criticism clusters mainly around the following three interconnected issues:

i)   the somewhat unclear nature of fundamental concepts such as *turn, floor* and *party*;

ii) the framework's inability to account for variation in turn-taking practices which stems from its supposedly ethnocentric foundation;

iii) as a consequence of the model's one-at-a-time principle, the failure to account for unproblematic overlaps and jointly authored turns.

The first point concerns underlying theoretical issues that are of equal relevance for all studies investigating turn-taking, regardless of the nature of the data that constitutes the empirical basis. As such it will not be discussed further in this paper (but see Wolfartsberger 2011 for a summary of the criticism of *turn* and *floor* and Santner-Wolfartsberger 2012 for a critical investigation into the concept of *party* in group interactions). For the research project at hand, issues ii) and iii) are arguably of greater significance, for these have to do with the kind of data analyzed.

The data for the research project described here consist of two authentic workplace meetings (totalling eight hours of audio-recorded interaction) that took place in two internationally operating business organisations. Each meeting includes seven participants, coming from a number of different European linguacultural backgrounds, who use English as a shared communicative resource. In contrast to much of the work on turn-taking carried out, which is concerned with the analysis of talk-in-interaction in monolingual – mostly white American – settings, this study hence investigates turn-taking in English as an international Lingua Franca.

Clearly, when studying turn-taking in English as a Lingua Franca situations, which are *per definitionem* situations of intercultural exchange, using an analytic framework that is based on established communicative conventions would be inadequate. The framework's supposedly ethnocentric foundation is therefore a crucial matter when dealing with ELF as a contact phenomenon bringing together speakers of various speech communities and different cultural backgrounds.

A review of the relevant literature reveals that a number of studies investigating interactional pragmatics in different ethnic groups, e.g. Reisman (1974) for the Antiguans, Moerman (1987) for the Thais, Kilpatrick (1990) for the Puerto Ricans and Szatrowski (1993) for Japanese conversations, have indeed voiced concerns about the universal applicability of the model. Reisman (1974: 113), for example, reports that in Antiguan conversation

> there is no regular requirement for two or more voices not to be going at the same time. The start of a new voice is not in itself a signal for the voice speaking either to stop or to institute a process which will decide who is to have the floor.

Makri-Tsilipakou (1994: 403) even goes as far as to argue that Sacks et al.'s model is "inoperative across different cultures".[19] This is not, however, the view taken in more recent research. A quantitative study by Stivers et al. (2009) investigating turn-taking in conversation across ten languages from diverse geographical regions suggests "a strong universal basis for turn-taking behaviour" (2009: 10589). While the authors acknowledge that they "do see measurable cultural differences" (Stivers et al. 2009: 10589), these differences are so small that they interpret them as "minor variation in the local implementation of a universal underlying turn-taking system, in which speakers aim to minimize the perceived gap before producing a following turn at talk" (Stivers et al. 2009: 10590). The authors admit, though, that "the differences involve a different cultural 'calibration' of delay" (Stivers et al. 2009: 10590). This culture-sensitive 'calibration', so the authors argue, could explain why speakers who are outsiders to a given cultural community may perceive turns as significantly 'delayed' or 'too early' even though the actual difference in timing is minimal. Summing up, one can say that the jury still seems to be out on the issue of cultural variation in turn-taking, even more so as Stivers et al. (2009) do not investigate variability in turn-taking behaviour in general (their title notwithstanding), but only in "question-answer sequences", based on the debatable assumption that these can be taken as "a reasonable proxy for turn-taking more generally" (Stivers et al. 2009: 10588).[20]

---

19 Moreover, Tannen (2005) has demonstrated impressively that certain turn-taking features may cause misunderstandings even among speakers from the same nation state. She gives the example of so called "machine-gun questions" (2005: 82ff.), which were employed by New Yorkers to show enthusiasm or interest, but were likely to be interpreted as interruptions by speakers from California who stopped talking and handed over the turn to the New Yorkers. Variation in turn-taking preferences is thus not only a matter of lingua-cultural membership, but also connected to different interactional styles. While this shows that variation in turn-taking is not limited to intercultural encounters, the question remains whether the turn-taking framework outlined in Sacks et al. (1974) constitutes a suitable model for the analysis of ELF interactions.

20 Their assumption that response times in question-answer sequences are representative of turn-taking more generally is backed up by a comparison of question-answer sequences with other types of speaker shift in a corpus of dyadic Dutch interactions, which yielded no statistically significant difference in turn-taking times between question-answer sequences and other types of speaker shift. The question remains, however, whether this would also be the case for other languages and/or for non-dyadic interactions. See e.g. Kerbrat-Orecchioni (2004: 4-5) on the differences between dyadic and polylogal interactions with regard to turn-taking.

The third issue mentioned above, i.e. the model's failure to account for unproblematic overlaps and jointly authored turns, is also of particular relevance for the
data analyzed in the present study. The interactions recorded for this case study
are characterized by a high density of *turn interventions*, i.e. "any utterance by a
member of the group which cuts into the ongoing speech of another, whether
or not it causes overlapping speech" (Watts 1991: 4). The notion of intervention
thus comprises phenomena such as interruptions, but also turn-completions or
otherwise jointly produced utterances. Therefore, it cannot simply be equated with
interruptions or *overlaps*. While it should be relatively clear that not all instances
of interventions – minimal responses like *yeah* and supportive completions being
cases in point – can justly be called *interruptions* (considering the "moral dimension" [Hutchby 2008: 227] inherent in this term), it probably requires further
explanation why interventions should also be distinguished from *overlaps*. An
example can be seen in extract 3 below:

1 S1: this is in this area we have two possibilities and we discussed this long (.) a::nd then we
2   s- we had to say yes we con- can extract for every let's say (.) erm (.) function like
3   marketing like sales like I T like (we) all the others (.) we can define (1) a OWN (.)
4   process like we have here for operations sales and so on (.) or we say no (.) this is a part
5   of the overall (.) process (.) it's included in the overall process because=
6 **S7: =it's not included in the overall process** in the overall process you will NEVER find
7   the C I O meeting the I M I T strategy meeting [...]

(Extract 3: author's data)

Here, S1 clearly is not finished with his turn (*because* projects turn continuation
giving one or several reason/s), but S7 nevertheless intervenes to voice his disagreement (line 7). Such an intervention can arguably be called an *interruption*,
but it notably does not involve any simultaneous speech. Ferguson (1977) calls
this a *silent interruption*, as it does not result in overlap. While this term may be
somewhat infelicitous, it points to the need to make a conceptual distinction between a purely acoustic phenomenon such as *overlap* and an evaluative concept
such as *interruption*, which clearly involves more than just two (or more) speakers
talking at the same time.

However, it is not always so obvious who is intervening in whose turn and
why. My data also includes stretches of talk where interventions occur in clusters
and so many utterances cut into the ongoing speech of an interlocutor that it
becomes virtually impossible to distinguish interventions from turns at talk, as
in the extract 4 below.

The example occurred during a meeting of the editorial board of an employee
magazine of an Austrian bank. It is a rather delicate situation: S3 conducted an

interview with one of the leading managers of the bank, which has already appeared in the magazine. In this interview said manager was quoted as having said
that his dream job was "early retirement". Quite understandably, the head of the
communications department was not amused, as this was not quite the message a
company's employee magazine should convey. Hence, in this extract the members
of the editorial board discuss how they could avoid such incidents in the future.
After a lively and quite emotional debate they assume that the incidence was a
result of the original text having been translated several times. They agree that
in the future all team members need to be vigilant and try to clarify any dubious
issues in the texts before the magazine gets published.

1 S5: and if somebody says his highest objective is to retire early yeah? then we should next
2 time call you and ask you is this really <1>**what he talked to us**</1> (.)
3 S1: <1>**and discuss it**</1>
4 S5: <2>**because everybody here was**</2> very er just er very curious (.)
5 S3: <2>**yeah which is not @@**</2>
6 S1: yeah
7 S5: and and erm so <3>**we (have) to ask you (.) and you should just take care**</3>
8 S3: <3>**but it-it's it's really pity that you didn't mention this**</3> earlier. right?
9 S4: mhm
10 S4: it's pity.
11 S5: yeah (.) <4>**yeah**</4>
12 S1: <4>**yeah**</4>
13 S3: so: <5>**please next time @ ask**</5>
14 S1: <5>**so it was a mistake**</5> yeah i-it was a mistake (.) and (.) so we […]

(Extract 4: author's data)

From an analytical perspective, it is hard to assign separate turns to individual
speakers in this passage, or sometimes even to decide who is occupying the
floor at which point in the interaction. Similar 'problems' are reported by Edelsky (1981), who concluded that the concept of 'floor' needs to be adapted in
order to accommodate such passages within the conversation analytic model of
turn-taking.

Passages like this are found quite frequently in both corporate meetings recorded for this study. What is characteristic for all of them is the fact that simultaneous
talk is a prominent feature for the analyst, and yet does not seem to be a 'noticeable event' for the participants themselves. Despite the overlaps being rather long
(e.g. lines 8-10 above), talking simultaneously is perceived as entirely normal by
the participants in such stretches of discourse, and is not sanctioned in any way, a
finding that is corroborated by Watts (1991), who reports the same for small talk

among family members. The only indication of a slight irritation caused by overlap is S3's repetition of "it's" in line 10 to 'outlast' the overlap (cf. Lerner 1996: 248).[21]

To a certain extent, the frequent use of simultaneous speech in this extract might be explained by the emotional involvement of the participants in the passage. However, there are also situations found in the data where there is not so much emotional involvement of the participants. Another possible explanation for this phenomenon, apart from the content discussed, might be the number of participants involved in the interactions. As Kerbrat-Orecchioni (2004: 5) points out,

> [t]he frequency of interruptions and simultaneous talk as well as the variety of ways in which these are carried out, increases in trilogies [i.e. interactions with three interlocutors], and a fortiori in multi-participant interactions.

The reason for this is their "variability in alternation patterns" with regard to turn-taking, which manifests itself in a "lack of balance in floor-holding, violations of speaker-selection rules, and interruptions and simultaneous talk" (Kerbrat-Orecchioni 2004: 4). She accounts for this by highlighting that in multi-participant interaction there "are more opportunities for a struggle for the floor, and for violations or failures in the functioning of the turn-system" (Kerbrat-Orecchioni 2004: 5) than in dyadic interactions. This, however, does not mean that group interactions are per se characterized by more competitive turn-taking behaviour than dyadic interactions: a "deeper analysis reveals the concerted organizations of these interruptions, which more often than not have a collaborative function" (Kerbrat-Orecchioni 2004: 5).[22]

In fact, such collaborative turn interventions have been described in the ELF literature and have sometimes even been considered a specific feature of English as a Lingua Franca interactions (e.g. House 2003: 569, 2006: 94). The fact that participants in ELF are communicating across different lingua-cultures makes constant feedback by the listener(s) in the form of minimal responses, agreement tokens, clarification requests and the like particularly important. Gramkow Andersen (2001: 157) therefore concludes from his study of dyadic ELF business phone calls that

> [i]n the future we shall have to emphasize the 'one speaker at a time' principle somewhat less than we have done so far, in the sense that the speakers, during simultaneous speech

---

21 The same strategy is described for ELF interactions by Gramkow Andersen (2001), who calls it 'outwaiting'.

22 This quote testifies to the confusion in terminology that prevails in the literature concerning the term *interruption*: Kerbrat-Orecchioni apparently uses the term here to encompass both interventions of a collaborative and a competitive kind.

passages, rarely orient to the fact that they are 'violating' the turn taking system. On the contrary they use it for their joint production of understanding and orient to the 'overlap-generating' devices as being collaborative and non-interruptive.

He therefore argues for a turn-taking model that is, in his own words, "quite radically different from SSJ [Sacks et al. 1974]" in a way that it "perceives so called 'violative' interventions by other speakers as normal and cooperative, provided that they are treated as such by the participants themselves" (Gramkow Andersen 2001: 157).

Such calls for an adaptation of existing theoretical models can be found repeatedly in research carried out on English as a Lingua Franca. Ehrenreich (2009: 130), for instance, reports that within the ELF research community "there is general agreement that established notions and frameworks may no longer be able to capture the new (socio-)linguistic realities of ELF communication adequately". The question thus arises whether we should try to fit ELF data into the traditional turn-taking framework at all costs; or whether we should look out for discrepancies between theory and practice and perceive them as indications that the theoretical framework might need to be adapted and developed further. After all, theoretical concepts are never set in stone. As Ford, Fox, and Thompson (2002: 6) maintain:

> The principles of turn taking and sequence organization that are fundamental to the CA enterprise [...] are always to be taken as *provisional, testable, and revisable* as further empirical research, *with new data, provides convergent or divergent cases* (emphasis added).

In light of what we can observe in ELF data, the chances are that these might be such "new data [that] provides [...] divergent cases" and thus help us to further refine the analytic tools and theoretical concepts we use in turn-taking research.

As with the other studies in this article, this again points to the need highlighted by ELF research and referred to in the introduction, to question established ways of thinking and so to shed new light on the old issues involving contact and conflict in communication.

References

Axelsson, Margaretha and Angela Hahn. 2001. 'The use of the progressive in Swedish and German advanced learner English – a corpus-based study'. *ICAME Journal* 25: 5-30.

Baskaran, Loga. 2004. 'Malaysian English: Morphology and syntax'. In: Bernd Kortmann, Edgar Schneider, Kate Burridge, Rajend Mesthrie, and Clive Upton (eds.), *A Handbook of Varieties of English 2: Morphology and Syntax*. Berlin/ New York: Mouton de Gruyter, 1073-88.

Biber, Douglas. 1999. *Longman Grammar of Spoken and Written English*. Harlow: Longman.

Collins, Peter. 2008. 'The progressive aspect in world Englishes: A corpus-based study'. *Australian Journal of Linguistics* 28:2: 225-49.

Comrie, Bernard. 1976. *Aspect: An Introduction to the Study of Verbal Aspect and Related Problems*. Cambridge: Cambridge University Press.

Crystal, David. 2003. *English as a Global Language* (2nd edn.). Cambridge: Cambridge University Press.

Dollinger, Stefan. 2008. *New Dialect Formation in Canada: Evidence from the English Modal Auxiliaries*. Amsterdam: John Benjamins.

Dorn, Nora. 2011. *Exploring –ing: The Progressive in English as a Lingua Franca*. Saarbrücken: VDM-Verlag Müller.

Eckert, Penelope and John R. Rickford (eds.). 2001. *Style and Sociolinguistic Variation*. Cambridge: Cambridge University Press.

Edelsky, Carole. 1981. 'Who's got the floor?'. *Language in Society* 10: 383-421.

Ehrenreich, Susanne. 2009. 'English as a Lingua Franca in multinational corporations – Exploring business communities of practice'. In: Anna Mauranen and Elina Ranta (eds.), *English as a Lingua Franca: Studies and Findings*. Newcastle upon Tyne: Cambridge Scholars Publishing, 126-51.

Ehrenreich, Susanne. 2011. 'The dynamics of English as a Lingua Franca in international business: A language contact perspective'. In: Alasdair Archibald, Alessia Cogo, and Jennifer Jenkins (eds.), *Latest Trends in ELF Research*. Cambridge: Cambridge Scholars Publishing, 11-34.

Eriksson, Andreas. 2008. *Tense and Aspect in Advanced Swedish Learners' Written English*. Göteborg: Acta Universitatis Gothoburgensis.

Ferguson, Nicola. 1977. 'Simultaneous speech, interruptions and dominance'. *British Journal of Social and Clinical Psychology* 16:4: 295-302.

Ford, Cecilia E., Barbara A. Fox, and Sandra A. Thompson. 2002. 'Introduction'. In: Cecilia E. Ford, Barbara A. Fox, and Sandra A. Thompson (eds.), *The Language of Turn and Sequence*. Oxford: Oxford University Press, 3-13.

Goffman, Erving. 1955. 'On face work: An analysis of ritual elements in social interaction'. *Psychiatry* 18: 213-31.

Goodwin, Charles. 1981. *Conversational Organization. Interaction between Speakers and Hearers*. New York: Academic Press.

Gramkow Andersen, Karsten. 2001. *The Joint Production of Conversation. Turn-sharing and Collaborative Overlap in Encounters between Non-native Speakers of English*. Aalborg: Centre for Languages and Intercultural Studies Aalborg University.

House, Juliane. 2003. 'English as a Lingua Franca: A threat to multilingualism?'. *Journal of Sociolinguistics* 7:4: 556-78.

House, Juliane. 2006. 'Unity in diversity: English as a Lingua Franca for Europe'. In: Constant Leung and Jennifer Jenkins (eds.), *Reconfiguring Europe. The Contribution of Applied Linguistics.* London: Equinox, 87-104.

Huddleston, Rodney and Geoffrey Pullum (eds.). 2002. *The Cambridge Grammar of the English Language.* Cambridge: Cambridge University Press.

Hülmbauer, Cornelia and Barbara Seidlhofer. 2013. 'English as a Lingua Franca in European multilingualism'. In: Anne-Claude Berthoud, François Grin, and Georges Lüdi (eds.), *Exploring the Dynamics of Multilingualism: The DYLAN Project.* Amsterdam: John Benjamins Publishing Company, 387-406.

Hülmbauer, Cornelia, Anita Santner-Wolfartsberger, Claudio Schekulin, and Astrid Ollinger. 2013. 'English language: English as a Lingua Franca'. *Year's Work in English Studies* 92:1: 124-40.

Hutchby, Ian. 2008. 'Participants' orientations to interruptions, rudeness and other impolite acts in talk-in-interaction'. *Journal of Politeness Research* 4: 221-41.

ICE-GB (2006), *The British Component of the International Corpus of English* (Release 2). Director: Bas Aarts. CD-ROM.

Joos, Martin. 1964. *The English Verb: Form and Meanings.* Madison: University of Wisconsin Press.

Kachru, Braj B. 1985. 'Standards, codification and sociolinguistic realism: The English language in the outer circle'. In: Randolph Quirk and Henry G. Widdowson (eds.), *English in the World: Teaching and Learning the Languages and Literatures.* Cambridge: Cambridge University Press, 11-30.

Kachru, Braj B. (ed.). 1992. *The Other Tongue: English across Cultures* (2nd edn.). Chicago: University of Illinois Press.

Kerbrat-Orecchioni, Catherine. 2004. 'Introducing polylogue'. *Journal of Pragmatics* 36: 1-24.

Kilpatrick, Paul W. 1990. 'Comprehension of simultaneous speech in conversation'. Paper presented at the 9th World Congress of Applied Linguistics, Thessaloniki, Greece, April 15-21, 1990.

Labov, William. 1984. 'Field methods of the project on linguistic change and variation'. In: John Baugh and Joel Sherzer (eds.), *Language in Use.* New York: Englewood Cliffs, 28-53.

Labov, William. 1994. *Principles of Linguistic Change. Volume 1: Internal Factors.* Oxford: Blackwell.

Lerner, Gene H. 1996. 'On the "semi-permeable" character of grammatical units in conversation: Conditional entry into the turn space of another speaker'. In:

Elinor Ochs, Emanuel A. Schegloff, and Sandra A. Thompson (eds.), *Interaction and Grammar.* Cambridge: Cambridge University Press, 238-76.

Mair, Christian and Marianne Hundt. 1995. 'Why is the progressive becoming more frequent in English?'. *Zeitschrift für Anglistik und Amerikanistik* 43: 111-22.

Makri-Tsilipakou, Marianthi. 1994. 'Interruption revisited: Affiliative vs. disaffiliative intervention'. *Journal of Pragmatics* 21: 401-26.

Meierkord, Christiane. 2000. 'Interpreting successful Lingua Franca interaction. An analysis of non-native/non-native small talk conversations in English'. *Linguistik Online* 5, 1/00. Accessible online at http://www.linguistik-online. de/1_00/MEIERKOR.HTM (26 March 2013).

Meyerhoff, Miriam. 2011. *Introducing Sociolinguistics* (2nd edn.). London: Routledge.

MICASE (2002), *The Michigan Corpus of Academic Spoken English.* Compilers: Rita Simpson, Sarah Briggs, Janine Ovens, and John Swales. Ann Arbor, MI: The Regents of the University of Michigan. http://micase. elicorpora.info/ (25 March 2012).

MICASE Website. 2013. 'Statistical overview of speakers and speech event'. http:// micase.elicorpora.info/micase-statistics-and-transcription-conventions/statistical-overview-of-speakers-and-spe/ (25 March 2013).

Millar, Neil. 2009. 'Modal verbs in TIME: Frequency changes 1923-2006'. *International Journal of Corpus Linguistics* 14:2: 191-220.

Milroy, Lesley and Matthew Gordon. 2003. *Sociolinguistics: Method and Interpretation.* Malden: Blackwell.

Moerman, Michael. 1987. *Talking Culture. Ethnography and Conversation Analysis.* Philadelphia: University of Pennsylvania Press.

Pitzl, Marie-Luise. 2010. *English as a Lingua Franca in International Business: Resolving Miscommunication and Reaching Shared Understanding.* Saarbrücken: VDM-Verlag Müller.

Prodromou, Luke. 2007. 'Is ELF a variety of English?'. *English Today* 23:2: 47-53.

Quirk, Randolph, Sidney Greenbaum, Geoffrey Leech, and Jan Svartvik. 1985. *A Comprehensive Grammar of the English Language.* London: Longman.

Ranta, Elina. 2006. 'The "attractive" progressive – why use the -ing form in English as a Lingua Franca?'. *Nordic Journal of English Studies* 5:2: 95-116.

Reisman, Karl. 1974. 'Contrapuntal conversations in an Antiguan village'. In: Richard Bauman and Joel Sherzer (eds.), *Explorations in the Ethnography of Speaking.* Cambridge: Cambridge University Press, 110-24.

Römer, Ute. 2005. *Progressives, Patterns, Pedagogy: A Corpus-driven Approach to English Progressive Forms, Functions, Contexts and Didactics.* Amsterdam: John Benjamins.

Sacks, Harvey, Emanuel A. Schegloff, and Gail Jefferson. 1974. 'A simplest systematics for the organization of turn-taking for conversation'. *Language* 50:4: 696-735.

Santner-Wolfartsberger, Anita. 2012. 'Parties, persons and one-at-a-time: Some fundamental concepts of conversation analysis revisited'. *VIEWS - Vienna English Working Papers* 21:1-24.

Scheffer, Johannes. 1975. *The Progressive in English.* Amsterdam: North-Holland.

Schegloff, Emanuel A. 2000. 'Overlapping talk and the organization of turn-taking for conversation'. *Language in Society* 29: 1-63.

Schegloff, Emanuel A. and Harvey Sacks. 1973. 'Opening up closings'. *Semiotica* 8:4: 289-327.

Schekulin, Claudio and Nora Dorn. 2014 (in print). 'English language: English as a Lingua Franca'. *Year's Work in English Studies* 93:1.

Schendl, Herbert. 2004. 'English historical code-switching in a European perspective'. In: Christine B. Dabelsteen and J. Normann Jørgensen (eds.), *Languaging and Language Practices.* Copenhagen: University of Copenhagen, 188-202.

Schendl, Herbert and Laura Wright (eds.). 2011. *Code-Switching in Early English.* Berlin/New York: De Gruyter Mouton.

Schmied, Josef. 2006. 'English in Zimbabwe, Zambia and Malawi'. In: Kingsley Bolton and Braj Kachru (eds.), *World Englishes* 2. London: Routledge, 181-99.

Seidlhofer, Barbara. 2011. *Understanding English as a Lingua Franca.* Oxford: Oxford University Press.

Seidlhofer, Barbara and Nora Dorn. 2012. 'English language: English as a Lingua Franca'. *Year's Work in English Studies* 91:1: 119-35.

Sidnell, Jack. 2001. 'Conversational turn-taking in a Caribbean English Creole'. *Journal of Pragmatics* 33:8: 1263-90.

Simpson, Rita, David Lee, Sheryl Leicher, and Annelie Ädel. 2007. *MICASE Manual* (version 3). Ann Arbor, MI: The Regents of the University of Michigan. http://micase.elicorpora.info/files/0000/0015/MICASE_MANUAL.pdf (25 March 2013).

Smith, Nicholas. 2002. 'Ever moving on? The progressive in recent British English'. In: Pam Peters, Peter Collins, and Adam Smith (eds.), *New Frontiers of Corpus Research: Papers from the Twenty First International Conference on English Language Research on Computerized Corpora.* Amsterdam: Rodopi, 317-30.

Stivers, Tanya, N. J. Enfield, Penelope Brown, Christina Englert, Makoto Hayashi, Trine Heinemenn, Gertie Hoymann, Federico Rossano, Jan Peter de Ruiter, Kyung-Eun Yoon, and Stephen C. Levinson. 2009. 'Universals and cultural variation in turn-taking in conversation'. *PNAS* 106:26: 10587-92.

Swan, Michael and Bernard Smith. 2001. *Learner English: A Teacher's Guide to Interference and Other Problems* (2nd edn.). Cambridge: Cambridge University Press.

Szatrowski, Polly. 1993. *Nihongo no danwa no koozoo bunseki-Kanyuu no danwa no sutoratezii no koosatu (Structure of Japanese Conversation-invitation Strategies)*. Tokyo: Kurosio Publishers.

Tagliamonte, Sali. 2012. *Variationist Sociolinguistics: Change, Observation, Interpretation*. Chichester: Wiley-Blackwell.

Tagliamonte, Sali and Jennifer Smith. 2002. '"Either it isn't or it's not": NEG/AUX contraction in British dialects'. *English World-Wide* 23:2: 251-81.

Tannen, Deborah. 2005. *Conversational Style. Analyzing Talk among Friends* (2nd edn.). Oxford: Oxford University Press.

Trudgill, Peter. 2010. *Investigations in Sociohistorical Linguistics: Stories of Colonisation and Contact*. Cambridge: Cambridge University Press.

VOICE (2009), *The Vienna-Oxford International Corpus of English* (version 1.0 online). Director: Barbara Seidlhofer; Researchers: Angelika Breiteneder, Theresa Klimpfinger, Stefan Majewski, and Marie-Luise Pitzl. http://voice.univie.ac.at (8 September 2010).

VOICE Project. 2007. *VOICE Transcription Conventions [2.1]*. http://www.univie.ac.at/voice/voice.php?page=transcription_general_information (25 March 2013).

VOICE Website. 2013a. 'News'. http://www.univie.ac.at/voice/page/news (25 March 2013).

VOICE Website. 2013b. 'VOICE online statistics'. http://www.univie.ac.at/voice/stats/ (25 March 2013).

VOICE Website. 2013c. 'Frequently asked questions'. http://www.univie.ac.at/voice/page/faq (26 March 2013).

Watts, Richard J. 1991. *Power in Family Discourse*. Berlin/New York: Mouton de Gruyter.

Winford, Donald. 2003. *An Introduction to Contact Linguistics*. Oxford: Blackwell.

Wolfartsberger, Anita. 2011. 'Studying turn-taking in ELF: Raising the issues'. Paper presented at the 4th International Conference of English as a Lingua Franca (ELF4), Hong Kong, China, May 26-28.

Yaeger-Dror, Malcah. 1997. 'Contraction of negatives as evidence of variance in register-specific interactive rules'. *Language Variation and Change* 9: 1-36.

Yaeger-Dror, Malcah. 2001. 'Primitives for a system of "style" and "register"'. In: Penelope Eckert and John R. Rickford (eds.), *Style and Sociolinguistic Variation*. Cambridge: Cambridge University Press, 170-84.

Yaeger-Dror, Malcah, Lauren Hall-Lew, and Sharon Deckert. 2002. '*It's not* or *isn't it*? Using large corpora to determine the influences on contraction strategies'. *Language Variation and Change* 14:1: 79-118.

Eva Duran Eppler

Language Contact, Culture Contact and Intergenerational Conflict

1. Introduction

Intergenerational conflict has been found to be more frequent and intense among immigrant families than in native households (Rosenthal 1984; Rosenthal et al. 1996). The greatest level of conflict is reported from families where the second generation is most assimilated to the host culture and language. Different rates of acculturation between parents and children, which result in an acculturation-gap, intensify this conflict (Dinh et al. 1994; Gil and Vega 1996; Kwak 2003; Nguyen and Williams 1989; Rosenthal et al. 1989).

Acculturation is the process of cultural change that occurs as a result of contact between members of two (or more) cultural groups (Berry 1990). Adult first generation immigrants tend to move in close-knit networks of fellow migrants and retain aspects of their culture of origin. They tend to have less interaction with the society of settlement and consequently acculturate more slowly than their children (Liebkind 1996). Children, by contrast, learn languages quickly, can therefore participate in the new culture more fully, and acculturate at a faster rate than their parents (Birman and Trickett 2001; Szapocznik and Kurtines 1980). The resulting differences between the generations can lead to misunderstandings and conflict between generations and has been proposed as an explanatory factor for why intergenerational conflict seems to be more frequent and pronounced in migrant than in non-migrant populations (Boman and Edwards 1984; Dinh et al. 1994; Kwak 2003; Landau 1982; Matsuoka 1990; Nguyen and Williams 1989; Nguyen et al. 1999; Rick and Forward 1992; Rosenthal 1984; Rosenthal et al. 1996).

The present paper contributes to the emerging literature on contact and conflict by exploring the effects of acculturation-gaps – and attempts to bridge them – on the relationship between a Jewish refugee from Vienna and her London-born daughter and grandson. It shows how rejection of the mother tongue and the loss of culture specific behaviour, exemplified on practices of food consumption, can lead to intergenerational conflict. It demonstrates that, when different cultural norms are projected onto the third generation, it too can get drawn into this conflict. More specifically, the study focuses on language maintenance/shift and culturally divergent practices of food consumption as expressions of different

acculturation strategies adopted by the mother and the daughter. The acculturation gap, widened by the mother opting for separation while the daughter chooses
assimilation, causes mis-understanding and friction between the two generations
of female Holocaust refugees.

As Eckert and McConnell-Ginet (1992) argue, to understand how language
interacts with culture requires us to look locally and closely observe linguistic
and cultural practices in the context of a particular community's social practices.
The current paper is therefore based on a detailed analysis of a ninety minute
sociolinguistic interview with three generations of Viennese Holocaust émigrés
on topics such as childhood and migration experiences, life in exile, language
choice and cultural identity. It explores why the mother chooses to keep on the
margins of British society, whereas her daughter and grandson are assimilated
into the host culture.

Section two presents the data and the participants. Section three outlines the
methodological approach. Section four establishes where the two central participants place themselves on the acculturation continuum. Section five focuses on
language shift and section six demonstrates how cultural aspects of food consumption have the potential to cause intergenerational conflict.

2. The data and the participants

The recordings this paper is based on consist of forty-six minutes of the central
participant DOR in discussion with the researcher EVA; twenty-two minutes
of DOR and EVA in conversation with DOR's daughter VIV. For the remaining
twenty-two minutes the three women are joined by VIV's son NIC. The recordings
provide rich and informative accounts of the central informant's (DOR) personal
(oral) history[1] as a first-generation Viennese Jewish refugee in London, while
DOR's daughter VIV gives her own perspective as a second-generation émigré
on many of the topics previously explored with DOR. The audio-recordings are
transcribed in the LIDES format (Barnett, Codo, and Eppler 2000). The audio
and transcription files are time-coded and linked; the files can be accessed on

---

1   Oral history is the collection (and study) of historical information about individuals,
     families, or everyday life using recordings and transcriptions of interviews. These in-
     terviews are conducted with people who participated in or observed past events and
     whose memories and perceptions of these are to be preserved. Oral history strives to
     obtain information from different perspectives, with special emphasis on information
     that cannot be found in written sources.

http://talkbank.org/media/BilingBank/Eppler. Duran Eppler (2010) provides more context for the recordings.

DOR, who was in her early seventies at the time of data collection, was one of approximately 206,000 Jews who left Austria between the *Anschluss* ('annexation') of Austria to the German Reich (May 1939) and November 1941. She came from an assimilated Jewish middle-class background, a social group that largely identified itself as Austrian in the national sense, German in the cultural and humanistic sense, and Jewish in the ethnic sense (Muchitsch 1992). DOR grew up in the Viennese villa district of Döbling, learnt German as her first language and attended a 'good' secondary school which she was expelled from in 1938 because she was Jewish. As the only member of her family who obtained a UK visa (as a domestic servant) before the war, DOR left Vienna for the UK in 1939. In London she mainly socialized at the Austria Centre, an organization around which much of Austrian refugees' social, cultural, and political life revolved in the early days of immigration. This is also where DOR met her Viennese husband. They had one daughter (VIV).

VIV was born in Hampstead, London, during World War II. When she was three, her maternal grandparents and aunt, who had survived the Holocaust, moved to London and in with her family. Her aunt soon returned to Austria, but her grandparents formed an integral part of the multi-generational household until their death. At the time of data collection VIV was in her early forties and worked as an office administrator in central London. VIV was married to an Englishman with whom she had one son, NIC. At the time of data collection NIC was a teenager.

3. Method

As this paper is based on language produced in authentic contexts by authentic speakers, the methodological framework that suggests itself is a sociolinguistic one. The study is mainly based on social constructionist approaches to identity (Bucholtz and Hall 2005), but also draws on socially/culturally orientated forms of discourse (Gumperz 1982) and conversation analysis (Auer 1984, 1988; Wei 1994, 2002).

Social constructionist approaches focus on identity as an "outcome of cultural semiotics that is accomplished through the production of contextually relevant socio-political relations of similarity and difference" (Bucholtz and Hall 2005: 382). How DOR constructs her gendered, ethnic, cultural and linguistic minority identity in interaction with her peers is the subject of Duran Eppler (2013). The current paper, which is based on different recordings, concentrates on the construction of similarity and difference between two generations of Holocaust émigrés. It takes macro-level categories (such as ethnicity, nationality, social role) into consideration, but focuses on the locally relevant identities the speakers construct, negotiate and affirm in the conversation. The analysis pays special attention to how the bilinguals use their different languages, language choice and code-switching to create stances vis-à-vis other speakers (see e.g. Williams' (2005) examination of a dispute between a mother and a daughter in a Chinese-American family). It demonstrates how different (aspects of) identities emerge/are highlighted in different parts of the interactions because these stances (and the resulting social alignments) are not fixed, but can shift, depending on social context.

From socially/culturally orientated strands of discourse analysis (DA) the present study draws on the concept that it is the "overtly marked separation between in- and out-group standards which perhaps best characterises the bilingual experience" (Gumperz 1982: 65). Based on this idea, Gumperz developed the notions of 'we' and 'they-code'. The we-code is the ethnically specific, minority language associated with informal activities in the bilinguals' repertoire; the they-code is associated with the majority language and more formal and out-group relations. Gumperz expects we and they-code to revert between the first and the second generation of migrants, but explicitly does not intend a straightforward association between the content of an utterance and the language in which it was uttered: the "association between communicative style and group identity is a symbolic one" (Gumperz 1982: 66). Despite this caveat, the we/they-code distinction has given rise to research that has been criticised as essentialist and naïve (Auer 1998; Stroud 1998). To obviate this, the current paper applies these notions in a carefully framed context (between a migrant mother and her daughter), to specific interactions, and within a social constructionist approach.

The other concept the current paper adopts from discourse strands of sociolinguistics is that code choice and code alternations can be put to pragmatic use. Code-switches can, for example, indicate a change of participant constellation, or mark reported speech, reiterations, side-comments and topic shifts. Codes have also been shown to mark topic/comment structure or indicate how speakers position themselves towards their utterance (personalisation vs. objectification). The potential for code-switching to be used in discourse related ways, however, depends on the systematicity of the code choice (e.g. among specific participants and/or contexts), the consistency of the switch direction, and the switch frequency. In heavily mixed data, changes in language are not only less marked as in near-monolingual data, but are also less likely to be associated with the (culture of a) code (Auer 1998). This is particularly pertinent when the data this study is based on are compared with natural language produced by DOR in a different contextual environment, i.e. among peers (Duran Eppler 2013).

By proposing code alternation and language choice as contextualisation cues, i.e. linguistic signals that provide an interpretive framework for the referential content of a message, Gumperz (1982: 131) also paved the way for conversation analytic (CA) approaches to code-switching. This paper draws on these approaches to show how participants use contextualisation cues to achieve interactional goals such as agreeing and disagreeing (see Bani-Shoraka (2005) for an analysis of an intergenerational argument in a bilingual family), and how bilinguals use language choice and code-switching to structure conversations. The main difference between CA and DA approaches to multilingual data is that the former aim to uncover the meanings that speakers themselves attribute to code-switching (rather than indexical relations between codes and the wider context). This can either be seen as an advantage, in that it precludes interpretative bias introduced by the researcher (Wei 1998), or as a weakness, in that it 'entextualises' by ignoring social context (Blommaert 2001). The data of this paper are rich enough to allow for both, a DA and a strict CA approach (social context is relevant only when it is demonstrably relevant to participants, see Schegloff 1997).

This paper aims to identify, through close linguistic analysis, the conflict between two generations of female Holocaust refugees, and its potential causes. To establish how and where the two women position themselves in relation to the home and host culture and language, an interdisciplinary approach has been chosen which draws on Berry's (1990) acculturation model, cross-cultural research (Rosenthal 1984; Rosenthal et al. 1996), and notions from cultural memory studies (e.g. Radstone 2008; Erll and Nünning 2008).

Migration causes change and migrants face two basic questions when dealing with this change, see Berry's Acculturation Model (1997) in Figure 1.

Figure 1: Acculturation Model (cf. Berry 1997: 10)

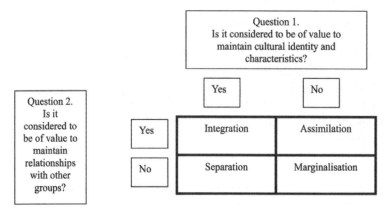

Depending on how migrants answer these questions, they will adopt different acculturation strategies. For the current study, assimilation and separation are most important. Individuals who do not wish to maintain their cultural identity and seek daily interaction with other cultures will assimilate to these cultures. Individuals who place value on holding onto their original culture, and wish to avoid interaction with others follow the separation strategy (Berry 1997). Naturally individual migrants can explore various strategies and may - but need not - settle on the most useful and satisfying one. Individuals can furthermore adopt different strategies, depending on the aspect (economic, sociocultural, psychological) and dimension (language, behaviour, values, etc.) of adaptation concerned.

Migrants are individuals who have developed in one cultural context and attempt to re-establish their lives in another. Culture, "whatever it is one has to know or believe in order to operate in community in a manner that is acceptable to its members" (Goodenough 1957: 167), is a powerful shaper of behaviour. Migration can therefore reveal a first generation migrant's behaviour, values and beliefs as inappropriate for the community of settlement. Alternatively, if cultural systems are not transmitted from generation to generation, a second generation migrant's behaviour, values and beliefs may become inappropriate for the community of origin. Incompatible behaviours may create difficulties and result in acculturative stress (Liebkind 1996), especially since the younger generation acculturates more rapidly than their parents (Matsuoka 1990; Rosenthal 1984). This generational discrepancy can lead to intergenerational culture conflict among immigrant families (Nguyen and Williams 1989; Rick and Forward 1992).

Processes of assimilation and acculturation are almost inevitably accompanied by language shift, the process by which one language displaces another in the linguistic repertoire of an individual or community (Fishman 1991). During language shift, individual speakers become less proficient in one language, they become semi-speakers or passive bilinguals, and more proficient in the language they shift towards. Language shift and language loss are influenced by individuals' attitudes toward the two languages and cultures. Bearman and Woodgate (2002: 235) note in relation to the German-speaking Jewish émigré community in London that "feelings and attitudes towards both the new and the old language are closely tied up with the individual's sense of identity [...] and their degree of integration into their adopted country".

Language shift tends to be accompanied by language contact phenomena (Thomason 2001). Two such phenomena that are prevalent in the speech of DOR are borrowing and code-switching. Lexical borrowings or loanwords are words from a language B that are frequently or conventionally used as part of a language A as a language contact. Code-switching is the non-conventionalised alternation between two languages in one sentence or discourse (Haspelmath and Uri 2009: 40). For the interpretation of the present data it is important that "the occurrence of code-switching is by no means universal in bilingual situations, and lexical borrowing is not in any way dependent on code-switching" (Haspelmath and Uri 2009: 42).

From memory studies the current paper mainly draws on the concept of *lieux de mémoire* (Nora 1989), i.e. mental tools or mnemonic devices which are not value-free, but ideological and national. This ideologization (of how things, events etc. are remembered) is proposed to happen as consequence of a

> particular historical moment, a turning point where consciousness of a break with the past is bound up with the sense that memory has been torn, but torn in such a way as to pose the problem of the embodiment of memory in certain sites where a sense of historical continuity persists. (Nora 1989: 7)

For the central participant and the first generation of Jewish refugees this historical moment was the Anschluss of Austria to the German Reich in March 1938.

The following three sections present extracts from recordings with DOR and VIV, representatives of the first and second generation of Austrian Shoah exiles in London. Although interdisciplinary in nature, the analysis is predominantly based on sociolinguistic methods. Language is taken as a discursive signifying system in which the speaking subject makes and unmakes itself in the course of telling its story. The analysis will focus on lexical, semantic, and structural properties of the participants' mono- and bilingual language use. The speech of the two generations of female Holocaust émigrés will be compared to reveal linguistic and cultural factors as causes for the tension between mother and daughter.

The next section looks at how and where the first generation mother and the second generation daughter place themselves in terms of acculturation, before two factors that seem to be particularly influential for the acculturation process in these two individuals are going to be investigated.

4. Acculturation strategies adopted by the first and second generation

This section takes a social constructionist approach to the participants' accounts of their acculturation processes. As we saw in the previous section, two choices seem to condition the acculturation paths of migrants: firstly, are cultural identity and characteristics considered to be important and is their maintenance strived for; secondly, to what extent do they remain among themselves or become involved in

other cultural groups (Berry 1997). The participants in this study were never explicitly asked these two questions, yet both provide clear and unequivocal answers
during the interview. This supports their centrality for acculturating migrants.

The central participant DOR left Vienna in 1939, aged nineteen. In the first
recording she explicates why she, unlike some of her fellow refugees, answers the
first question in the affirmative.

Extract 1[2]
DOR: **but I** [//] ich hab(e) sehr schöne Zeiten gehabt [in Wien].
      [I have had very good times in Vienna]
DOR: ich war sehr **happy** so +...
      [I was very happy]
DOR: jeder sagt +" Gott du hast eine gute # Erinnerung [//] **memory**.
      [everybody says =" God, you've got a good memory]
DOR: **but yes # because** es sind schöne Zeiten gewesen.
      [they were good times]

Extract 1 is predominantly in German, but contains quite a few English language
elements. This is not the norm among the German-speaking refugees in London,
but quite common among those who mainly socialize in émigré circles (Duran Eppler 2010). Frequently operating in bilingual mode may impact on DOR's ability
to conduct conversations in 'pure' variants of each of her two languages (Meeuwis
and Blommaert 1994; Auer 1998), but this is not at issue here. What is important
is that DOR was free to choose the language of the interview, did not feel obliged
to adhere to monolingual norms, and chose to be recorded in her vernacular, the
code-switched speech that is most closely associated with her locally based community (Eckert 2000). Once this has been established, DOR's bilingual language
use becomes available for analysis in terms of signaling identities (Bhatt 2008).

The English elements in extract 1 are, on the one hand, "sequentially dependent elements which bracket units of talk" (Schiffrin 1987: 31), like the discourse
markers *but* and *but yes # because*. *But* marks the first line as a contrast. The anti-
Semitism and 'bad times' of pre-WWII Vienna are not explicitly mentioned, but
implicitly contrasted with "good times" (spending time with friends and family,
going out etc.). In this sense, *but* may also cancel what DOR correctly assumes
to be her interlocutor's expectation (Blakemore 2002). The other elements DOR
borrows in extract 1 are key meaning-carrying units, such as *happy* and *memory*.

---

2 Transcription conventions: +... trailing off, +" quotation follows, [//] retracing, xxx
   unintelligible speech, +^ quick uptake, + self-completion, [/-] false start, # pause.

Both types of elements are essential in constructing oral history and their use demonstrates that DOR needs both her languages to convey it.

The English discourse markers not only frame extract 1 but also DOR's life in exile. All narrative is based on memory (cf. Kristeva 2000: 54), and in retirement DOR and her friends relish the memory of the good times they had as adolescents in Vienna, and "reassemble [...] [their] identit[ies] out of the refractions and discontinuities of exile" (Said 2001: 179). DOR is, however, aware that many of her peers would rather forget some of their childhood memories and place less value on the maintenance of their Austrian cultural identity and characteristics.

With regard to the second question, i.e. did she seek relationships with host culture representatives and what shaped her decision to remain primarily among her community of origin, DOR explains:

Extract 2
DOR: sie haben uns am anfang [//] sie haben uns **rejected in the beginning**.
      [they [the English] have us in the beginning [//] they have us
DOR: **you know ## foreigner # it doesn't matter** von wo man kommt #
      [where you come from]
      man is(t) immer der auslaender.
      [one is always the foreigner]
DOR: **and** [//] und darueber hat man sich eine eine waffe +/.
      [and one turned it against them]
DOR: +" ich hab(e) sie auch nicht gern(e)".
      [I don't like them either]
DOR: **you know**, es ist so [//] es war so automatisch
      [it happened so automatically]

DOR does not go into detail about why she felt rejected by "them", the English, but the broader national context (the outbreak of World War II, the invocation of the Alien's Act, internment and deportation) is likely to have contributed to the formation of an us/them way of thinking.

Extract 2 is still predominantly in German and the types of elements borrowed are similar to those already encountered in extract 1: sequential discourse markers such as *and* and *you know*. Key-concepts such as *rejected* and *foreigner* are not regularly expressed in English, not even in the Jewish refugee community; neither are idiomatic expressions such as *it doesn't matter* or entire prepositional phrases such as *in the beginning*. These elements are not in sentence initial position and are syntactically linked with the remainder of the utterance; they are neither discourse markers nor borrowings/loanwords but code-switches. The syntactic junctures at which DOR switches, however, are so 'natural'/grammatical that the two languages virtually blend into each other. As in extract 1, there is no straightforward association between the meaning of the borrowed elements and the language in which they are uttered, nor do they index macro-level social context. When in conversation with the Austrian researcher (extracts 1 and 2), the main function of the English language elements in DOR's speech is not to signal in- vs. out-group membership through language use, but to explain it. This analysis is further corroborated by the switches being bi-directional and frequent.

DOR's relationship with host culture representatives also frames extract 3, in which she explicates why she remained among her community of origin.

Extract 3

DOR: aber wir waren nie mit richtigen Engländer zusammen, nicht?
[but we never mingled with genuinely English people, did we?]

DOR: man hätte können # man hat nicht wollen.
[we could have # we did not want to.]

DOR: **because** man fühlt sich mit den eigenen Leuten wohler.
[because one feels more comfortable with one's own people]

DOR: **you know**, wir haben die selbe Sprache, die selbe **mentality**.
[You know, we have the same language, the same mentality.]

DOR: wir haben **different** [///] die selben **idea**-en eigentlich # wie wir sie als Kinder gehabt haben.
[we have different (//) the same ideas, really, # which we had as children.]

DOR: so # man hat nicht so viel **in common** mit den Englaendern.
[so # one does not have so much in common with the English.]

By opting for cultural maintenance and against participation in the host culture society, DOR chose separation as the most satisfying acculturation strategy. This, however, does not mean that separation is the only strategy DOR explored, and that she chose the same strategy for all domains. Economically DOR contributed to the war effort by running a shop, but for the private sphere she clearly opted for separation.[3] Separation is an option for DOR because her ethno-cultural group is dense and sizeable, and enough members share in the wish to maintain their cultural heritage ("separation is collective", Berry 1997: 11). She only had to adapt to the socio-cultural context that resulted from migration in the public sphere.

In extract 3, however, DOR does much more than elicit her acculturation strategy. She consolidates the we/they dichotomy by identifying her cultural in-group (*die eigenen Leute* 'one's own people'), those who one shares *idea-en* (*idea*-PL$_{G;}$

---

3   "Ich habe lauter österreichische Freunde, **hardly any** Engländer, **because** mein Mann war auch ein Wiener **and** meine Eltern sind nach dem Krieg gekommen **and** meine Schwester" [all my friends are Austrians, hardly any English people because my husband was Viennese, too, and my parents came after the war and my sister.]

'idea-s'), language and mentality with, as the German-speaking Jewish refugees from Vienna. The cultural Other are *richtige Engländer* ('genuinely English people'), who one doesn't have so much *in common* with.

Like in extracts 1 and 2, the English elements in extract 3 (and the example quoted in footnote 3) structure the conversation (the discourse markers *aber* 'but', *and*, *because* are all utterance initial), serve pragmatic/discourse functions (*because*, for example, also signals a causal relationship between the utterances in lines 1 and 3), and help achieve interactional goals (*you know*, for example, marks shared knowledge between the speaker and the hearer), or are near synonyms *mentality* and *idea-en*. The other English elements, *different, hardly any* and *in common* are not borrowings or loanwords, but they are code-switched phrases. The argument that DOR may be unable to express these concepts in German (Meeuwis and Blommaert 1994) is invalid, because the English elements do not fill lexical gaps (DOR is on record using translation equivalents of *because* = *weil, you know* ~ *weisst, different* = *anders, in common* = *gemeinsam; hardly any* ~ *kaum; and* = *und;* files *IBro, Jen1, 2 and 3*). DOR's speech is bilingual, but in conversation with the researcher, no indexical relations between languages and the wider context seem to be intended; this is, the codes do not mark in-/out-group membership.

In extract 4 DOR provides the ultimate answer to the identity question and introduces the next topic: factors that influence language maintenance. The base language has changed to English because DOR's daughter VIV has joined the conversation, and VIV, according to DOR, "understands everything, but doesn't want to speak German" (file IBro, line 2459333).

Extract 4

EVA: **it [language maintenance] always depends on how far you identify with the country where you are living.**

VIV: **obviously none of you lot did identify, did you?**

DOR: **no.**

VIV: **you still talk of home as Austria.**[4]

DOR: **ja, it's true.** *(Activities: DOR laughing)*

DOR: **when [/] when we say, we go home, we don't mean** [London, UK] +...

VIV: **which is [/] is really quite sad.**

DOR: **yes # but we all do.**

VIV: **I know # but you +/.**

DOR: **she [VIV] can't understand but xxx.**

VIV: **no I don't understand.**

---

4   "DOR: jedes mal wenn ich fahr(e) nach Wien # fühl(e) ich mich wie zu haus. [every time when I go to Vienna # I feel I am at home]" (file IBro, line 1410058)

Extract 4 is entirely composed of adjacency pairs, two turns in which the first part conditions the production and interpretation of the second part. This even seems to extend to language choice: DOR's confirmation *ja* 'yes' appears to be triggered by VIV's mention of Austria in the preceding assertion. The shift in dynamic modality from general ability/possibility *can't* in DOR's utterance to VIV's non-epistemic *don't* in the last adjacency pair summarises the first and second generation's position on the acculturation question. VIV was born in London, UK, and therefore cannot and does not (want) to understand that home is still Austria for her mother, whose life in the UK is marked by separation from the host culture.

VIV summarises her own cultural identity as follows: "I am the English child of # of a foreign family". For a member of the second generation of Austrian Jewish refugees to summarise her cultural identity like this, acculturation, assimilation and abjection[5] (Kristeva 1982) must have taken place. In- and out-group (Gumperz 1982), home and host culture (Berry 1997), we and they-code (Gumperz 1982) have reversed. VIV clearly does not wish to maintain her (grand)parents' Austrian cultural identity. She is supportive of her mother, by, for example, accompanying her to events organised by refugee organisations, but does not actively seek daily interaction with first or second generation members of the German-speaking central-European Jewish refugee community in London. She chose assimilation and draws a clear line between herself and her mother. Language choice and culture-specific forms of behaviour are the most obvious markers of this line.

The next two sections explore these two aspects and analyse how they contribute to the acculturation gap and cause dissonance between the mother and daughter.

5. Language shift

DOR's first language, like that of the vast majority of Vienna's Jews (Berghan 1988; Mallet and Grenville 2002), was German (not Yiddish or Hebrew). This was a consequence of the 1781 'Edict of Tolerance' (*Toleranzedikt*), which required the Jewish population of the Austro-Hungarian monarchy to educate their children in German medium schools. As a further consequence, Viennese Jews had started identifying themselves as Austrians in the national sense and as Germans in the cultural and humanistic sense by the second half of the nineteenth century (Wistrich 1989: 16).

---

5   Abjection are "attempts to release the hold of *maternal* entity […] thanks to the autonomy of language. It is a violent, clumsy breaking away, with the constant risk of falling back under the sway of a power as securing as it is stifling" (Kristeva 1982: 13).

On arrival in the UK, DOR moved to Hampstead (NW London). Unlike the traditional Jewish settlement area of London, the working-class and Yiddish-speaking East End, Hampstead was gentile, middle-class, popular with artists, and English-speaking. Due to the influx of a growing number of German-speaking exiles in the 1930s, however, German became a kind of *lingua franca* in NW London. In extract 5 DOR sketches the predominant language use patterns in the public and private domains in Hampstead in the 1940s.

Extract 5
DOR: hier in Hampstead # auf der Strasse # man hat nur Deutsch gesprochen.
      [here in Hampstead # in the street # people only spoke German]
DOR: zuhause haben wir doch auch nur Deutsch gesprochen.
      [at home we also only spoke German]

DOR's depiction of language use in Hampstead is well attested (Berghan 1988), yet surprising, given that German was the language of the enemy during World War II and Jewish refugee organisations had published advice not to speak German in public (see Muchitsch 1992: 33). Extract 5 furthermore indicates that language maintenance was not an issue for DOR (*nur, doch auch nur*). Not so for the next generation.[6] Extract 6 testifies to language choice having been a sensitive issue on DOR's domestic front, too.

Extract 6
DOR: das einzige # mit meiner Tochter # mit meinem Enkerl muss ich Englisch sprechen.
      [only # with my daughter # with my grandson I have to speak English.]
DOR: und sie [VIV] hat sie [die Grosseltern] gezwungen, dass sie Englisch lernen.
      [and she (VIV) forced them (her grandparents) to learn English.]
DOR: sie hat immer gesagt +" **you are in England # you have to speak English** +."
      [she always said, "you are in England # you have to speak English."]

There is a lot of resentment in extract 6 (*I have to speak English*; VIV *forced them to learn English*) and DOR clearly disapproves of the second generation shifting from German to English.

With the exception of the direct quote, extracts 5 and 6 are entirely in German. Reported speech is a well attested discourse function of code-switching (Gumperz 1982; Gardner-Chloros 2009) and in extract 6 DOR most probably quotes her daughter in the original language, the we-code for VIV, but the they-code for her

6   "I was terrified my parents spoke German in the street, especially during the war. I would sort of crawl away - 'I don't belong to them' sort of thing". (Mallet and Grenville 2002: 237)

mother. The message VIV apparently wants to convey to her (grand)parents is that separation is not an option: "you are in England", if you want to become involved in English society, "you have to speak English". Extract 6 moreover testifies to the duration of the conflict over language between the generations: VIV apparently never understood her (grand)parents' decision not to become involved in the mainstream cultural group (Berry 1997), and opted for assimilation at a young age.

VIV's choice of acculturation strategy may also explain why she was as reluctant to speak German as her (grand)parents were to speak English:

Extract 7
DOR: sie [VIV] hat muessen Deutsch sprechen mit meinen Eltern.
      [she (VIV) had to speak German with my parents]
DOR: hat sie müssen verstehen; hat sie müssen sprechen, ob sie wollen hat oder nicht.
      [she had to understand; she had to speak (German), whether she wanted to or
      not.]

Resentment over language choice cut both ways in DOR's family, but she was not the only parent who struggled to pass her mother tongue onto the second genera-tion (see e.g. file Iariel.cha, line 1334 for a similar statement by participant EAR).

Passive bilingualism, the ability to understand but not actively speak a lan-guage, is widespread among the second generation of Jewish refugees (Bearman and Woodgate 2002) and more generally among migrant communities that are undergoing language shift (Cheshire 2005; Clyne 2003). What is unusual about the German-speaking Jewish refugee community is that language shift happened so rapidly and is virtually complete with the third generation. DOR regrets that this also applies to her own family (file IBron.cha, line 469331).

Why was VIV and the second generation so adamant to shift to English, despite demographic factors (such as family and community structure) and personal factors (DOR's desire to pass her cultural/linguistic identity on) favouring main-tenance? The broader national context (World War II), institutional (e.g. school) and governmental factors (e.g. the Alien's Act) clearly also affected DOR's family. These factors seem to have shaped VIV's attitudes, so that she adjusted her values, beliefs and modes of behaviour to the host culture from an early age. Two aspects of acculturation are particularly important to VIV: good English and good man-ners (IBron, lines 968550, 972823, 976166, 1049727 and extract 11).

Language and culture, including 'good' social behaviour, are held in high es-teem in many Jewish households. Mother (DOR) and daughter (VIV) share simi-lar values, but migration put some of these values on different settings. For DOR 'good' language and 'good' social behaviour mean good German and good Aus-trian manners; for VIV, they mean good English and good English manners. The extracts analysed so far have shown that migration and the impact of differential acculturation have polarised the two generations on issues such as language choice and culture-specific forms of behaviour. Discrepancies between culture-specific value settings have led to intergenerational conflict in this immigrant family. The acculturation gap, broadened by DOR having chosen separation and VIV having chosen assimilation, has resulted in intergenerational disharmony, non-understanding, resentment and embarrassment, as illustrated by the next extract.

Extract 8
VIV: **when you used to ring me at work +, you know # (be)cause there were very [/-] sort of # very well spoken English people there.**
VIV: **and they said +"VIV a foreign lady is on the phone for you".**
VIV: **it's my mother!**

VIV hedges (*sort of*) the fact that her mother is not a "very well spoken English" woman, but she was not the only member of the second generation who felt like this. Participant MON recalls that the children were a bit embarrassed that their migrant parents "speak so with a heavy /eksent/" (mimicking a German accent) (file Imon.cha, lines 955-9). Extract 8 furthermore ties directly back to VIV's self-characterisation as "the English child of # of a foreign family" (Section 4). DOR's traceable German language origin renders her foreign in her daughter's English world, and VIV is left to reconcile the *foreign lady* with her *mother*.

6. Culture loss

In section 5 we established that DOR's Austrian cultural and linguistic identity is important to her and that she wishes to maintain it. She can do so because other German-speaking Jewish refugees share in this wish, and because demographic conditions allow them to maintain strong ties. Extract 9 underlines the importance of demographic factors for language and culture maintenance (see extract 5), and introduces food as a new factor.

Extract 9
DOR: [Hampstead] ist ja **more** eine **bohemian** [//] so # **you know.**
         [[Hampstead] is more of a bohemian district (//) right # you know.]
DOR: deswegen sind wir doch alle hier,- weil es war nicht so typisch Englisch.
         [that's why we are all here -. +^ because it wasn't so typically English.]
DOR: da waren so, **you know, continental** Geschäfte und das Essen +...
         [there were, you know, continental shops and the food +...]

Extract 9 combines several themes which have already emerged from previously analysed data. DOR's experience as a migrant is characterised by a strong sense of separation between in- and out-group (Gumperz 1982): *we* [us Jewish refugees from central Europe] *are all here* [in Hampstead] *because it wasn't so typically English* [the cultural and linguistic Other]. DOR illustrates her point with examples from the culture of food consumption, *continental* shops and food.

In terms of language use, DOR once again borrows the discourse markers (*you know* marks out explanations and exemplifications of important information) and key-words from the host language. The latter are not just any high frequency words, but adjectives with culture-specific nuances of meaning, *mot justes*. *Continental* is a typically English way of referring to anything "characteristic of mainland Europe" (*OED*); *bohemian* refers to "a socially unconventional person, especially one who is involved in the arts" (*OED*). *Bohemian* thus not only characterizes Hampstead with its high concentration of artists, but also DOR's own social standing in England; she is "socially unconventional" because she is not assimilated. DOR (indirectly) indicates her social position in the UK through attributes ascribed to her chosen area of settlement and the shops she purchases food in: she is a central European living at the margins of the society of settlement.

The relevance of food and the culture of food consumption for identity building resurfaces in extract 10, which - in its original context (IBron, 347473- 347524) is embedded in an oral narrative (Labov 1972). In the abstract and orientation (see extract 3) the central enigma (cultural and linguistic sameness and difference), the main characters ("one's own people") and the cultural Other are introduced. Before the evaluation, "one does not have so much in common with the English" (extract 3), DOR provides an example of culture-specific behaviour from the area of food consumption: *Wiener Kaffeehauskultur* ('Viennese Coffee House Culture').

Extract 10
DOR: **we enjoy** [///] wir gehen gerne ins Kaffeehaus # noch immer.
          [We enjoy [///] we enjoy going to the coffee house # still.]
DOR: **you know**, wir sitzen da für Stunden +...
          [You know, we sit there for hours]
(Activities: joint laughter DOR and Eva)

Viennese coffee houses are described on UNESCO's Intangible Cultural Heritage web-site (2011) as places "where time and space are consumed, but only the coffee is found on the bill". *Wiener Kaffeehauskultur* involves meeting friends in public space, a coffee house, spending hours talking, reading the papers, and drinking coffee. The English 'High Tea', by contrast, is by invitation only, frequently takes place at family homes, and is strictly limited in time by the onset of dinner/supper. In a contemporary Austrian context, *Kaffeehauskultur* is a cultural stereotype; for Austrian Jewish refugees in London, however, it has become a *lieu de mémoire* (Nora 1989). The Holocaust created an irrevocable break with the past for Viennese Jews. DOR and her friends therefore had to recreate *Kaffeehauskultur* in a reconstruction of a Viennese coffeehouse in London. Viennese Coffee House Culture has become ideological: real environments of memory, *milieux de mémoire*, have become sites of memory, *lieux de mémoire*. Sitting and talking in a coffee house for hours, DOR and her friends preserve, mend and reinvigorate their "torn" memories (see Nora 1989: 7) and "reassemble [...] [their] identit[ies] out of the refractions and discontinuities of exile" (Said 2001: 179).

DOR's rendition of *Kaffeehauskultur* triggers joint laughter between the interviewee and the interviewer. This type of turn pair, response solicitor followed by laughter, frequently occurs at the end of sequences (Coates 1996: 145), and has been said to mark mutual understanding in female same-sex conversations (Coates 1996; Tannen 1993). The *you know* in extract 10 prefaces a repair (it is followed by a false start and retracing in the other language), and marks clarification/explanations/exemplifications.

The next extract, a narrative, also features joint laughter and another Austrian cultural 'institution', the *Würstelstand* ('hot-dog stand'). It describes how, on return from a trip to Austria with his grandparents, NIC, the third generation, gets caught in the culture conflict between his mother and grandmother because of the manner in which he consumes *Wiener Würstel* ('sausages'). We have already seen in section 4 that, as part of the socially recognized British cultural norms, *good* (English table) *manners* are priorities for VIV. Conflict between the first and the second generation culminates when VIV realises that DOR had seized the opportunity of the trip to Austria to convey culture-specific forms of food consumption onto her grandson NIC. All three generations and the interviewer are present during this part of the recording.

Extract 11

DOR: **we went, you know [//] we went to** Salzburg **and the(re)** den   Würstelstand
[We went, you know (//) we went to Salzburg and there the hot-dog stand.]

DOR: **so I said +**"NIC **you have to eat it [the sausage] with** der Hand, **because** das schmeckt ganz anders."
[Nicolas you have to eat it with your fingers, because it tastes very differently.]

DOR: das muss man mit der Hand essen, es schmeckt ganz anders.
[you have to eat it with your fingers, it tastes very differently.]

DOR: so wie er nach Haus gekommen is(t), hat er (e)s in die Hand genommen.
[so when he came back home, he ate it [the sausage] with his fingers.]

DOR: sagt die VIVien "**what are you doing?**"

DOR: sagt er, „es schmeckt ganz anders."
[says he (NIC), "it tastes very differently"]

(Activities: EVA and DOR laughing)
VIV: xxx **tragedy** xxx **you know** xxx.
VIV: **you know, all the things I was trying to do** xxx **good manners**
VIV: **you know, that's what I'm saying in reverse**
VIV: **as if she didn't like, what you are doing.**

The language of the conversation is English when the story about the *Würstelstand* is recounted. The first German word in this narrative is the cultural borrowing *Würstelstand*.[7] *Hot-dog stand* does not seem to appropriately express the reality pertaining to her associations with *Würstelstand* and DOR borrows the German lexical item. A *Würstelstand* is a fast food kiosk (but not a take-away) where people eat hot sausages, usually with different kinds of bread, mustard and beer, as if standing at a bar. Visiting a *Würstelstand* is part of popular culture and means much more than simply having a snack. *Würstelstände* are places of communication, they are open until late in the night or even early in the morning. The similarities between Viennese coffee house-culture (extract 10) and *Würstelstand*-culture are as striking as the differences to English High Tea and fish and chip shops, *the* English fast food place. At fish and chip shops, one purchases the ready meal and consumes it in the privacy of one's home; at *Würstelstände* and Viennese coffee houses, by contrast, one stays to consume the purchased goods in company, talking.

Borrowing the term *Würstelstand* may also function as a "proper-name allusion"[8] (Leppihalme 1997: 3) directed at the other cultural in-group member, the researcher, in extract 11. DOR and EVA know that at a *Würstelstand* there is only one culturally appropriate, unmarked way of consuming *Würstel,* namely "*with der Hand*" ('with one's fingers'). The full meaning of this borrowing is culturally determined and can only be understood if its use evokes the referent *and* some characteristic features linked to it (such as conversing with the proprietor and other customers). This interpretation is supported by the joint laughter between the two participants, which, as we have already seen, has been interpreted as an indicator of female solidarity by Edelsky (1993: 220) and Coates (1996: 145). As at the end of extract 11, DOR thus indirectly divides her audience into cultural and linguistic in- and out-group members: herself and EVA form the

---

7   The place-name *Salzburg* cannot really be avoided, as it forms part of the orientation (Labov 1972). The American English term *hot-dog stand* only approximately covers the concept of *Würstelstand.*

8   An allusion that presupposes specialised knowledge or interest and is "recognised by a small minority of receivers only" (Leppihalme 1997: 4).

'us/we', her daughter (VIV) the cultural Other or the 'they'; her grandson (Nic) is drawn between the two.

The topic and the first two German words in extract 11, *Salzburg* and *Würstel-stand*, consequently trigger frequent intra-sentential code-switching. The 'explanation/reason' why it is important for DOR to consume *Würstel* in a culturally appropriate way is already given in an almost entirely German clause *because das schmeckt ganz anders* (that tastes completely differently). This, of course, is no causal reason and only makes sense in the context of DOR maintaining her Austrian cultural identity as a Jewish refugee in London, i.e. when *Würstelstand* is interpreted as a *lieu de mémoire*. With the English conjunction *because*, DOR is literally reconnecting her grandson NIC with the elementary taste for the flavours of food from her own cultural background (Bourdieu 1984).

DOR obviously enjoys telling this particular part of the story and repeats the entire previous utterance, which also constitutes the peak of the narrative, translated into German, and she does not bother to switch back to English for the next transition in the narrative. By adhering to her language choice, DOR may not exclude VIV from her audience, but most probably Nic. As if to heighten the language and culture conflict between herself and her daughter, DOR reverts to English to quote VIV's shocked reaction to her son's newly acquired Austrian manners. Gumperz (1982) stresses that it is the contrast between we and they-codes that is important in code-switched direct quotations (and not the faithful representation of language). DOR quotes her own daughter in English. NIC, on the other hand, who has just been taught an Austrian culture trait, is quoted in German. By choosing to represent her daughter in the they-code, DOR highlights the fact that her daughter embraces different cultural norms and excludes her from the cultural in-group. Conversely, VIV interprets her mother's attempts at teaching NIC some Austrian cultural behaviour as unwelcome interference with her own educational goals: to raise her son as a well-spoken and well-mannered Englishman. DOR provokes conflict with her daughter by actively counteracting culture and language loss across generations, and by attempting to revive her own culture of food consumption in the third generation.

7. Conclusion

The conversations between DOR, a first generation Jewish refugee from Vienna, and her London born daughter VIV support studies which have shown that intergenerational conflict can be pronounced in migrant populations (Dinh et al. 1994; Kwak 2003; Landau 1982; Nguyen and Williams 1989; Nguyen et al. 1999; Rosenthal 1984; Rosenthal et al. 1996) and that different rates of acculturation between parents and children can intensify this tension (Lee et al. 2000; Rick and Forward 1992; Rosenthal et al. 1996; Szapocznik and Kurtines 1993).

In the ninety minute sociolinguistic interview DOR explicates why her Austrian cultural identity and her mother tongue German are important to her and why she wishes to maintain them. A high density of German-speaking refugees from central Europe in NW London allowed her to maintain her mother tongue and her cultural identity, and to become involved with the host cultural group in the economic domain only; i.e. DOR opted for separation (Berry 1990, 1997). Her daughter VIV, on the other hand, chose acculturation and assimilation at an early age. She tried to convince her parents and grandparents of the need to acculturate, and led the language shift to English in her family. The fact that answers to Berry's (1997) questions about cultural maintenance as well as contact and participation emerge from the recordings despite not having been explicitly asked, support their centrality to the migrant experience.

Most of the research on intercultural conflict in migrant populations focuses on parent – adolescent relationships. This current paper shows that intergenerational conflict firstly, need not be confined to adolescence, and secondly, may remain unresolved for decades. According to the participants' accounts the culture gap between the generations became apparent in the 1940s; the data demonstrate that the tension between the generations over issues of acculturation was still unresolved forty years later. Not only is the conflict unresolved, mother and daughter even drag the third generation, DOR's grandson NIC into it. Future research could investigate whether intergenerational conflict in migrant populations persists in this and other migrant populations.

The two main factors that emerged from the data as causes of the conflict between mother and daughter are language shift (Zhu 2008) and culture-specific ways of food consumption. Both factors are related to the acculturation strategies the two generations of women adopt. DOR's English is adequate for the domains in which she has contact with the host culture, such as business, but she prefers to speak German with her parents, her husband and her closest friends. She would also prefer to speak German with her daughter and grandson (extract 5). "Good" English, however, is a priority for the next generation (VIV) and DOR "has to" speak English with VIV and NIC, despite her desire to transmit her mother tongue onto the next generations in her family (Section 6).

Culture maintenance is the other factor that emerges from the data as a cause for conflict between the generations. *Kaffeehauskultur* is an intangible cultural heritage that is difficult to pass on to future generations in London. DOR and her refugee-generation friends seem content to use replicas of Viennese coffee houses to satisfy their need to relish the memory of the good times they had as adolescents in Vienna and to reassemble their identities out of the refractions and discontinuities of exile. Through forced migration, a *milieu de mémoire* has become a *lieu de mémoire*. When given the opportunity to pass Austrian ways of consuming food, for example *Würstel*, onto her grandson, DOR relishes it without much further consideration of her daughter's educational priorities. When she tells the story about the *Würstelstand* to another cultural in-group member, however, the conflict between the generations resurfaces in their language use. DOR uses the 'we' and 'they-codes' to create a stance vis-à-vis her acculturated daughter. Unlike in the recording with the other cultural in-group member, the researcher, she uses her two languages to construct divergent linguistic and cultural identities and to mark/encode the intergenerational conflict. The sad thing is that it is the Holocaust that forced a different language and distinct cultural norms of food consumption on the first generation mother and the second generation daughter and triggered this conflict.

References

Auer, Peter. 1988. 'A conversation analytic approach to code-switching'. In: Monica Heller (ed.), *Codeswitching: Anthropological and Sociolinguistic Perspectives*. Berlin: Mouton de Gruyter, 187-215.

Auer, Peter (ed.). 1998. *Code-Switching in Conversation: Language, Interaction and Identity*. London: Routledge.

Bani-Shoraka, Helena. 2005. *Language Choice and Code-Switching in the Azerbaijani Community in Tehran: A Conversation Analytic Approach to Bilingual Practices*. Uppsala: Elanders-Gotab.

Barnett, Ruthanna, Eva Codo, and Eva Eppler. 2000. 'The LIDES coding manual'. *International Journal of Bilingualism* 4:2: 131-270.

Bearman, Marietta and Erna Woodgate. 2002. 'Postwar: The challenges of settling down'. In: Marian Malet and Anthony Grenville (eds.), *Changing Countries: The Experience and Achievement of German-speaking Exiles from Hitler in Britain, from 1933 to Today*. London: Libris, 217-46.

Berghan, Marion. 1988. *German-Jewish Refugees in England. Ambiguities of Assimilation*. Oxford: Berg.

Berry, John W. 1990. 'Psychology of acculturation'. In: John J. Berman (ed.), *Cross-cultural Perspectives: Nebraska Symposium on Motivation*. Lincoln: University of Nebraska Press, 201-34.

Berry, John W. 1997. 'Immigration, acculturation, and adaptation'. *Applied Psychology* 46: 5-34.

Bhatt, Rakesh. 2008. 'In other words: Language mixing, identity representations, and third space'. *Journal of Sociolinguistics* 12: 177-220.

Birman, D. and Edison J. Trickett. 2001. 'Cultural transitions in first-generation immigrants: Acculturation of Soviet Jewish refugee adolescents and parents'. *Journal of Cross-Cultural Psychology* 32: 456-77.

Blakemore, Diane. 2002. *Relevance and Linguistic Meaning. The Semantics and Pragmatics of Discourse Markers*. Cambridge: Cambridge University Press.

Blommaert, Jan. 2001. 'Context is/as critique'. *Critique of Anthropology* 21:1: 13-32.

Boman, B. and M. Edwards. 1984. 'The Indo-Chinese refugee: An overview'. *Australian and New Zealand Journal of Psychiatry* 18: 40-52.

Bourdieu, Pierre. 1984. *Distinction: A Social Critique of the Judgement of Taste*. Cambridge, MA: Harvard University Press.

Bucholtz, Mary and Kira Hall. 2005. 'Identity and interaction: A sociocultural linguistic approach'. *Discourse Studies* 7: 585-614.

Cheshire, Jenny. 2005. 'Age and generation-specific use of language'. In: Ulrich Ammon, Norbert Dittmar, Klaus J. Mattheier, and Peter Trudgill (eds.), *Sociolinguistics: An International Handbook of the Science of Language and Society*. Berlin: Mouton de Gruyter, 1552-63.

Clyne, Michael. 2003. *Dynamics of Language Contact*. Cambridge: Cambridge University Press.

Coates, Jennifer. 1996. *Women Talk*. Oxford: Blackwell Publishers.

Dinh, Khanh T., B. R. *Sarason*, and I. G. *Sarason*. *1994*. 'Parent-child relationships in Vietnamese immigrant families'. *Journal of Family Psychology* 4: 471-82.

Duran Eppler, Eva. 2010. *Emigranto*. Vienna: Braumüller.

Duran Eppler, Eva. 2013. 'A bisserl ('little') English, a bisserl Austrian, a bisserl Jewish, a bisserl female: Minority identity construction on bilingual collabora-tive floor'. *International Journal of Bilingualism* 17:1: 23-42.

Eckert, Penelope. 2000. *Linguistic Variation as Social Practice*. Oxford: Blackwell.

Eckert, Penelope and Sally McConnell-Ginet. 1992. 'Think practically and look locally: Language and gender as community-based practice'. *Annual Review of Anthropology* 21: 461-90.

Edelsky, Carole. 1993. 'Who's got the floor?'. In: Deborah Tannen (ed.), *Gender and Conversational Interaction*. Oxford: Oxford University Press, 189-227.

Erll, Astrid and Ansgar Nünning (eds.). 2008. *Cultural Memory Studies: An International and Interdisciplinary Handbook*. Berlin/New York: De Gruyter.

Fishman, Joshua. 1991. *Reversing Language Shift*. Clevedon: Multilingual Matters.

Gardner-Chloros, Penelope. 2009. *Code-Switching*. Cambridge: Cambridge University Press.

Gil, A. G. and W. A. Vega. 1996. 'Two different worlds: Acculturation stress and adaptation among Cuban and Nicaraguan families'. *Journal of Social and Personal Relationships* 13:3: 435-56.

Goodenough, William H. 1957. 'Cultural anthropology and linguistics'. In: P. L. Garvin (ed.), *Report of the 7th Annual Round Table Meeting on Linguistics and Language Study*. Washington, DC: Georgetown University Press, 167-73.

Gumperz, John J. 1982. *Discourse Strategies*. Cambridge: Cambridge University Press.

Haspelmath, Martin and Tadmor Uri (eds.). 2009. *Loanwords in the World's Languages: A Comparative Handbook*. Berlin: De Gruyter Mouton.

Kristeva, Julia. 1982. *Powers of Horror. An Essay on Abjection*. New York: Columbia University Press.

Kristeva, Julia. 2000. *The Sense and Non-Sense of Revolt: The Powers and Limits of Psychoanalysis*. New York: Columbia University Press.

Kwak, Kyunghwa. 2003. 'Adolescents and their parents: A review of intergenerational family relations for immigrant and non-immigrant families'. *Human Development* 46: 115-36.

Labov, William. 1972. 'The transformation of experience in narrative syntax'. In: William Labov, *Language in the Inner City*. Philadelphia: University of Pennsylvania Press, 354-96.

Landau, Judith. 1982. 'Therapy with families in transition'. In: M. McGoldrick and J. K. Pearce (eds.), *Ethnicity and Family Therapy*. New York: Guilford, 552-72.

Lee, Richard M., J. Choe, G. Kim, and V. Ngo. 2000. 'Construction of the Asian American family conflicts scale'. *Journal of Counseling Psychology* 47: 211-22.

Leppihalme, Ritva. 1997. *Culture Bumps*. Clevedon: Multilingual Matters.

Liebkind, Karmela. 1996. 'Acculturation and stress: Vietnamese refugees in Finland'. *Journal of Cross-Cultural Psychology* 27: 161-80.

Mallet, Marian and Antony Grenville (eds.). 2002. *Changing Countries. The Experience and Achievement of German-Speaking Exiles from Hitler in Britain, from 1933 to Today*. London: Libris.

Matsuoka, Jon K. 1990. 'Differential acculturation among Vietnamese refugees'. *Social Work* 35: 341-5.

Meeuwis, Michael and Jan Blommaert. 1994. 'The 'Markedness Model' and the absence of society: Remarks on codeswitching'. *Multilingua* 13: 387-423.

Muchitsch, Wolfgang. 1992. *Österreicher im Exil. Grossbritannien 1938-1945*. Wien: Bundesverlag.

Nguyen, Nga A. and H. L. Williams. 1989. 'Transition from East to West: Vietnamese adolescents and their parents'. *Journal of the American Academy of Child and Adolescent Psychiatry* 28: 505-15.

Nguyen, Huong, L. A. Messe, and G. E. Stollak. 1999. 'Toward a more complex understanding of acculturation and adjustment: Cultural involvements and psychosocial functioning in Vietnamese youth'. *Journal of Cross- Cultural Psychology* 30:1: 5-31.

Nora, Pierre. 1989. 'Between memory and history: Les lieux de mémoire'. *Representations* 26: 7-24.

Radstone, Susannah. 2008. 'Memory studies: For and against'. *Memory Studies* 1: 31-9.

Rick, K. and J. Forward. 1992. 'Acculturation and perceived intergenerational differences among Hmong youth'. *Journal of Cross-Cultural Psychology* 23: 85-94.

Rosenthal, Doreen. 1984. 'Intergenerational conflict and culture: A study of immigrant and nonimmigrant adolescents and their parents'. *Genetic Psychology Monographs* 109:1: 53-75.

Rosenthal, Doreen, R. Bell, A. Demetriou, and A. Efklides. 1989. 'From collectivism to individualism? The acculturation of Greek immigrants in Australia'. *International Journal of Psychology* 24: 57-71.

Rosenthal, Doreen, Nadia Ranieri, and Steven Klimidis. 1996. 'Vietnamese adolescents in Australia: Relationships between perceptions of self and parental values, intergenerational conflict'. *International Journal of Psychology* 31: 81-91.

Said, Edward W. 2001. *Reflections on Exile and Other Literary and Cultural Essays.* London: Granta Books.

Schegloff, Emanuel A. 1997. 'Whose text? Whose context?'. *Discourse and Society* 8:2: 165-87.

Schiffrin, Deborah. 1987. *Discourse Markers.* Cambridge: Cambridge University Press.

Stroud, Christopher. 1998. 'Perspectives on cultural variability of discourse and some implications for code-switching'. In: Peter Auer (ed.), *Code-Switching in Conversation: Language, Interaction and Identity.* London: Routledge, 321-48.

Szapocznik, Jose and W. Kurtines. 1980. 'Acculturation, biculturalism and adjustment among Cuban Americans'. In: A. M. Padila (ed.), *Acculturation: Theory Models and Some New Findings.* Boulder, CO: Westview, 139-59.

Szapocznik, Jose and W. M. Kurtines. 1993. 'Family psychology and cultural diversity: Opportunities for theory, research, and application'. *American Psychologist* 48: 400-7.

Tannen, Deborah. 1993. *Gender and Discourse*. New York/Oxford: Oxford University Press.

Thomason, Sarah. 2001. *Language Contact*. Edinburgh: Edinburgh University Press.

UNESCO. 2011. Intangible Cultural Heritage web-site for Austria. http://immaterielleskulturerbe.unesco.at/cgi-bin/unesco/element.pl?eid=71 (accessed 26/06/2014).

Wei, Li. 1994. *Three Generations Two Languages One Family: Language Choice and Language Shift in a Chinese Community in Britain*. Clevedon: Multilingual Matters.

Wei, Li. 1998. 'The 'why' and 'how' questions in the analysis of conversational code switching'. In: Peter Auer (ed.), *Code-Switching in Conversation*. London: Routledge, 156-76.

Wei, Li. 2002. 'What do you want me to say? On the Conversation Analysis approach to bilingual interaction'. *Language in Society* 31: 159-80.

Williams, Ashley M. 2005. 'Constructing and reconstructing Chinese American bilingual identity'. In: James Cohen, Kara T. McAlister, Kellie Rolstad, and Jeff MacSwan (eds.), *ISB4: Proceedings of the 4th International Symposium on Bilingualism*. Somerville, MA: Cascadilla Press, 2349-56.

Wistrich, Robert S. 1989. *The Jews of Vienna in the Age of Franz Josef*. Oxford: Oxford University Press.

Zhu, Hua. 2008. 'Duelling languages, duelling values: Codeswitching in bilingual intergenerational conflict talk in diasporic families'. *Journal of Pragmatics* 40: 1799-816.

Julia Averill

Hip Hop Discourse: Identity Formation and Tirolean Youth

1. Introduction

This ethnographic study investigates how Austrian adolescent boys engage in hip hop discourse to forge social identities in light of global forces that are exerted upon local contexts. The purpose of this study is to contribute to a growing understanding of the impact of American hip hop practices on cultures globally, particularly focused upon the adaptation of adolescent identities and language. At a broader scope, this study contributes to studies of globalization and in particular the relationship of the local and the global.

2. Theoretical framing

In order to frame the concepts and methods of this study, I look to three key theoretical constructs which present noticeable overlap. Each of these include a discussion of identity – a concept central to my main source of inquiry. As this study seeks to interrogate the relationships between language production and identity formation, the three concepts, including sociolinguistic ethnography, humanistic linguistics, and performative theory, play critical roles in guiding the methods of inquiry and giving shape to analysis and interpretation.

2.1. Sociolinguistic ethnography

First, this study is organized following principles of sociolinguistic ethnography as expressed by Gumperz (1982), Hymes (1974), and Johnstone (2000), particularly regarding standards of evidence and ethnographic procedures. Gumperz (1982) offers a series of tools with which to frame the study. What is most applicable to my research is his insistence that communication does not rely on speech alone, rather it is the positionality within social context that creates meaning. He further states that "conversationalists thus rely on indirect inferences which build on background assumptions about context, interactive goals and interpersonal relations to derive frames in terms of which they can interpret what is going on" (Gumperz 1982: 2). Related scholarship includes Hymes' (1974) references to Sapir (1933) who asserted that the thrust of research is becoming more divergent from positivist approaches that yield static models and products for analysis. Instead, he acknowledges a trend that explains the concern of sociocultural studies with context and networks of exchange. He further attests that these movements have shifted in intent from former abstractions of categories and fixed norms toward strategic assessment of social engagement as fluctuating and dynamic.

Hymes further places emphasis on language use in the context within which it is used to reveal meaning and contends that

> one cannot take linguistic form, a given code, or even speech itself, as a limiting frame of reference. One must take as context a community, or network of persons, investigating its communicative activities as a whole, so that any use of channel and code takes its place as part of the resources upon which the members draw. (1974: 4)

Hip hop discourse provides these resources as a global phenomenon allowing participants to draw from what is called by hip hoppers, the "Hip Hop Nation" (see Heath 2006; Alim 2006). Although the participants are negotiating frames for their localized, community-based hip hop practices, they do not limit their scale of engagement to that of the local. Rather, Hip Hop Nation insists that locally situated participation shapes and perpetuates a broader, encompassing, recursive transnational movement which is by way of participation, constantly re-imagining itself. In this way, any study of hip hop discourse must examine the proliferation of networks that connect global movements to local practices, thus expanding the potential for meaningful contact, appropriation, and reciprocation. Language plays a vital role in these processes and communicates the aesthetics and ideologies of the Hip Hop Nation and how participants identify themselves as local practitioners.

2.2. Humanistic linguistics

Analyzing linguistic intention is essential in linking participants' usage to their identity formation. Providing a conceptual tool for viewing these relationships is the theoretical vantage of humanistic linguistics, whose key proponents include Becker (2000) and Tannen (1989). As these scholars contend, language is in a constant state of negotiation and is referential in function, indexing meaning to the circumstances of its context and grounding the meaning of an utterance or sign. As such, humanistic linguists consider the social dimensions of communication, noting the active process of unpacking and reassembling recognizable indices for a personalized construction of meaning.

To consider language as a process requires problematizing previous assumptions of static and isolable constructions. Becker (1988: 25) reconsiders the term "language" as a correct description of what actually happens in everyday social interaction and instead proposes the term "languaging". He explains that this "shift from the word 'language' to the word 'languaging' [...] is one of the easiest ways [...] to make the shift from an idea of language as something accomplished [...] to the idea of languaging as an ongoing process". This removes language from abstraction and places it firmly in action, acting in personal ways by individuals and their own imaginations. It is this personalization that both Becker and Tannen explore to reveal the intellectual and emotional content embedded in the languaging people do.

In order to examine this content, Tannen offers a humanistic analysis of the inner workings of utterances. She connects the value of aesthetic representation in successfully engaging the listener in shared principles of "involvement strategies" (1989: 19). An effective strategy consists of enlisting shared, pre-patterned tropes and conventions, allowing what she calls "coherence". She furthers that "[t]he familiarity of the strategies makes the discourse and its meaning seem coherent, and allows for the elaboration of meaning through the play of familiar patterns" (Tannen 1989: 13). She further examines how speakers break those conventions leading to innovative ways of achieving creativity and illustrates how these patterns are consciously and unconsciously manipulated to allow for inventive speech. In her view, Becker's description

> suggests that language is less freely generated, more prepatterned, than most current linguistic theory acknowledges. This is not, however, to say that speakers are automatons, cranking out language by rote. Rather, prepatterning (or idiomaticity, or formulaicity) is a resource for creativity. It is the play between fixity and novelty that makes possible the creation of meaning. (Tannen 1989: 37)

Tannen and Becker furthermore argue that it is this creativity that promotes meaning making particular to each listener and each event. Tannen extends this notion to enlist what she calls "constructed dialogues" in stating:

> Dialogue is not a general report; it is particular, and the particular enables listeners (or readers) to create their understanding by drawing on their own history of associations. [...] Constructing dialogue, moreover, is an example of the poetic in everyday conversation. In the terms of Friedrich (1986), it is a figure that fires the individual imagination. The creation of voices occasions the imagination of alternative, distant, and others' worlds by linking them to the sounds and scenes of one's own familiar world. (Tannen 1989: 133)

Becker argues for the importance of the particular in regard to uses of languages and indicates that this particularity is found inherently between speaker and listener. Of exchanges, he contends that "we can often not predict how they will change: in the dimension of structure, the coherence of things, the ways things are put together" (1988: 26). Hence, individuals internalize messages particular to their own sets of experiences and not necessarily based upon what was uttered. In this light, particularity can be seen in the ways that global ideologies are perceived, modified, and internalized in local contexts and how individuals respond to these processes in ways that affect identity.

2.3. Performative theory

Tannen's theorizing of pre-patterning in speech can be extrapolated to a broader scale in relation to the tenets of Butler's performative theory. While Tannen applies this notion to language, Butler advances these structures as foundational for identity formation and adopts the nomenclature of 'citationality'. That is, she describes the iterative function of identity building/altering based upon a preconceived norm. Hey (2006: 440) describes this process noting that identity "is the result of an illusion sustained by the incessant replication of norms that materialise that which they govern" and furthers of Butler that "[s]he argues that this fiction is produced by compulsive (but alterable, also potentially subversive) repetition".

Butler would argue that the circumstances which individuals index are presumed to be stable and, therefore, essentialized. Warikoo (2007) maintains that established norms can be reconsidered and manipulated to form alternate identities based on performance, a concept furthered by Butler. Butler identified the mutability of identities through a process she called "performativity" whereby tropes are actually performed according to notions of authenticity (a concern within hip hop communities). To borrow from Tannen's notion of pre-patterned tropes, Butler would argue that these scripts can be multiple and sometimes conflicting, calling individuals to perform them in novel and potentially unharmonious ways.

Interrogating scripts and performing highly personalized iterations that, too, are mutable, places communication in action and through a matrix of humanistic linguistics, the salience of language is revealed as a prime vehicle for identity. In the case of this study, I will be looking at how the participants access knowledge of global hip hop discourse, and the ways that they enact or perform aspects of this discourse in their local lives. As global hip hop discourse is exerting notions of authenticity upon its participants, Stromquist and Monkman (2000) indicate that local groups are faced with decisions of how to reorient themselves in light of trends and ideologies. Identity work then becomes less static and proliferates in a multiplicity of instantiations.

Framing my interrogations with these three theories provides more informed articulation of the phenomena I observe. Consequently, this approach supports natural occurrences of overlap where data may compliment or conflict with one another.

These zones of overlap help to locate the participants' construction and adaptation of local identities, particularly as they are revealed by the linguistic choices they make.

3. Methodology

Chiefly, it is important to note that this study is organized as an ethnographic study. Regarding this approach, Hammersley and Atkinson state:

> in terms of data collection, ethnography usually involves the researcher participating overtly or covertly, in people's daily lives for an extended period of time, watching what happens, listening to what is said, and/or asking questions through informal and formal interviews, collecting documents and artefacts – in fact, gathering whatever data are available to throw light on the issues that are the emerging focus of inquiry. (2007: 3)

The organization of my research protocol illustrates the epistemological arc of qualitative processes aimed to capture the mutability of meanings and the complex networks at play as participants account for their participation in multiple contexts. As an ethnography of communication this study approaches speech events through a number of vehicles that may be later triangulated to analyze the use and purposes for which the participants perform hip hop identities. Hammersley and Atkinson define triangulation as

> involv[ing] the comparison of data relating to the same phenomenon but deriving from different phases of the fieldwork, different points in the temporal cycles occurring in the setting, or the accounts of different participants (including the ethnographer) differentially located in the setting. (2007: 183)

With this in mind, my approach, as discussed above, includes a number of the strategies suggested in order to capture multiple facets of participants' engagement in an attempt to bring to bear the goal of triangulation.

4. Data collection

As is rendered above, the study is theoretically underpinned by ethnographic concepts of what constitutes responsible approaches to qualitative research. However, Hammersley and Atkinson (2007) define specific descriptions of how these theories shall be put into practice. I approach the methodology in this study to be reflective of these precepts. The study is based upon the participation of five adolescent male students in Innsbruck, Austria. In the interest of cultivating strong, ongoing relationships with the participants, I chose to limit the sample to this size and carry out multiple interviews over an extended period of time. Maintaining a small research group supports the notion that approaching authenticity can be better anticipated with a small sample and multiple interventions over time. Longitudinal studies allow the researcher to be immersed in the contextual surroundings within which they act. The interview period spanned ten months, however, I was in a working capacity within their high schools and therefore, made other contact with them and was able to document their school behaviors. Being an actor in the schools allowed me to track them over two academic years and research protocols were performed in the familiar contexts of those schools. In selecting that setting, I attempted to minimize those affective barriers that may hinder their capacities for breadth in their responses while encouraging forthcomingness and spontaneity in their contributions. I believe that given those factors, the assertions of Hammersley and Atkinson (2007) are most evident in the structuring of my ethnographic research plan. The fundamental principles as noted below underscore the method of inquiry of my study by the following criteria:

> (1) people's actions and accounts are studied in everyday contexts, rather than under conditions created by the researcher [...] research takes place "in the field", (2) data are gathered from a range of sources, (3) data collection is, for the most part, relatively "unstructured", in two senses. First it does not involve following through a fixed and detailed research design specified at the start. Second, the categories that are used for interpreting what people say or do are not built into the data collection process through the use of observation schedules or questionnaires. Instead, they are generated out of the process of data analysis, (4) the focus is usually on a few cases, generally fairly small-scale, perhaps a single setting or group of people, and (5) the analysis of data involves interpretation of the meanings, functions, and consequences of human actions and institutional practices, and how these are implicated in local, and perhaps also wider, contexts. What are produced, for the most part, are verbal descriptions, explanations, and theories. (Hammersley and Atkinson 2007: 3)

Given those elements which constitute an ethnographic agenda, I organized my data collection to include: (1) an opinion survey, (2) a lexical survey, (3) video recorded individual interviews ranging between 15 and 75 minutes per session, (4) small focus groups, (5) student directed and recorded videos of their out of school lives and practices, and (6) extensive field notes observing the students in and out of school contexts as well as documentation of the research process overall including my own reflections of my shifting positioning as engagement among the participants changed over time.

Self-recorded videos allow participants to report on their own vision of how their lives are affected through hip hop practices which, as a byproduct, involves them in a meta-analysis of their affiliation which may lead to a better understanding of how they choose to participate. For research purposes, this provides me insight into social milieux and other cultural spaces to which I may not otherwise have had access as a researcher. To date, the self-recorded videos include participants' daily happenings where hip hop music is played, as well as a video tutorial instructing how the beat generating software MPD is used to create hip hop tracks, and a series of videos recording a tour of Innsbruck graffiti along with a demonstration of how to tag. The students have approached these videos as an expression of the particularity of their engagement in hip hop discourse which provides further basis upon which to assess their manners of appropriation and the choices they make based on these affinities.

5. Data analysis

Ethnography can be considered messy and unwieldy in that it considers a broad scope of sources and situates each according to local contexts. However, "the analysis of data involves interpretation of the meanings, functions, and conse-quences of human actions and institutional practices" and may result in drawing connections between individual and broader generalizations (Hammersley and Atkinson 2007: 3).

In order to classify findings, I employ thematic analysis as outlined by Glaser and Strauss (1967), Glesne (2006), and Wolcott (1994). Thematic analysis is per-tinent to my research study as the dominant data collection method consists of video recorded interviews and student-recorded videos. Thematic analysis allows me to examine the transcripts for patterns and similarities which can be coded and categorized to discover and identify any underlying ideas located in the data. Glesne summarizes coding as,

> a progressive process of sorting and defining and defining and sorting those scraps of collected data (i.e., observation notes, interview transcripts, memos, documents, and notes from relevant literature) that are applicable to your research purpose. By putting like-minded pieces together into data clumps, you create an organizational framework. (2006: 152)

As my study involves a small group of participants, I am able to not only compare an individual participant's responses against himself over time, but I can draw linkages between group members to gain a multi-layered perspective of their be-liefs and practices. In this way, the research analysis is 'grounded' in the data and can be used to generate understanding of how these group members experience the role of global hip hop in local milieux. 'Grounding' is used here in the sense of Glaser and Strauss's Grounded Theory (1967) whose purpose is to "demonstrate relations between conceptual categories and to specify the conditions under which theoretical relationships emerge, change, or are maintained" (Charmaz 2002: 675; as cited in Glesne 2006: 12). Glesne further discusses the connection between the data and the generation of theory and cites Wolcott (1994), who distinguishes "*description, analysis,* and *interpretation* as three means of data transformation" (Glesne 2006: 164). While description involves staying close to the original form of the data, analysis follows with "the identification of key factors in the study and the relationships among them" (Glesne 2006: 164) and leads necessarily to interpretation, which takes place when deeper analysis "transcends factual data and cautious analysis and begins to probe into what is to be made of them" (Wolcott 1994: 36; as cited in Glesne 2006: 165).

6. Participants

In order to establish relationships to the data discussed later, I will introduce the participants in the order that they joined the study. The first participant recruited was Flo, both an abbreviated name for Florian, and also a nickname mimicking "flow", an important feature of rap performance. Flo's knowledge of hip hop is extensive and consists mainly of European – particularly German language – rap. He is 18 years old and completing his fourth of five years at the high school. Flo is an only child and has a close relationship with his mother and father. They are both professional musicians who are classically trained and perform traditional Austrian music throughout the world. Flo has had the opportunity to accompany his parents on some of their trips, including a lengthy stay in Japan. This exposure to world cultures has provided him a worldview that allows him to be open to multiple possibilities and has developed in him a deep appreciation for music. He claims to have moved through a variety of phases of musical styles and "ended up" at hip hop where he claims to be satisfied by its versatility and vibrance. His appreciation for the music encouraged him to expand his listening to include multiple styles of hip hop, though he admits a preference for what has to either "be aggressive or question something". His disposition is well aligned with vigorous questioning. He displays great introspection and moves flexibly through analytical challenges. As a graphic artist he enjoys participating in street art and graffiti, one element of hip hop culture, particularly stenciling. He exhibits some pride in being a part of the study and has contributed the most interviews of all participants. He is also responsible for introducing me to his friend, Marco, whom he recommended as a potential asset to the program.

The second to participate is Simon, a 15 year old whose primary engagement with hip hop culture is dance. He, like all of the participants, has a great appreciation for rap music, particularly contemporary American rap. He practices a style of dance called "jerkin", which is relatively new in the hip hop dance landscape. His participation is sporadic, since he is often absent from school and often reluctant to commit time to interviews. Nevertheless, his commitment to each interview is focused and he is eager to share his knowledge and expertise. Simon lives in a village outside the city and claims that there was a greater hip hop scene in the smaller village of Telfs than what he finds in the city of Innsbruck. Simon primarily listens to American hip hop with very little attention paid to German language rap. He asserts that hip hop is an American cultural phenomenon by right of origin. Simon often travels to nearby Munich, Germany to visit his cousin who is also a jerker and hip hop consumer. Simon says that he and his cousin were not particularly close until Simon brought up hip hop music which was also an affinity of his cousin. In the beginning of this new relationship, Simon says that they mostly related to one another around hip hop, but that they are much closer in other respects now that they have spent time together over a shared interest.

Hannes is the third participant to join and was recruited based on his style of dress which is in keeping with the commonly and historically accepted hip hop style consisting of baggy pants, oversized t-shirts, and basketball shoes. Hannes is 16 years old and is active in the graffiti scene in Innsbruck. Hannes' musical interests reside mostly with what is called consciousness-raising and underground. His favorite artists produced music between 1990 and 2000, though his tastes fall outside those lines in certain cases. In addition, his preference is for American hip hop and rap. He can list only one or two German language rappers that he enjoys because he thinks they are aggressive and mostly only participate in braggadocio. Hannes is an imposing figure, being over six feet tall and broad shouldered. His attitude, however, is peaceable and relaxed. His command of English is competent, however, compared to the other participants, he often code-switches between German and English to communicate more conceptual matters.

The next participant to join the study is Marco, who is called Macko, by his friends. The alias Macko is a reference to a hip hop term, mack, which is a person with credibility and savvy within the hip hop community. Macko is 18 years old and also in his fourth of five years of high school. He was introduced to the study by his long-time friend and aforementioned participant, Flo. He, like Hannes, is involved in the graffiti scene in Innsbruck and has been interested in hip hop since he was nine years old. Like Simon and Hannes, he listens primarily to American hip hop and tends to appreciate the West Coast style over East Coast. He is also very interested in the lyrics of rap music and takes time to research any meanings that are unclear. He claims that this has helped his academic English substantially and reckons that he is the top student in his English class. Macko, like the others, has a calm demeanor during the interviews and despite his brevity, appears to be forthcoming with his responses.

The final participant is Orcun, a 16 year old Innsbrucker with Turkish background. This is significant as there is a stigma attached to people of Turkish descent in Austria. However, as Hannes' best friend, he has had no trouble participating in hip hop discourse as it is experienced by other hip hoppers of Austrian heritage. Interestingly, he approached me about participating in the project. I was at a different school and teaching an English lesson. At the end of the lesson, he raised his hand and asked, "Do you know Hannes? From the other HTL?" When I saw the oversized headphones wrapped around his neck, I knew which Hannes he meant (as it is the same accessory he sports). "He's my best friend", he stated. He met me at the door after class and I asked him if he was "into hip hop", which he replied with an enthusiastic "yes, I love it". I asked if he would like to participate and he immediately agreed. This display of enthusiasm is indicative of his level of commitment to the project. He has preempted my asking him for another interview on a few occasions and has offered to meet me at other locations. He is able to use his school studies of electronics to master the rather tedious and difficult software program MPD. This program, and special equipment, is used by professional hip hop producers to create the beats heard under vocal tracks. In this way, he has taken up the role of deejay as he cuts and mixes together samples from rather obscure sources to mash up intricate and danceable beats. He has a willingness to cooperate and always demonstrates a polite nature in his verbal and email correspondences with me.

7. Overview of findings

The following section breaks down the preliminary analyses into discrete subsections. In doing so, I wish to touch upon the main areas concerning this study while demonstrating that there is some discontinuity and some appearance of disjointedness when the categories are juxtaposed. I believe this reflects some of the imbalances that exist in globalized popular culture and can become a robust space for deeper analysis. The issues introduced below each warrant further exploration if research wishes to address a genre that keeps pace with the expanding networks of global youth culture. Looking at the everyday practices of the participants may expose these issues for wider scrutiny, particularly the dynamics of what takes place when global forces and local forces come into contact.

7.1. Student knowledge of hip hop discourse

All of the participants are not only consumers of hip hop music and video, but they are deeply tied to at least one of the four main elements comprising hip hop culture. This involvement indicates a critical distinction related to two predominant metaphors in educational theory – noting that learning often follows either an acquisition model or a participation model. During an interview with Hannes, he succinctly defined the difference between them. I asked him about other hip hoppers and he asked whether I meant people who listen to hip hop or people who are hip hop. In identifying them he noted that to be in (or participate in) hip hop, one must not only know the music, but "he must also beschäftigen [be involved in it] – he's a rapper, he's a beat boxer, he's a sprayer". This defines their level of involvement and dedication to the genre and certainly speaks of the recurrent construction of hip hop as they know it and how they express it within their own communities of practice (Lave and Wenger 1991).

A further attempt to understand how these participants identify themselves as hip hoppers questions how they use language to engage in these activities. As avid consumers of hip hop music, they each go to great lengths to learn the lyrics of the songs they enjoy, including more elusive slang terminology and unconventional English usage. However, when asked whether or not they use this language, each confirmed that they do, but only among closed circles. Also, when asked how to identify a hip hopper, they agreed that clothing was no longer a reliable determinant, but that how one speaks is indicative of a hip hop affiliation. But, when asked why they don't use it, questions of authenticity arose. Bearing in mind the tensions surrounding authenticity, the participants' approach to hip hop language reflects the struggle to understand which behaviors are permissible and in which settings. To express their understanding and engagement with the music and its various other activities, one critical factor we discussed was the relationships with the language forms used to participate in these activities. While on the one hand, the participants agree that language is a reliable marker for identifying one's affiliation with hip hop music and culture, they each stated that they seldom use it. When asked if they understood the slang that they hear in English language rap music they each said yes and added that when they do not understand certain terms, they research them on the internet or ask friends for clarification. Their reluctance to use hip hop language is then not due to a lack of interest or facility with the language, rather it may express a common concern shared by the participants that those outside the rap scene may not fully understand what is communicated. In the case of these participants, transparency of communication is a priority which may discourage hip hop language except among those few of their peers who share a common vocabulary. Knowing the appropriate settings and audience for using hip hop language is central to the ways the participants speak.

In light of this, each participant has a unique relationship to the language governing engagement in that discourse. Flo admitted that he had previously used hip hop language somewhat loosely in school with his friends and in English class. He reported that he suffered some academic repercussions for doing so causing him to not only drop it in class, but withdraw from it except on very specific occasions. Simon indicated that he does not use hip hop language with most of his friends in Innsbruck, though he did admit to using it often with other dancers he meets and a cousin who lives in Munich. Hannes explains that he rarely uses the language – except with some "homies" in the graffiti community – because it is street language and he doesn't come from the streets, therefore, it would be a misrepresentation of both himself and the language as he feels it was meant to be used. As well, Macko reiterated this concern, although he had previously used hip hop language often among a group of Chechen immigrants who were also involved in hip hop. As he withdrew from the group, he withdrew from social use of hip hop language.

7.2. Authenticity and credibility

The pertinent hip hop phrasing related directly to the notion of authenticity is called "keepin' it real". This notion is a persistent challenge to American performers and consumers to represent their affiliations to street culture; however, on a broader scale, it is also applied to validate transnational idioms in maintaining a hip hop aesthetic. When describing the impact of hip hop in the Netherlands, Pennycook (2007a: 98) states,

> [h]ere is a perfect example of a tension between, on the one hand, the spread of a cultural dictate to adhere to certain principles of what it means to be authentic, and on the other, a process of localization that makes such an expression of staying true to oneself dependent on local contexts, languages, cultures and understandings of the real.

As a consequence of these concerns, one participant felt that it would be inauthentic to use hip hop language as it is a reflection of American street life. And given his social and economic positioning, he would be misrepresenting both himself and the language by using it.

7.3. Hip hop communities

Both Simon and Hannes speak of strong local connections reinforced through close contact with other hip hoppers in their respective communities. These connections are also reinforced through the flow of transnational media that they use to gain information, inspiration, and expand their skills. Through these transnational channels, the participants become integrated into, as described above, the Hip Hop Nation. They argue that hip hop is a movement constituted across borders and in a constant state of flux as individuals contribute, shift, and reconceptualize an overarching hip hop identity. As mentioned above, each of the research participants is active in one of the four elements of hip hop discourse. Through this participation, each student contributes to the growth and evolution of the Hip Hop Nation. In this sense, globally, hip hoppers are connected by affinity and often seek similarly oriented individuals with whom to share social practices.

To demonstrate this sense of community, Simon and Hannes illustrate these relationships through examples of the processes involved in establishing an affinity group (Gee 2000). Simon identifies himself as a "jerker", a new trend in hip hop dance. We discussed whether he feels that hip hoppers are connected both locally and globally. He told a story of him and his cousin in Munich jerkin' at a corner in the city which an hour later, became a group of seven as one by one, other hip hoppers passed by and jumped in. He enthusiastically discussed the shared community to which he belongs as a consequence of his dance and musical preference and how he continues to learn and practice hip hop discourse through these relationships. Similarly, Hannes spoke of his identification with the graffiti presence in Innsbruck. He states that "it's one community, it's vernetzt [connected], only people get together and draw and spray, it's family, in prinzip [principle]". I inquired, "how did this family grow?" To which he described a gradual inculcation process as, "yeah, at first you are alone, you have no one. Then you get up and up. You meet other people who do it and you go 'immer mehr hinein' [...] Immer mehr in die Szene. [always further in, always further in the scene]" And of the camaraderie that develops, he adds, "It's like you are süchtig [addicted]". Communities can provide the structure to maintain global authenticity within the scope of local contexts, fostering unity of a hip hop aesthetic and a stable positioning from which new ideas may be expressed. Members of the Birmingham school dealing with subcultures note that communities cohere when "there is a shared set of social rituals that define them as a group instead of a mere collection of individuals" (Maira 2011: 208). Affinity draws together hip hoppers in local communities and virtual worlds. Indeed, a communal experience of hip hop discourse summons a shared worldview which further nurtures participation in these communities.

7.4. Appropriation of hip hop discourse in the local setting

As exhibited by the research participants, notions of global hip hop are refashioned to reflect the circumstances of local ideologies and cultural norms. This relates to Alastair Pennycook's explication of the nexus of local and global forces and what constitutes authenticity. He first establishes that "[l]ocalization inevitably involves complex relations of class, race/ethnicity and language use" (2007a: 98). As such, localization is supported as a transformation resulting from the contact between two or more cultural forces. In the case of this study, I am looking at the ways that the globalization of American hip hop is received, interpreted and adapted by these five adolescents.

This sentiment calls forth an investigation of the spaces inhabited by transnational hip hoppers and the questions of validity they confront as they take up various hip hop activities outside the United States. In particular, they are concerned with the credibility of local participation within a global hip hop idiom. From this conflict, the participants seek meaning by piecing together facets of hip hop that speak to "real" Innsbruck, and "real" contributions to hip hop culture as they are constructed in their communities. These contributions reach beyond the immediate community to shape a global Hip Hop Nation which transcends borders real and imagined. As such, hip hoppers create and recreate a hip hop ideal that provides access to participants around the world – access which allows transnational hip hop ideologies to merge and carve out active spaces for local participants worldwide.

8. Discussion

In choosing to identify themselves as hip hoppers, the adolescents in this study are making decisions which blur the boundaries demarcating local cultural practices from those outside. These findings are similar to those found in Warikoo's (2007) discussion on boundary work as it pertains to adolescents. As the findings show, local contact with global channels can influence the ways that individuals conceptualize these borders and can cause those borders to become less clearly defined. With the technological and linguistic resources they possess, the participants readily locate globalized information about hip hop music, videos, publications, and other elements which enhance their overall knowledge of hip hop discourse and ideologies. When asked how they find this information, they each answered that they use the internet almost exclusively.

One advantage to the internet as a resource is that the participants have access to all aspects of global hip hop discourse. As the internet provides global availability, the only limits to how they can participate are their own skills and interests. Further, with the ease of the internet, the participants are free to try on this discourse and its multiple dimensions and make decisions as to what they can identify with and then tailor the discourse to fit in with their wants and desires. In this way, they are given the ability to experiment with aspects of their identities and cultivate a hip hop persona that resonates with their own understandings of themselves and their environments.

The participants seem to grasp that they are negotiating their identities against the broader, more pervasive, and hegemonic presence of an American ideal in hip hop discourse. They are highly aware (and constantly reminded) of the influences of American hip hop in their choices. For example, the beat tracks that Orcun develops on his highly specialized production equipment are samples and cuts pulled exclusively from American songs. He is creating Innsbruck hip hop, but he uses American produced and performed music as his sole resources. In this way, Orcun is appropriating global hip hop and easily localizing it to match an Innsbruck aesthetic.

Another example is Graffiti. Graffiti in Innsbruck, for example, has elements of traditional American designs, most evident in the tags that sprayers develop and use to establish territory. However, the works I have seen here possess an aesthetic departure from the predominant American style when looking at lettering and line. But, perhaps the greatest departure is found in the topics and themes they address. Innsbruck graffiti tends toward decidedly more political and social commentary than the majority of what one encounters in an American city. To demonstrate this, I allude to a work that I discovered overnight at my bus stop in Innsbruck. Sprayed in black across a stark white wall is the phrase, "Welt Untergang" [End of the world]. What is of note is the foreground features a black and white painting of a small girl who herself is painting over the phrase in red paint the word "Cancelled", in English. This form of social commentary is common among Innsbruck graffiti. For some sprayers, graffiti is still about keenly artistic depictions of their sprayer name. But, for many others, it is a platform to typify social and political dissonance. In these interpretations, Innsbruckers are attempting to fuse two worlds, filtering global hip hop discourse through the lens of their local circumstances. What appears to be simple expressions are actually difficult decisions made about appropriation.

Given the delicate work of appropriation, a common theme that seemed to be of concern to each of the participants was legitimacy or credibility. Acknowledging the value placed on authenticity, Pennycook further expands the argument that for some,

> African American hip-hop is the only real thing and that all other forms are inauthentic deviations; others insist that hip-hop must be a culture of the streets [...] some insist that to be authentic one needs to stick to one's 'own' cultural and linguistic domain, to draw on one's own traditions, to be overtly local; [...] for others, being authentic is a matter of just speaking from the heart: the expression of one's own feelings [...] yet another position suggests that authenticity is a question of style and genre, of finding ways to tell a story that resonates with an audience, of achieving agreement about what matters; and some suggest that any recontextualization of language and culture renders it authentic anew. (2007a: 14)

The position taken by Flo, as mentioned above, resonates Pennycook's proposal that "being authentic is a matter of just speaking from the heart". As Flo succinctly stated, any hip hop is authentic so long as the artist "has love for the thing". As Pennycook's explication of the multiple contentions discussed among the hip hop community indicates, the point of contact between the global dictates of "real hip hop" and the reworking of what is real in local consciousnesses is the site where authenticity is negotiated. Therefore, authenticity plays a strong role in assessing the outcomes of adaptations. Pennycook's rubric explains the proximity of the global to the local and what value is placed on that proximity. In the case of this study, there are varying degrees of proximity that are played out by the participants, and each seems to have realized his position within that matrix. This leaves the concerns of authenticity up to the individual in that one can reconcile his or her own synthesis of global and local ideals.

The participants embody the complexities of negotiating identities on the edges of local iterations of globalized ideals. This conflict comes to the surface in the decisions they are asked to make in order to position themselves favorably amid questions of authenticity and self-representation. The idea of hip hop discourse as a source of identification is a stark contrast to that typified in their local setting, including demands placed on them to carefully select which forms of self they wish to promulgate. How they situate themselves is related to the relationships found between both competing and complementing ideologies and speaks to the broader notion of how globalization impacts remote contexts worldwide. Drawing conclusions becomes particularly unwieldy as the messages communicated to these participants are often in conflict with themselves, and therefore, in conflict with the cultures where they are represented – particularly regarding "keepin' it real". As is evinced by the experiences of the participants, Flo's summation of the contact between global and local hip hop most forcefully suggests that authenticity is achieved when one "has love for the thing". The personalization of each student's story is indication that there is indeed love and an eagerness to take his place among the Hip Hop Nation.

References

Alim, H. Samy. 2006. *Roc the Mic Right: The Language of Hip Hop Culture*. New York/London: Routledge.

Becker, A. L. 1988. 'Language in particular: A lecture'. In: Deborah Tannen (ed.), *Linguistics in Context: Connecting Observation and Understanding*. Norwood, NJ: Ablex Publishing Corporation, 17-36.

Becker, A. L. 2000 [1995]. *Beyond Translation: Essays Toward a Modern Philology*. Ann Arbor: University of Michigan Press.

Friedrich, Paul. 1986. *The Language Parallax: Linguistic Relativism and Poetic Indeterminacy*. Austin, TX: University of Texas Press.

Gee, James Paul. 2000. 'The new literacy studies: From 'socially situated' to the work of the social'. In: David Barton, Mary Hamilton, and Roz Ivanic (eds.), *Situated Literacies: Reading and Writing in Context*. London: Routledge, 180-96.

Geertz, Clifford. 1973. *The Interpretation of Cultures: Selected Essays*. New York: Basic Books.

Glaser, Barney G. and Anselm Leonard Strauss. 1967. *The Discovery of Grounded Theory: Strategies for Qualitative Research*. Piscataway, NJ: Rutgers University Press.

Glesne, Corrine. 2006. *Becoming Qualitative Researchers: An Introduction* (3rd edn.). Boston, MA: Allyn and Bacon.

Gumperz, John J. 1982. *Discourse Strategies*. Cambridge: Cambridge University Press.

Hammersley, Martyn and Paul Atkinson. 2007. *Ethnography: Principles in Practice*. New York/London: Routledge.

Heath, R. Scott. 2006. 'True heads: Historicizing the hip-hop 'nation' in context'. *Callaloo* 29:3: 846-66.

Hey, Valerie. 2006. 'The politics of performative resignification: Translating Judith Butler's theoretical discourse and its potential for a sociology of education'. *British Journal of Sociology of Education* 27:4: 439-57.

Hymes, Dell H. 1974. *Foundations in Sociolinguistics: An Ethnographic Approach*. Philadelphia: University of Pennsylvania Press.

Johnstone, Barbara. 2000. *Qualitative Methods in Sociolinguistics*. New York/Oxford: Oxford University Press.

Johnstone, Barbara. 2008. *Discourse Analysis* (2nd edn.). Oxford: Blackwell.

Lave, Jean and Etienne Wenger. 1991. *Situated Learning: Legitimate Peripheral Participation*. Cambridge: Cambridge University Press.

Maira, Sunaina. 2011. *Youth Cultures, Language, and Literacy. Review of Research in Education*. Washington, DC: AERA.

Pennycook, Alastair. 2007a. *Global Englishes and Transcultural Flows*. New York/London: Routledge.

Pennycook, Alastair. 2007b. 'Language, localization, and the real: Hip-hop and the global spread of authenticity'. *Journal of Language, Identity, and Education* 6:2: 101-15.

Stromquist, Nelly P. and Karen Monkman (eds.). 2000. *Globalization and Education: Integration and Contestation Across Cultures*. Washington, DC: Rowman and Littlefield.

Tannen, Deborah. 1989. *Talking Voices: Repetition, Dialogue, and Imagery in Conversational Discourse*. Cambridge: Cambridge University Press.

Warikoo, Natasha. 2007. 'Racial authenticity among second generation youth in multiethnic New York and London'. *Poetics* 35: 388-408.

Wolcott, Harry F. 1994. *Transforming Qualitative Data: Description, Analysis, and Interpretation*. Thousand Oaks, CA: Sage Publications.

DAVID FULLER

'There is no method …'?
Contact and Conflict in Interdisciplinary
Studies

«J'ai la passion de comprendre les hommes», wrote Jean-Paul Sartre.[1] It is a fundamental drive of the intellect and a passion that cannot be compartmentalised. What in an academic context is dignified as 'interdisciplinarity' is the natural bent of the mind not corralled by frameworks of education.

This natural bent is illustrated *in parvo* by literary criticism. Despite immense, contested methodological variety, literary criticism is usually and rightly conceived as having a disciplinary 'core': attention to language in all its historical and formal aspects. Wallace Stevens: "In poetry you must love the words […] with all your capacity to love anything at all".[2] In poetry, and in all literary art. While the kind of attention and love may vary with genre (poetry, prose, drama, 'literary' non-fiction), ears attuned by wide reading to the multiple resonances of language are central. But literary criticism is also inherently a subject without boundaries, freewheeling – 'interdisciplinary'. Creative fluidity – methodological chaos – is among the things that make it so interesting. To the interpretation of texts anything can be relevant. As well as issues that are obviously literary – language, form, genre – there are always issues that potentially engage with other disciplines – knowledge of society and politics, of the other arts, and of all areas of intellectual and spiritual life. "There is", as T. S. Eliot puts it, "no method except to be very intelligent".[3] And as with any discipline, refreshing the methods of literary criticism by testing them through engagement with other modes of thought, or opening up kinds of thinking not readily conceivable within accepted assumptions of criticism, can also be a source of more vivid perception and creative articulation. Anybody whose natural intelligence has not been entirely channelled and compartmentalised by the rigidities of systematic education will scarcely take a solemn view of disciplinary boundaries, which are certain to vary

---

1   Jean-Paul Sartre, *Saint Genet, comédien et martyr* (Paris: Gallimard, 1952), p. 158.
2   Wallace Stevens, "Adagia", in Samuel French Morse, ed., *Opus Posthumous: Poems, Plays, Prose* (New York: Knopf, 1957), pp. 157-82, p. 161.
3   T. S. Eliot, "The Perfect Critic", in *The Sacred Wood: Essays on Poetry and Criticism* (London: Methuen, 1920), pp. 1-16, p. 11.

with fashion and must be transcended or dissolved by any education the effects of which pass into life beyond institutions of learning. (There is a method other than that prescribed by Eliot – the method of relying on special knowledge to limit the demands on intelligence and saying more or less what other professionals say. Viewed positively, this may be seen as the academic world well attuned to the needs of contemporary society; viewed negatively, it is the herd instinct. Whether it leads to comforting reflections on one's deathbed is a question not to be asked.)

However, though thinking beyond disciplinary boundaries is natural to unfettered intelligence and inherent in criticism, creative contact with other disciplines in an academic context can be fraught with difficulties. More than many other forms of study, and in part because of its inherent interdisciplinarity, literary criticism is situated knowledge – knowledge that depends on the cultural situation and personal choices of the critic, and on the critic's view of the needs of readers. Method must, therefore, be eclectic. This can make collaboration with disciplines in which the cultural construction of knowledge plays a lesser role and method is more generally agreed variously problematic. Science may be fragmented, so that only a small number of people are abreast of advanced thinking in each area at a given moment; but fundamental scientific method, testing hypotheses by experiment, constructing experiments to obtain relevant data, is universal. The precise methods by which this is best done in a given case will admit debate; but of science one could not say what Eliot says of criticism. While problems of collaboration between disciplines therefore sometimes reflect relatively superficial differences of training, they may also reflect deeper and revealing differences of substance, difficulties that can sometimes be reconciled, but must sometimes remain (perhaps valuable) sites of conflict.

I should say that I did not expect to become so involved in interdisciplinary studies as I have. I am an aesthete. 'Immediate need of Pater' is my mantra. To me, music is the art of arts, to which all others aspire. With any work by which I am fully engaged, beauty is the first consideration and the last. Much of what I do in teaching and writing aims to clear away the sort of intellectualising typical of institutional study of the arts that gets in the way of taking pleasure in beauty. It is a predisposition often associated with formalism, and so at first I supposed it. Teaching and writing have become for me more interdisciplinary, not as the result of a plan to make them so, but by a gradual process, as I have evolved a more eclectic view of criticism. This has come about as I have more and more accepted and tried to work from my basic feeling of how fundamentally incommensurate with critical formulation art often is, so almost anything may be brought to bear on understanding the mysteries. While beauty in art is first and last, between that alpha and omega there may be many necessary detours. Art works of any depth will be amenable to being seen in many different ways. The perception of any work can be deepened by placing it in a variety of human contexts – that is, by reaching out into the worlds in which it was made and the worlds in which it has had and now has meanings. What Keats called "the true voice of feeling" (Letter, 22 September 1819) is often not easily heard. Still, however intellectually demanding it may be, criticism should not preen itself. However grand the intellectual superstructures – and interdisciplinary work sometimes tends to the grand or grandiose – criticism remains a second-order activity. Its function is to focus and, having focussed, to evaporate. Criticism that hubristically implies any claim beyond this – there the art work, the partial articulation; here the critical account, the full revelation – misconceives criticism and art. But criticism's focussing mechanisms may be, as well as delicate, elaborate and various.

If the discourses of criticism need constantly to be refreshed from beyond their usual boundaries, really new perception may require shifts of viewpoint more radical than are suggested by the academically inward-looking implications of 'interdisciplinary'. Criticism may also engage with new forms of understanding through contact with non-academic practitioners: writers, directors, performers. It may be that there are limits to the transactions possible between creative and critical work. The modes of knowledge are in some ways different. There is no reason why creative writers, directors or performers should be able both to practise their arts and describe what they do discursively. Nevertheless, in recent years my own teaching and writing have engaged with the performance of drama and poetry, and with the creation of new work, in ways that have helped me understand aspects of art I would not have perceived without these engagements. While the discursive knowledge of conscious reflection and the more intuitive knowledge associated with creation and performance may mean there cannot be direct translation, creative, non-discursive, performance interactions can help to generate forms of knowledge in the arts that would not be prompted by more usual academic means. There is no simple distinction between discursive and intuitive knowledge. Criticism renders intuitive understanding more conscious. Creation involves conscious reflection and judgement about intuition. For a literary critic, discussion with a poet or novelist is at least as likely to be constructive as discussion with a historian or biologist.

An extended prefatory caveat: in all understanding and study of the arts it is important not to overrate the new. One fundamental aim of Arts and Humanities, of making the past live in the present, often involves taking new views – acts of re-interpretation as aspects of the past are foregrounded or shown in some new light by aspects of contemporary culture. The twentieth century saw huge changes in the dissemination of knowledge. No previous age had made such an attempt to see world culture as a whole, and this has given a new sense of the relativity of experiences and values to cultural contexts. Arising from this new sense of the relativity of values to culture, there has been a major effort to see the past afresh in terms that are based in the present – in the West, the new place of women, and of racial and sexual minorities. One consequence of this has been conflict of interpretation between people who see such re-viewings as revelatory and those who see them as impositions on the past from the present. The issue here is the relation of literary criticism to historical and social studies. The more various the relationships one creates for a literary work, the more various and the less stable its potential meanings, and the more one may also tend to dissolve its status as an artefact that constructs meanings in special kinds of ways, through formal devices and generic conventions, with special – aesthetic – effects. I am keen to encourage a wide view of relationships, in the past and the present, but this needs to be done in ways compatible with maintaining a proper sense of the special nature and status of aesthetic objects, without which art is not art. The effects of art on consciousness mean that literary criticism can be an agent of social change, but it should not be an instrument of political agendas. Eliot may be right that "[l]iterary criticism should be completed by criticism from a definite ethical and theological standpoint".[4] But it must be literary criticism first. That is, criticism with its own standards of judgement about a work's nature and quality as art: judgement should not (unconsciously) leak into that from ethical, theological or any other perspective. And ethical and other perspectives should not be independent of one's reading of imaginative literature. Critics who know what life is, not from the records of human experience preserved in art, but from some other source of wisdom they regard as finally giving an organising perspective on these have a false hierarchy of modes of knowledge. If ethics, theology et al. are not learning from the arts, they should be.

It is important, then, not to overrate the new. One should not overstress re-interpretation. Works of art continue to mean potentially, to the present, all they have meant to past cultures, and it is of primary importance to what the Humanities do that we attempt to see works of art in their own terms, not just in ours. The grasping of difference, as well as similarity, is of central importance. One function of studying the Arts and Humanities is to pass on living traditions. 'Living' means that traditions may take new forms; but if traditions are simply transformed to conform to contemporary tastes – which often means subordinating art to some social agenda

---

4   T. S. Eliot, "Religion and Literature", in Frank Kermode, ed., *Selected Prose of T. S. Eliot* (London: Faber, 1975), pp. 97-106, p. 97.

– one central function of the Arts is lost: helping to make people less emotionally and imaginatively parochial, better able to recognise that life might be substantially different from what the accidents of history and geography have contrived to suggest. No method except …? For criticism really to address the mysteries of art, scepticism about methodology is fundamental. Strait-jackets of method are for people focussed on criticism, not on art. I am embedded in an English tradition that is pragmatic and anti-theoretic, of which my myriad-minded teacher, William Empson, is a good representative.

> I don't believe in having any [critical] Credo; a critic ought to trust his own nose, like the hunting dog, and if he lets any kind of theory or principle distract him from that, he is not doing his work. […] All the same, there is clearly a need for such theories; for one thing, without a tolerable supply of handy generalisations you can't stretch your mind to see all round a particular case. And the theory alters the feelings no less than the feelings alter the theory.[5]

Though in some ways characteristically English, Empson, who worked in Japan and in China and was as much interested in Buddhism (which he admired) as Christianity (which he abhorred), promulgated what he praised in Yeats: that criticism should be "world-minded".[6] As his 'no-Credo' creed implies, in relation to method criticism is properly paradoxical. Eclectic pragmatism, theoretical self-consciousness: each requires the complement of the other. It is a dynamic natural to the partly uncharted interactions inherent in interdisciplinary work, which has constantly to allow a mutually stimulating friction between considering the full range of what one might think about in given areas and, through leaps of informed intuition, making specific actual connections. This is Empson's theoretic-pragmatic dynamic – theory alters feeling, feeling alters theory; interaction between received ways of thinking stretched to their limits and specific perceptions that do not fit recognised paradigms. It is congruent with the paradoxical stance of the great Romantic polymath Friedrich Schlegel:

> Es ist gleich tödlich für den Geist, ein System zu haben, und keins zu haben. Er wird sich also wohl entschliessen müssen, beides zu verbinden.[7]
> [It is equally fatal for the spirit to have a system and to have no system. It will just have to decide to combine the two.]

5   William Empson, "The Verbal Analysis" (1950), in John Haffenden, ed., *Argufying: Essays on Literature and Culture* (London: Chatto, 1989), pp. 104-9, p. 104.
6   William Empson, "The Variants for the Byzantium Poems", in *Using Biography* (London: Chatto, 1984), pp. 163-88, p. 164.
7   Friedrich Schlegel, "Athenäums-Fragment Nr. 53" (1798), in Wolfdietrich Rasch, ed., *Kritische Schriften* (München: Hanser, 1956), p. 30.

Method and non-method: in literary criticism and in interdisciplinary work both are essential.[8]

One underlying reason for this, which makes for problems of interaction between literary criticism and more purely objective forms of knowledge, is the creative and situated nature of understanding in the arts. Meaning is not simply inherent in a work of art. The reader (audience, viewer) is always and quite properly actively engaged in the construction of meaning. This is not a recipe for entirely freewheeling response: the reader must interact with what is genuinely present in the work. But for the work really to come alive to the reader's experience there must be an interaction, the parameters of which are set not only by relatively objective aspects of the reader's cultural situation but also by subjective elements of individual predisposition. Henry James's analogy of perceiving 'the figure in the carpet' may be helpful, so long as one realises that the figure is not simply there: it is a Rorschach test. Real response opens the reader to himself/ herself as well as to the work. A great deal about the nature of criticism flows from this that can be difficult for more positivist forms of knowledge to engage with or even to understand, both about the kind of situated knowledge that criticism is and the forms of writing in which understanding is best formulated and conveyed.

Recognition of the reader or viewer's creative engagement is present in the earliest modern formulations of a sophisticated theory of criticism – as in G. E. Lessing's *Laokoon* (1766): "Dasjenige aber nur allein ist fruchtbar, was der Einbildungskraft freies Spiel lässt" [that alone is significant and fruitful which gives free play to the imagination].[9] Free play of imagination: that is the crucial element – and Lessing's elaboration is also important. The imagination by adding more finds more: "Je mehr wir sehen, desto mehr müssen wir hinzu denken können. Je mehr wir dazu denken, desto mehr müssen wir zu sehen glauben" [the more we see, the more must we be able to add by thinking. The more we add by thinking, the more we believe ourselves to see]. Even more than with Lessing, with Schiller (*Über die ästhetische Erziehung des Menschen*, 1794) this element of the reader's freedom of response is only one aspect of a complex and elaborate argument about the nature and value of art. But Lessing's term, *Spiel*, is also a crucial word in Schiller's aesthetic vocabulary, and Schiller makes fundamentally the same point about art

---

8   For a more methodologically self-conscious view of interdisciplinary studies (largely concerned with science and social science), see Catherine Lyall, Ann Bruce, Joyce Tait, and Laura Meagher, ed., *Interdisciplinary Research Journeys: Practical Strategies for Capturing Creativity* (London: Bloomsbury, 2011).

9   Gotthold Ephraim Lessing, *Laokoon* (1766), ed. Dorothy Reich (London: OUP, 1965), § 3, p. 71.

and imaginative freedom: "Freiheit zu geben durch Freiheit ist das Grundgesetz dieses Reichs" [to bestow freedom by means of freedom is the fundamental law of this kingdom] – that is, the kingdom of the aesthetic impulse.[10]

The creative engagement of the reader in constructing meaning is one of many elements basic to the proper variousness of method in criticism that Eliot, Empson, and Schlegel enjoin. While this makes criticism in one way fundamentally congruent with the necessarily trial-and-error, educated-intuition nature of eliciting experimental interdisciplinary relationships, it makes many specific forms of interdisciplinary study problematic, because in interdisciplinary study criticism is often related to intellectual disciplines in which method is more regulated and understanding has a more straightforwardly objective existence.

Different fundamental conceptions, different working methods, and equally crucial may be a different idea of writing. Criticism is a kind of creative writing. As a form of art, criticism has some of the formal qualities of art. Most forms of intellectual discourse work with a paradigm of a more objective style of presenting argument. The concomitant of the fundamental connection of style and meaning is fully to take that connection into account in how criticism is written. As Schlegel (again) has it:

> Poesie kann nur durch Poesie kritisiert werden. Ein Kunsturteil welches nicht selbst ein Kunstwerk ist, entweder im Stoff […] oder durch eine schöne Form […] hat gar kein Bürgerrecht im Reiche der Kunst.
> [Creative writing can only be criticised by way of creative writing. A work of art criticism which is not itself a work of art, either in substance or in the beauty of its form, has no civil rights in the realm of art.][11]

Schlegel's critical aphorisms are indeed works of art, expressive in form and hugely generative in their multivalent eloquence. But the idea of creative form need not be taken with a simple literalism – Goethe's discussion of *Hamlet* through the semi-autobiographical hero of *Wilhelm Meisters Lehrjahre*; W. H. Auden writing a commentary on *The Tempest* in the form of a series of monologues spoken by its characters (*The Sea and the Mirror*); T. S. Eliot writing (in imitation of Dryden) a critical dialogue in which various points of view clash unresolved ("A Dialogue on Dramatic Poetry"). The varied and expressive discursive rhetorics of Northrop Frye, William Empson, and F. R. Leavis (to take three of the most influential critics

---

10 Friedrich Schiller, *Über die ästhetische Erziehung des Menschen, in einer Reihe von Briefen* (1794), ed. Elizabeth M. Wilkinson and L. A. Willoughby (Oxford: Clarendon, 1967), Letter 27, § 9, pp. 214-15.

11 Friedrich Schlegel, "Lyceums-Fragment Nr. 117" (1797), in *Kritische Schriften*, p. 21.

of the last century) are equally forms of *Poesie*: all three polymaths with broad cultural interests, all naturally not self-consciously interdisciplinary, all highly distinctive as stylists, and distinct one from another. Frye, magisterial, as befits his 'above the fray' stance of criticism as a descriptive science; Empson, unusual in his use of personal anecdote and comedy, congruent with his exaltation of the relaxed liberal ethics of Fielding and Joyce; Leavis, with his mode of earnest Puritan-tradition iconoclastic polemic: all use language, not of disinterested reason, but coloured by inflections that convey implicitly relations to the work and the world; all illustrate that style and content are not separable, that engagement with works of imagination cannot be other than in language of highly varied rhetorical and imaginative resource. The discourses of many areas of intellectual life imply that matter is everything, manner has no meanings, that language is a transparent pointer to the world, or that the discourse of the intellect is necessarily impersonal. But in criticism, as in art, what you say is how you say it. How that 'voice' of a personal and culturally situated point of view is carried over into negotiations with fundamentally different disciplines, disciplines that may quite properly aim for a greater impersonality of utterance, means that problems of style can be central.

Before going on to examples of actual interdisciplinary work and their precise problems I should acknowledge that there may be here too much discussion about 'disciplines' as though 'literary criticism' (or History, or Maths) identifies a coherent and unified body of activities. In fact, specialisation of focus, in sub-subject and in method and competition between competing fashions means that people working in academic departments often understand little about what their colleagues do or – as in debates of the 1980s and 90s about the place of critical theory in literary education – are actively hostile to it. It is the mildest index of this fragmentation that a colleague invited to lecture on Shelley should respond, as though to a pleasant tease (the request could not be intended seriously), "you know I am a 1790s person"; or a Milton specialist, interviewed for a post in Renaissance literature, asked if he could teach more widely – for example, Shakespeare? – should affirm, with more righteous emphasis (professional contempt of amateurism), that that surely could not be expected. In this world, 'English Studies' is interdisciplinary in a less admirable sense – that if people within it work together at all, it is by relating sub-subjects and methodological antagonisms across divisions that make 'world-mindedness' seem more than a distant ideal, and from within a view of specialisation that, measured by such an ideal, will seem a mad waste of educational resource and distortion of human potential. The pressures that make this an ordinary feature of academic life are as likely to enforce such patterns in Sciences or Social Sciences, in which advanced knowledge is often equally specialised, perhaps with better reason than in literary studies, where knowledge is necessarily comparative.

This kind of narrowed focus is now regularly promoted as 'research-led teaching', that is, Arts and Humanities teaching drawing on a science model of research specialisation, not (as the slogan implies) so that teaching can be up-to-date and high-powered, but so that teaching causes minimal diversion from the activity that generates income. It might more closely reflect the reality to call this 'research-distorted teaching'. The result is typically a narrowing of the syllabus, which ceases to include areas of a discipline previously thought essential – as in a Music Department near me where the Western tradition is now scarcely taught (its students cannot study Bach, Mozart, Beethoven, etc.) because its (income-generating) research success is in Ethnomusicology. As for the wider educational value and cultural effects of not teaching music students their own traditions and teaching instead traditions that have little if any relation to their own, or of teaching a syllabus made up from the vagaries of a department's research interests rather than fundamental elements of a subject, though the value of teaching the Arts and Humanities in higher education may be seriously compromised by such distortions, income-generation often overwhelms every other consideration.

The inertly powerful shaping force of funding can be felt at every point. One reason for the current interest in interdisciplinary studies in the UK is that, in a context where state funding has been largely withdrawn, Arts and Humanities subjects are expected to pay for themselves on a model long practised in the Sciences. Arts subjects have limited ability to attract the necessary kind of funding independently and can more readily do so if they devise projects with a scientific aspect. As with teaching patterns, research interests are presented as intellectual where the moving force is economic. But directions of research should not be generated or governed by opportunities for funding. Funding is for what is fashionable, and fashion is scarcely more congruent with real need in intellect than in clothing. Fashion is generated by a pseudo-need for the new, which is the stuff of which careers are made, not knowledge and understanding. And this is not only an issue about current funding patterns. It reflects the status of the sciences in a university context, where they are often an unduly powerful model, distorting non-scientific studies. Using creatively the conditions of the environment in which one is cast requires understanding its distorting pressures and doing what one can to turn them towards intellectual interests with which they may be – and with the arts in higher education often are – at odds.

The simplest problems of interdisciplinary collaboration arise from misunderstanding literature as a mode of knowledge. When people whose primary interests are not literary want, perhaps for the most large-minded reasons, to draw literature into the service of their branch of study they seem often inclined to take their reading too literally – to have an inadequate sense of how variously literary texts signify, as if all fictions are unmediated reflections of individual feeling or social reality. This is reading as a fundamentalist, with an insufficient sense of the symbolic, the stylised, or the meanings of genre or form. It is often difficult for people who do not have a strong aesthetic sense to feel the force of the idea that in art style and meaning are inextricably bound together and that meaning is not simply to be identified with subject-matter. As W. H. Auden puts it, "a painting of the Crucifixion is not necessarily more Christian in spirit than a still life, and may very well be less".[12] For historians, theologians, people reading with some primarily non-literary agenda, subject matter, content in the simplest sense, often looms too large.

And of course I can identify in myself comparable blindness – a lack of feeling for style. While I have done my best not to acquiesce in a natural dullness, I do not have a strong feeling for visual art. Paintings I like are usually of something that is itself, before it was painted, beautiful; so my pleasure is as much in the subject as in the painting. When I read a great art critic like Ruskin, I am interested to try to imagine what he sees, but I cannot myself have that experience of seeing – which is instructive about the limits of what criticism can do, and the limits of understanding one can hope for, even in a willing and sympathetic collaborator. One fruit of interdisciplinary study is to learn to listen where one cannot hope to do more than listen – one cannot hope fully to learn. But finally there may also be a level of proper resistance to the presuppositions of another discipline. I regard all history as cultural history. I have little sense of the material circumstances of daily life in the past, and I am not persuaded that such circumstances much affect what interests me in literature. The efforts of historians who suppose themselves literary-minded to make them appear so seem to me a particularly annoying and accursed form of error. One cannot hope to accommodate everything, and one should not. The world is wide, and genuine flexibility of mind is always to be admired. But flexibility that has no definite points of resistance is merely flabby.

If your interests are, as mine are, primarily aesthetic, and if you take the view, as I do, that the real existence of a work of art lies in the interaction between the work and an individual responsive consciousness, one way of addressing difficulties of interdisciplinary collaboration is to be one's own collaborator. No distraction from the aesthetic; no dissipation of the artwork-mind interaction. I would perhaps not have supposed I could do this in more than a limited way (literature and music) without several years of trans-disciplinary engagement throughout

12 W. H. Auden, "Postscript: Christianity and Art", in *The Dyer's Hand and Other Essays* (London: Faber, 1963), pp. 456-61, p. 458.

my university presenting candidates for honorary degrees. Learning to describe, in terms suited to a lay audience, the fundamental nature of subjects ranging from theoretical anthropology to cosmology to international jurisprudence, and the relation of these to the work of an individual graduand, was a liberal education. Writing for the voice and for the ear, and writing in a variety of styles suited to different subjects and occasions, was a training in rhetoric. Could this be put to use in literary criticism? I have tried recently in the multi-disciplinary aspects of a book on Shakespeare's Sonnets.[13] The book is an experiment which involved, in the first part, writing in other disciplines (philosophy, visual art, music, and film), and, in the second part, writing about performance and performing (the book is accompanied by a complete recording of the Sonnets). The aim is to prompt a more experientially engaged reading of poetry by setting the Sonnets to resonate with a variety of materials that have a broad congruence with the love poems addressed to the young man – materials from philosophy (Plato), visual art (Michelangelo), music (Benjamin Britten), and film (Derek Jarman), as well as from other poetry and prose fiction. Whatever the method's success or failure, it exemplifies a natural connection between criticism's methodological openness and interdisciplinary thinking.

In working with other disciplines one central desideratum is sympathetic collaborators who are capable of addressing one's inevitable ignorance by thinking about their subjects in ways that are not just those of experts handling its normal currency for other experts. This may be as good for them as for you. I recently had the pleasure of working on a ballet based on Marlowe's *Edward II* with help from its choreographer, David Bintley.[14] My aim was to get away from thinking about drama in the way in which literary people mostly experience it, as text, to think in terms of what one sees on stage, an embodied sequence conveying narrative and character. My problem was that, while I have long loved dance, I know nothing about dance technically. One should not overrate intellectual innocence, but there are virtues to groping in the dark. Ignorance of the technical aspects of an art is no more always a limitation than familiarity with an art's normal discourse always enables freshness of perception. No sophisticated art can appeal with full subtlety to people not familiar with its conventions, but neither is any art intended only for its practitioners. Most of the time, in most disciplines, people are talking to

---

13 David Fuller, *The Life in the Sonnets* (Shakespeare Now!, London: Continuum, 2011); with a complete recorded reading of the Sonnets available at <http://www.continu-umbooks.com/resources/9781847064547> (18 September 2013).

14 David Fuller, "Love or Politics: The Man or the King? *Edward II* in Modern Performance", *Shakespeare Bulletin* 27:1 (2009), pp. 81-115.

others who know the discourse. This is normal and, within limits, enabling, but it is not unproblematic: in handling the usual currency people are not pressed to consider fundamentals, to think beyond existing frameworks, or even to consider with fresh perception what the existing frameworks really mean. Whatever I was able to make of it, considering narrative, embodiment, and tableau in drama through a ballet based on a play was an opportunity to think in some unusual ways. And this is what one looks for with interdisciplinary work: that it should challenge accepted discourses, and open up lines of thought not available within the usual frameworks of a single discipline.

Somewhat different from groping in the dark with the help of a sympathetic collaborator – though here too I had the help of discussion with the composer – was recent work on a new opera about Alzheimer's disease, *The Lion's Face*, with a score by Elena Langer and libretto by Glyn Maxwell.[15] The opera was launched at the Brighton Science Festival, and there was considerable emphasis on the medical input, from health care workers, patients and carers, and a group of researchers at the Institute of Psychiatry, King's College London. My role was to provide aesthetic evaluation of the libretto and the score.[16] The problematic issue was somewhat like that with literalists who assume that all fiction is unmediated reflection of social reality – the relation of dramatic to documentary aspects of the project. Most problematic, because fundamental to the drama and the science, was the opera's presentation of what constitutes research into Alzheimer's disease. The importance given to investigating the central patient's recurrent memory implied a psychoanalytic model of the illness, which is distinctly different from the biochemical investigations actually employed in current research. The main scientific consultant was in fact happy that one research model should do duty for another: he took the view that in a dramatic context the precise nature of (offstage) research is less important than the dilemmas to which the needs of research (whatever its nature) give rise – problems about consent with a patient who is not self-responsible; problems about treatment (the good of the individual) in relation to research (the good of the community). Science accommodated aesthetics. The compromise with documentary realism could be justified by the gain in terms of drama – but this required considerable accommodation on the part of the scientists involved.

---

15 *The Lion's Face: Music Meets Science in a New Opera*, <http://thelionsface.wordpress. com/> (18 September 2013).
16 David Fuller, "Dementia at the Opera: *The Lion's Face*", *The Opera Quarterly* 27:4 (2011), pp. 509-21.

Equally about the production of a new multi-media work, but more experimental in its co-operative working methods, 'The Faerie Queene Now!' brought together poets, a novelist, a theologian, a priest, an imam, literary scholars, a dramaturge and a composer.[17] The main focus again was creative work, writing a new liturgy, drawing from Book I of Spenser's poem, for use in Anglican contexts, but inclusive and non-sectarian.[18] My own primary interest was tangential to this, in Protestant Christianity presented as militant righteousness in opposition to Roman Catholic Christianity and Islam. Could we consider the paradoxical contemporary relation of this to post-Enlightenment Western culture in which aspects of that fundamental situation are reversed? – Christian militancy historic; Spenser's form of Protestantism (uneasily) allied to Roman Catholicism; militant religion now Islam. In the event, we made little of this. There may have been a natural reluctance to consider whatever complex and sensitive analogies there might be between militant Protestantism in the sixteenth century and militant Islam in the aftermath of 9/11 and the second Iraq War, given their different relations to colonial, post-colonial and global political power. Given that Spenser's militant Protestantism also has in itself many controversial aspects (especially his role in the exercise of English power in Catholic Ireland), even when not compounded by possible relationships with contemporary Islamic militancy, the literary and historical issues would in any case have been too complex a diversion from the group's main focus, which was creative: the composition of a liturgy. Nevertheless, issues that remained part of freewheeling, finding-our-way preliminary discussion suggest the kind of interdisciplinary literary-historical-theological project that might, by means of contemporary analogies, give a more vivid sense of Spenser's Christianity in its contexts. And one never knows what excitements new perspectives may prompt. The British liberal-left newspaper The Guardian ran an article about the project incorporating comments on, and a poem for, the liturgy by Andrew Motion – a national and representative figure because he had recently been the British Poet Laureate.[19] The issue of how the project treated the questing figure of St George – who (drawing on a mural in one of the hosting venues, Manchester

---

17 The Faerie Queene Now: Remaking Religious Poetry for Today's World, <http://www.rhul.ac.uk/english/faeriequeene/> (18 September 2013).

18 For the liturgy and reflections on the process of its composition, see Ewan Fernie, ed., Redcrosse: Remaking Religious Poetry for Today's World (London: Continuum, 2012).

19 Dalya Alberge, "Poets enlist for quest to pull St George from jaws of far right: Exlaureate Andrew Motion joins exploration of Englishness in works that redefine patron saint in 'agnostic liturgy'", The Guardian (24 Jan. 2011), <http://www.guardian.co.uk/books/ 2011/jan/24/poets-enlist-st-george-liturgy> (18 September 2013).

Cathedral) was updated as black British – was then taken up by organs of a less liberal tendency. As a result, members of the right-wing British National Party began sending threatening hate-mail to the organisers. So while some potential interdisciplinary aspects of interesting controversy remained undeveloped, for an academic project '*The Faerie Queene* Now!' attracted an unusual degree of attention. It more than amply demonstrated that working with creative writers can take academics into new and exciting areas.

I have so far scarcely strayed beyond discussing kinds of work that, with whatever limitations, I understand by having attempted them. The Alzheimer's opera and its medical underpinning apart, this is to leave out of account kinds of work which for a variety of intellectual and institutional reasons – from the attention of neuroscience to affect to the funding needs of the Humanities – are in current circumstances particularly likely to attract interdisciplinary projects: work with the sciences. The classic backgrounds to this, the 'two-cultures' debate in England between C. P. Snow and F. R. Leavis, and the more internationally conducted arguments about the social construction or objectivity of science that culminated in the 1990s in the so-called 'science wars', both, by their violence, indicate the uneasy local and international contexts in which arts-science interdisciplinary work often takes place.[20]

Both controversies revealed more than their fair share of stereotyping, which is often a problem with interdisciplinary work: just as mutual respect breaks down barriers, so mutual hostility or suspicion builds them up. It is, however, genuinely difficult to see different forms of thought other than through the mind-set evolved by one's own; and the stereotypes that disciplines have of one another may produce conflict because they expect to find it – perhaps with some validity. Are there, as well as strictly disciplinary differences about method, characteristic disciplinary mind-sets? Are bio-scientists commonly atheists? (Nature is a mechanism; everything is a mechanism.) Are physicists commonly religious? (The universe is finally incomprehensible; all theories of cosmology require undemonstrable postulates – acts of faith based on rational inference.) Do social scientists (living too exclusively in the present?) tend to hold views that might be characterised from the point of view of traditionally-minded critique as 'politically correct'? With the present as their element, are they subdued (on another view, elevated)

---

20 C. P. Snow, *The Two Cultures* [1959, 1964], ed. Stefan Collini (Cambridge: CUP, 1993); F. R. Leavis, *Two Cultures? The Significance of C. P. Snow, with an Essay on Sir Charles Snow's Rede Lecture by Michael Yudkin* (London: Chatto, 1962); Guy Ortolano, *The Two Cultures Controversy: Science, Literature and Cultural Politics in Post-War Britain* (Cambridge: CUP, 2008); Andrew Ross, ed., *Science Wars* (Duke, NC: Duke UP, 1996).

to what they work in? Do those working in historical disciplines place excessive emphasis on perspectives of which the contemporary world has ceased to see the point? Are they characteristically more likely to be impressed by the relativity of values to culture? That disciplinary stereotypes need to be viewed with scepticism need not mean that they are wholly devoid of accurate perception. As Blake's devils have it (*The Marriage of Heaven and Hell*, proverbs): "everything possible to be believed is an image of truth" – though truth may, of course, be seen obliquely. Differences of method need not be inflammatory. Differences of mind-set, particularly if they are linked to professional investments, are perhaps – as the 'two cultures' and 'science wars' controversies suggest – likely to be more tricky to negotiate. Interdisciplinary work is often demanding – of imagination about how one perceives a different point of view; of tact about how one responds to its perceived limitations.

I should like finally to consider some fully arts-science interdisciplinary work, current Durham University projects in which close colleagues are involved. One is concerned with the mathematical metaphor of 'tipping points', co-ordinating inputs from Mathematics, Economics, Earth Sciences, English Studies, and a conglomerate concerned with Hazard and Risk, funded by the Leverhulme Trust.[21] The other is a project on Voice Hearing, co-ordinating inputs from Psychology, Medicine, Philosophy, Theology, and English, funded by the Wellcome Trust, and with participation from the Hearing Voices Movement, a movement which has altered how the experience of supposed auditory hallucination is perceived, severing links with pathology and enabling voice-hearers to speak in terms of their own self-understanding.[22]

The 'tipping point' problem is that the metaphor has been applied to different kinds of phenomena (physical and socio-economic) that do not work in directly comparable ways. Though human intentionality may influence their development once observed, in physical systems the crucial elements of change do not act with intent. Though human intentionality may produce effects neither intended nor observed, in socio-economic systems it is present from the beginning. The aim of the interdisciplinary project is to provide detailed inputs from a variety of disciplines so as to reflect on the issues in a representative range of areas. The problem of the study epitomises a central problem of interdisciplinary work: the differences between studying physical phenomena, with which interpretation

---

21 *Tipping Points: Mathematics, Metaphors and Meaning*, <http://www.dur.ac.uk/ihrr/tippingpoints/> (18 September 2013).

22 *Hearing the Voice*, <http://www.dur.ac.uk/hearingthevoice/> (22 September 2013).

relates largely to objective information, and phenomena that are a consequence of human agency, with which interpretation is more dependent on point of view. The differences that are potentially most illuminating are just those that make the methodologies of their comparative study difficult to relate.

'Hearing the Voice' is concerned with understanding the experience of hearing voices in the absence of any external stimuli – what the experience is actually like; how it is interpreted in different cultural contexts; how it is to be understood in terms of cognitive neuroscience; and how this research can inform its therapeutic management. The project also aims to evolve working methods that might apply to other interdisciplinary work, though how far this might be possible is at present far from clear. The input from a variety of disciplines and from the Voice Hearing Movement indicates the high degree to which context and point of view bear on interpretation, offering perspectives other than those usual in modern study, where assumptions about schizophrenia, and hence of disvaluing the voice, are pervasive. The project's main difficulty so far has been precisely its interdisciplinary range – integrating the cognitive neuro-science with the arts-based activities.

Of course, with both these projects, methods have been described to the funding bodies in good faith. But with really investigative interdisciplinary work it is inevitable that there will be a considerable element of methodological experiment – that the most fruitful methods of relating kinds of knowledge and discourse not usually brought together are bound to be partly evolved in the process of working with one another. With ways of thinking that are really new, or unusual, bringing together disciplines the discourse and knowledge norms of which are different, the only method for collaboration is to work from existing methods (probably existing methods in the separate disciplines) expecting these to be at the very least modified by collaboration. This may not quite mean that 'the only method is to be very intelligent', but the more the interaction is substantial, the more it is likely at times to feel like that. That something like this methodological experimentation is regularly involved in literary criticism makes it a natural partner.

For interdisciplinary work there are no short cuts: to engage seriously with others, any discipline has to understand and make constructive responses to their characteristic methods and modes of thought. One discipline may suggest critiques of another, but if the process is not reciprocal there is unlikely to be worthwhile interaction. Even narrowly conceived – discrete areas of knowledge with their characteristic boundaries and procedures – work between different disciplines can have many values: clarifying assumptions otherwise tacit; reversing the narrowness consequent on specialisation; re-engaging the inwardly-looking 'academic' with worlds beyond those of specialists addressing specialists; perhaps even discovering that disciplines which from outside appear separate, factual and positivist, are, just as much as literary criticism, resistant to closure, various in discourse, open to interpretive choice. But interdisciplinary work may also suggest something beyond what are ultimately lesser or greater adjustments of compartmentalised norms. It may be a reminder of, and recall to, the drive to understand that is sceptical of boundaries, *la passion de comprendre les hommes* – in the Arts and Humanities, seeing focussed and realised in the multifariousness of great works a seething life, and, not satisfied by known methods of representing this, conceiving the possibility of understandings more fully realised, experiences more adequately articulated. It may be that with any area of intellectual life an 'interdisciplinary' agenda – recognising that discipline boundaries are often artificial creations – is always potentially present. The proper driver of invention is a due sense of the mysteries.

SABINE COELSCH-FOISNER AND CHRISTOPHER HERZOG

The Two Cultures Revisited: Strategies in Science Drama, with an exemplary reading of Caryl Churchill's *A Number* (2002) and Elfriede Jelinek's *Kein Licht* (2011/12)

1. Introduction: Is there science in the theatre?

The Salzburg Research Group ALiEN (Alternative Lives in Experimental Narratives), initially a project funded by the Austrian Science Fund, has dedicated its work for over a decade now to phenomena and strategies of the fantastic in a wide range of cultural contexts. The fantastic is taken to include all artistic forms and modes of expression that disrupt the mimetic and, by so doing, shed light on what we know and experience in real life. A more recent research axis in this project deals with so-called *science plays* – stage plays that take their point of departure in scientific findings, premises or concerns. Initially, it was research on science fiction that had pointed the way to drama for us, and this is precisely the context in which recent criticism has sought to define science plays – *ex negativo*. Major critics in this field are Judy Kupfermann,[1] Kirsten Shepherd-Barr,[2] Carl Djerassi,[3]

---

1   Judy Kupfermann, "Science in Theater", *All About Jewish Theater* (2003), <http://www.jewish-theatre.com/visitor/article_display.aspx?articleID=485&pagenumber =1> (31 July 2013).

2   Kirsten Shepherd-Barr, *Science on Stage: From 'Doctor Faustus' to 'Copenhagen'* (Princeton: Princeton UP, 2006). See also Kirsten Shepherd-Barr, "*Copenhagen*, Infinity, and Beyond: Science Meets Literature on Stage", *Interdisciplinary Science Reviews* 28:3 (Fall 2003), pp. 193-9; "*Copenhagen* and Beyond: The 'Rich and Mentally Nourishing' Interplay of Science and Theatre", *Gramma: Journal of Theory and Criticism* 10 (2002), pp. 171-82.

3   Carl Djerassi, "Contemporary 'Science-in-Theater': A Rare Genre", *The Homepage of Carl Djerassi*, <http://www.djerassi.com/sciencetheatre.html> (1 August 2013); "When is 'Science on Stage' Really Science?", *American Theatre* 24:1 (January 2007), pp. 96-103; and "Science-in-Fiction ist nicht Science Fiction: Ist sie Autobiographie?", in Wendelin Schmidt-Dengler, ed., *Fiction in Science – Science in Fiction: Zum Gespräch zwischen Literatur und Wissenschaft* (Vienna: Hölder-Pichler-Tempsky, 1998), pp. 71-104. See also Chloe Veltman, "Carl Djerassi: From Pill to Quill – An Award-Winning Chemist Takes His Science to the Stage", *American Theatre* 19:6 (July/August 2002), pp. 53-4.

and Eva-Sabine Zehelein.[4] These studies are, no doubt, indicative of the current interest both in science and in works of art foregrounding (mainly spectacular) innovations or, conversely, failures in science. Besides, the sheer number of performances of plays dealing with science in one form or another and their immense popularity with audiences strengthen the impression of a new dramatic genre. Yet, the problem in all these efforts to map science plays is precisely *how* science can be represented in non-scientific contexts. This is an issue of profound epistemological impact, and it is in this context that we should like to point out the striking connections between science fiction and science drama, rather than presupposing, like Shepherd-Barr, Djerassi and Zehelein, the 'truth value' of science in science plays. As these critics specify (mainly thematic) criteria in order to set up a canon of science plays (despite differences in their respective theories, there is surprising agreement as to which plays constitute science plays and which not), they rely on a facile connection between knowledge and theatre, as if drama was a container in which to pour science. The criteria they list are: scientific content (the representation of 'real' science, scientists, and history of science), discursive and performative aspects of knowledge transfer, and didacticism.[5]

---

4   Eva-Sabine Zehelein, *Science: Dramatic: Science Plays in America and Great Britain 1990-2007* (Heidelberg: Winter, 2009). Subsequently abbreviated as *SD*.

5   For further criticism dealing with science and theatre, mainly in the form of shorter case studies, see Heinz Antor, "The Arts, the Sciences, and the Making of Meaning: Tom Stoppard's *Arcadia* as a Post-Structuralist Play", *Anglia* 116:3 (January 1998), pp. 326-54; Silvana Barbacci, "Science and Theatre: A Multifaceted Relationship between Pedagogical Purpose and Artistic Expression", *The Pantaneto Forum* 19 (July 2005), <http:// www.pantaneto.co.uk/issue19/barbacci.htm#_top> (31 July 2013), and "From the Golem to Artificial Intelligence: Science in the Theatre for an Existential Reflection", *Jekyll.comm* 3 (September 2002), pp. 1-26, trans. Elisabetta Maurutto, <http://citeseerx.ist.psu. edu/viewdoc/summary?doi=10.1.1.194.8341> (31 July 2013); Michael Chayut, "Tragedy and Science", *History of European Ideas* 25:4 (1999), pp. 163-77; Irit Degani-Raz, "Theatrical Fictional Worlds, Counterfactuals, and Scientific Thought Experiments", *Semiotica* 157:1/4 (2005), pp. 353-75; William W. Demastes, "Of Sciences and the Arts: From Influence to Interplay between Natural Philosophy and Drama", *Studies in the Literary Imagination* 24:2 (Fall 1991), pp. 75-89; Cara Gargano, "The Starfish and the Strange Attractor: Myth, Science, and Theatre as Laboratory in Maria Irene Fornes' 'Mud'", *New Theatre Quarterly* 13:51 (1997), pp. 214-20, and "Complex Theatre: Science and Myth in Three Contemporary Performances", *New Theatre Quarterly* 14:54 (May 1998), pp. 151-8; Martin Matthew, "Stephen Poliakoff's Drama for the Post-Scientific Age", *Theatre Journal* 45:2 (May 1993), pp. 197-211; Robert Myers, "Science, Infiltrating the Stage, Puts Life under the Microscope", *New York Times* (5 Dec. 1999), pp. 2, 7; Sidney Perkowitz, "Science Treads the Boards", *Physics*

Science in the arts (whether fiction, performative or visual art) is not a quantifi-able category, as we shall demonstrate, and it is, therefore, not adequate to define 'science plays' on the basis of these criteria, let alone demarcate them against science fiction and fantasy,[6] as claimed by Shepherd-Barr and Zehelein. Still, the question remains why playwrights (and theatre managers) obviously consider

---

World 17:11 (November 2004), pp. 16-17, <http://physicsworldarchive.iop.org/index. cfm?action=summary&doc=17%2F11%2F phwv17i11a20%40pwa-xml&qt=> (31 July 2013); Cory A. Reed, "'No está olvidada la ciencia': Science, Chaos Theory, and Tragedy in 'El medico de su honra'", *South Central Review* 13:1 (Spring 1996), pp. 26-39; Robert P. Reno, "Science and Prophets in Dürrenmatt's *The Physicists*", *Renascence* 37:2 (Winter 1985), pp. 70-9; Giuseppina Restivo, "*Melencolias* and Scientific Ironies in *Endgame*: Beckett, Walther, Dürer, Musil", *Samuel Beckett Today* 11 (2001), pp. 103-11; Dietrich von Engelhardt, "Macht und Ohnmacht des Forschers: Mary Shelleys *Frankenstein oder Der moderne Prometheus*", in Norbert Elsner and Werner Frick, ed., '*Scientia Poetica*': *Literatur und Naturwissenschaft* (Göttingen: Wallstein, 2004), pp. 227-42; Hart Wegner, "The Work of the Devil: Anti-Faustian Tendencies in Twentieth Century Drama and Film", *West Virginia University Philological Papers* 27 (1981), pp. 8-14.

6   There are several case studies or shorter essays broaching the intersection of sci-ence fiction and the stage, but as yet, there are no comprehensive critical maps. See e.g. Joseph Krupnik, "'Infinity in a Cigar Box': The Problem of Science Fiction on the Stage", in Patrick D. Murphy, ed., *Staging the Impossible: The Fantastic Mode in Modern Drama* (Westport, CT: Greenwood Press, 1992), pp. 197-219; Christopher Innes, "Science on the Stage", *Anglistik und Englischunterricht* 64 (2002), pp. 95-105; Wolfgang Biesterfeld, "Friedrich Dürrenmatts Hörspiel *Das Unternehmen der Wega* (1955) und die Tradition der Science Fiction", *Literatur für Leser* 30:4 (2007), pp. 241-61; Brian Stableford, "*Henceforward*: SF in the Theatre", *New York Review of Science Fiction* 7 (1989), pp. 1, 3-4; Peter J. Heck, et al., "Three Views of Two Guys: *Two Guys from the Future* and Other Plays: An Evening of Science Fiction Theater by Terry Bisson", *The New York Review of Science Fiction* 47 (1992), pp. 1, 3-6; K. V. Bailey, "Archetypal Eagles, Operatic Sparrows", *Foundation: The Review of Science Fiction* 39 (1987), pp. 5-20; Merritt Abrash, "R.U.R. Restored and Reconsidered", *Extrapolation: A Journal of Science Fiction and Fantasy* 32:2 (1991), pp. 184-92; Robert Appleford, "'That Almost Present Dream of Tomorrow': Daniel David Moses' *Kyotopolis* as Native Canadian Science Fiction/History Play", in Marc Maufort and Franca Bellarsi, ed., *Crucible of Cultures: Anglophone Drama at the Dawn of a New Millennium* (Brussels: Lang, 2002), pp. 199-207; Moonyoung Chung, "Stage as Hyperspace: Theatricality of Stoppard", *Modern Drama* 48:4 (Winter 2005), pp. 689-705. See also Shepherd-Barr, *Science on Stage*, pp. 7-8; Marjean D. Purinton, "Theatricalized Bodies and Spirits: Techno-Gothic as Performance in Romantic Drama", *Gothic Studies* 3:2 (2001), pp. 134-49, and "Science Fiction and Techno-Gothic Drama: Romantic Playwrights Joanna Baillie and Jane Scott", *Romanticism on the Net* 21 (2001), pp. 1-27.

drama and science such an intriguing combination in our time:[7] from Michael Frayn, Mark Ravenhill, Tom Stoppard, and Caryl Churchill to Austria's Nobel-Prize winner Elfriede Jelinek. In fact, the combination extends well into the past, if we only consider Mary Shelley's *Frankenstein*, which was put on stage immediately after its publication (in 1818) in the form of a melodrama, its extraordinary success actually triggering a whole range of melodramatic adaptations.[8]

What we are suggesting is that the crucial question in science plays is not what or how much science they contain but: what makes science interesting from a dramatic, or melodramatic, theatrical standpoint? In order to gain a foothold on this new genre we shall first consider major definitions of science plays and show how attempts to quantify the science content in science plays fail to understand these plays in terms of *plays*. To this end, we shall probe into some of Carl Djerassi's plays and study Caryl Churchill's *A Number* (2002),[9] a play commonly considered to be a science play. Speaking about 'science drama', we cannot, of course, take Churchill's play as *pars pro toto*, but it furnishes a prime example of how science is used to make sense in drama and how drama transforms or reconfigures science. Moreover, the dramatic strategies employed by Churchill are strikingly congruous with Elfriede Jelinek's more radical texts *Kein Licht* (2011)[10] and its *Epilog?* (2012),[11] which are not commonly classified as science drama. Both are

---

7   Cf. Harry Lustig and Kirsten Shepherd-Barr, "Science as Theater: From Physics to Biology, Science is Offering Playwrights Innovative Ways of Exploring the Intersections of Science, History, Art and Modern Life", *American Scientist* 90 (Nov./Dec. 2002), pp. 550-5.

8   Cf. Albert LaValley, "The Stage and Film Children of Frankenstein", in George Levine and U. C. Knoepflmacher, ed., *The Endurance of Frankenstein: Essays on Mary Shelley's Novel* (Berkeley: U of California P, 1979), pp. 243-89; Pedro Garcia, "Beyond Adaptation: Frankenstein's Postmodern Progeny", in Mireia Aragay, ed., *Books in Motion: Adaptation, Intertextuality, Authorship* (Amsterdam: Rodopi, 2005), pp. 223-40; William St. Clair, "The Impact of *Frankenstein*", in Betty T. Bennett and Stuart Curran, ed., *Mary Shelley in Her Times* (Baltimore: Johns Hopkins UP, 2000), pp. 38-63; Steven Earl Forry, *Hideous Progenies: Dramatizations of 'Frankenstein' from the Nineteenth Century to the Present* (Philadelphia: U of Pennsylvania P, 1990); *Romantic Circles*, <http://www.rc.umd.edu/ editions/peake/apparatus/earlyversions.html> (30 July 2013).

9   Caryl Churchill, *A Number* (London: Nick Hern Books, 2002).

10   Elfriede Jelinek, *Kein Licht* (2011), <http://www.elfriedejelinek.com/> (30 July 2013).

11   Elfriede Jelinek, *Fukushima – Epilog? Eine Trauernde. Sie kann machen, was sie will:* (2012), <http://www.elfriedejelinek.com/> (30 July 2013).

apt examples to illustrate the obvious inadequacies of defining science plays in terms of science content and science teaching.

2. The hazards of defining science plays: Djerassi's science-in-theatre and Zehelein's taxonomy

Efforts to define science plays must be seen in the context of debates about the relation between the arts and the sciences, calling to mind the concept of the *two cultures*, which has been as frequently criticised as it has been employed. The crux in defining science plays lies in the hazards of defining science, on the one hand, and art, on the other,[12] and in the epistemological uncertainties connected with science and the ways in which it is embedded in history and has evolved in the course of time, as Mike Vanden Heuvel convincingly argues in a short essay entitled "Playing Science".[13] Science plays need to be seen in their respective historical context, thus constituting a highly dynamic genre – like science fiction. What is not considered science or scientific by contemporary standards may very well have fulfilled the role of modern science in earlier times: notably that of a culturally sanctioned form of knowledge along with the cultural practices related to it:

> Most modern scientists would not consider, for instance, the dialogue in John Redford's medieval *The Play of Wit and Science* to even approximate the concerns, methodologies, or forms of inquiry that today would be termed science, yet in its time it might well have represented the cutting edge of the science play. Earlier still, when the distinctions between science and other forms of knowledge were not so explicit, the brief appearance in Aristophanes' *The Birds* of the geometer Meton (complete with geometric instruments) might indicate at least a casual interest in bringing mathematical perspectives to bear on the playwright's excoriating critique of sophist thought. Any number of Latin and medieval plays, as well as early modern masques, featuring human and extra-human representatives of learning, wisdom, and natural philosophy (as in, for instance, Marianus Capella's *On the Marriage of Hermes and Philology*, that includes The Seven Liberal Arts as characters) might also be considered science plays within this more expansive definition. And even these broader categories leave out work [sic], both scientific and imaginative, that use dialogue to communicate scientific thought in lively dramatic manner (Galileo's *Starry Messenger*, Fontanelle's "Conversations on the Plurality of Worlds"). (Vanden Heuvel, p. 203)

---

12 See Jürgen Mittelstraß, "Kunst und Wissen: Plädoyer für einen offenen Wissensbegriff", in Sabine Coelsch-Foisner, ed., *TATORT Kultur: Atelier Gespräche II* (Salzburg: Verlag Anton Pustet, 2013), pp. 80-9.

13 Mike Vanden Heuvel, "Playing Science", *Revista Canaria de Estudios Ingleses* 50 (2005), pp. 201-12.

While critics taking into consideration the historical dimension of science agree that, in the course of past centuries, the element of science has been given ever wider attention, they disagree as to how to define such plays. The two dominant studies in this field, Shepherd-Barr's *Science on Stage* (2006) and Eva-Zehelein's *Science: Dramatic* (2009), actually represent the two diametrically opposed positions in current genre debates: Shepherd-Barr argues that, in the course of centuries, the representation of science has moved from the margin to the centre and has come to determine the structure of the plays. While in the earliest examples she mentions (e.g. Shakespeare's *Coriolanus*, Christopher Marlowe's *Doctor Faustus*, Ben Jonson's *The Alchemist*) science was metaphorical and marginal, most recent plays, according to her, represent scientific concepts both at a discursive and performative level, incorporating science in the structure of the play. As examples she cites amongst others Friedrich Dürrenmatt's *The Physicists*, Brian Friel's *Molly Sweeney*, Michael Frayn's *Copenhagen*, Margaret Edson's *Wit*, Tom Stoppard's *Arcadia*, or Timberlake Wertenbaker's *After Darwin*. She continues to argue that plays like *Copenhagen* or *Arcadia* "are performative in the classic Austinian sense that they do the thing they talk about; they bring into being a material enactment of an abstract idea under discussion through a speech act".[14] In *Copenhagen* – a play about Heisenberg and quantum physics –

> ... the dialogue [...] is one long speech act that performs the uncertainty principle in a way that only the liveness and immediacy of theater can bring about. Through their corresponding movement and speech acts the actors demonstrate that exact measurement of position and momentum is not possible, because the observer affects the act of measurement. The dialogue does not merely reflect the principle; it makes it happen, with the audience participating in that act of creation. (Shepherd-Barr, pp. 35-6)

To substantiate her claim, Shepherd-Barr refers to the vision of the director of the play's première, Michael Blakemore: "'I felt that if we had the actors moving rather like particles within an atom, there would be times when this could be instructive and other times when as a metaphor it might be quite interesting'" (qtd. in Shepherd-Barr, p. 104). Scientific themes are thus considered to determine the form of the play.

In a similar vein, Vanden Heuvel stresses that research should not be limited to dramatic *texts* (p. 203), but include both science opera and science dance (p. 203) as well as experimental theatrical forms largely excluding the discursive

---

14 Shepherd-Barr, *Science on Stage*, p. 35.

level in favour of performative qualities.[15] Even when analysing conventional science plays, he argues, non-discursive elements, such as "movement, body kinesics and proxemics, and design elements in [...] the *mise-en-scène*" (p. 204) need to be taken into consideration, since all these contribute to the communication of scientific concepts, ideas, and models.

Zehelein, by contrast, holds that science plays are mainly traditional plays and, for this reason, are to be approached as "text theatre", i.e. discursively.[16]

While Shepherd-Barr, Djerassi, and Zehelein widely agree on there being an element of science communication inherent in science plays, the very notion of *communication* requires critical reflection. As George Lakoff and Mark Johnson have stressed, communication does not work in a manner that ideas are conceptualised as objects, linguistic expressions as containers, and the process of communication as sending "them (along a conduit) to a hearer who takes the idea/ objects out of the word/containers."[17] The problem with this so-called 'conduit-metaphor' is that it simplistically assumes that meaning exists "independent of any context or speaker".[18] The concept of communication in Djerassi, therefore, requires special consideration.

For, what is particularly disturbing in theories of science plays is the assumption that science *can* be 'communicated' on stage in an objective and unmodified way. Here too, form determines content, as Damien Broderick has argued when distinguishing between literary and scientific writing. For him, the key difference is that "literary writing aims to create ambiguity, scientific writing to disambiguate".[19] In this respect, the stage would invariably not qualify as a forum for transferring knowledge about science. The crux is that theatre disrupts the auctorial perspective of scientific discourse by multiplying voices and having them speak in dialogue, or even in a chorus – either in harmony or in discord. Multiplicity of voices is not an effective means for rendering scientific information.

---

15 Shepherd-Barr, for example, discusses among such experimental forms Théâtre de Complicité's *Mnemonic* (2001) and John Barrow's *Infinities* (2002). See *Science on Stage*, pp. 128-54.

16 See Zehelein, *SD*, particularly pp. 13, 63, 76-7, 80-1, 97-8, 111, 320-1.

17 George Lakoff and Mark Johnson, *Metaphors We Live By* (Chicago and London: U of Chicago P, 1980), p. 10.

18 Ibid.

19 Victoria Stewart, "A Theatre of Uncertainties: Science and History in Michael Frayn's 'Copenhagen'", *New Theatre Quarterly* 15:4 (1999), pp. 301-7, p. 306. See also Damien Broderick, *The Architecture of Babel: Discourses of Literature and Science* (Melbourne: Melbourne UP, 1994), p. 102. See also Vanden Heuvel, pp. 204, 211.

Even though some critics[20] observe that science plays, especially those fore-grounding the non-discursive element, do *not* serve the function of popularising or communicating science but, on the contrary, tend to defamiliarise scientific content, there are to date no systematic attempts to explore the semiotics of theatre in science plays and map them according to dramatic properties.

Despite the tradition of the Socratic dialogue with its overtly didactic purpose, and despite the fact that many science plays employ epic, narrative, and diegetic elements (monologues, dialogues, stage directions, multimedial presentations, etc.) to discuss scientific issues, which Zehelein calls didactic "mini-lectures" (*SD*, p. 6), all approaches attempting to reduce science plays to pop-science, i.e. to a mere mode of science communication and science teaching are problematic in that they suggest a hierarchy of science and art, deprecating the theatre as subser-vient to science[21] instead of exploring its full potential as a form of art.

It is in this ideological-critical climate that we need to see typologies of science plays, which are predicated either on the individual fields of science tackled or on the amount of science treated in them, the scale ranging from 'central' to 'peripheral'.[22] Djerassi's dogmatic approach is a case in point, his professed aim being the education of theatre audiences in science – more pre-cisely, in his views of the social and ethical benefits of scientific practices. Pre-ferring plays that have a high science content, he, not surprisingly, cites his own plays as prime examples of his theory (e.g. *An Immaculate Misconception*, 2000; *Oxygen*, 2001; *Calculus*, 2003; *Phallacy*, 2005; *Taboos*, 2006; or *Four Jews on Parnassus*, 2008). In order to define his concepts 'science-in-theater' and 'science-in-fiction', Djerassi establishes four categories: a) accuracy of the sci-ence represented or involved; b) realistic representation of the scientist and/ or the scientific community; c) science constituting the 'core' of a work, and d)

---

20 See William Storm, "On the Science of Dramatic Character", *Narrative* 19:2 (May 2011), pp. 241-50; Paul Edwards, "Science in *Hapgood* and *Arcadia*", in Katherine E. Kelley, ed., *The Cambridge Companion to Tom Stoppard* (Cambridge: CUP, 2001), pp. 171-84; Alan Brody, "Operation Epsilon: Science, History, and Theatrical Narrative", *Narrative* 19:2 (May 2011), pp. 253-7. See also Vanden Heuvel, pp. 201-11; Stewart, "A Theatre of Uncertainties"; and Tonie L. Stolberg, "Communicating Science through the Language of Dance: A Journey of Education and Reflection", *Leonardo* 39:5 (October 2006), pp. 426-32.

21 A controversial issue occasionally broached in this context is the funding of plays overtly dedicated to the 'propagation of science'; see e.g. Shepherd-Barr, *Science on Stage*, p. 11; and Vanden Heuvel's critique of propagandist science plays, p. 209-11.

22 See Vanden Heuvel, p. 210.

didactic function.[23] Literature, if acknowledged at all as an aesthetic practice, is at best considered a corollary, at worst a marketing strategy apt to spice up science with "the occasional sexy metaphor".[24] His typology results in binary oppositions, such as expert/layman, science/art, the sciences/the humanities, each implying value judgments ready to provoke hostility between the *two cultures* rather than addressing stagecraft, more positively, as an imaginative response to science with a great potential to affect audiences in multiple, and different, ways.

Zehelein, who for the most part supports Djerassi's views, distinguishes four groups of science plays in her own taxonomy: a) plays which primarily communicate a scientific topic to the audience, b) plays which describe the respective field of science and represent scientists, c) plays which focus on the history of science, d) plays which are border cases in that they do not really contain science (see *SD*, pp. 14-15). The first two categories are largely identical with Djerassi's categories, the latter two complement his. In all four groups of plays, science is treated as a quantifiable criterion, which, according to Zehelein, serves as a demarcation line between science plays (representing 'real science' or representing science 'realistically') and science fiction, which disrupts reality. The flaws of this distinction become apparent in her own reading of Djerassi's plays.

While emphasising their genuine function of educating through entertaining, Zehelein argues that these plays also deal with the ethical, socio-cultural and legal consequences of contemporary science (Zehelein, "CDS", pp. 62-4), major concerns being chemistry and the public perception and esteem of scientific innovation (*Oxygen*, 2001), general science and the life and public perception of scientists (*Calculus (Newton's Whores)*, 2003), (assisted) reproductive technologies (ART) and in-vitro fertilisation (such as ICSI, Intra-Cytoplasmic Sperm Injection), which are coupled with politics in the Near East (*An Immaculate Misconception*, 2000), sexuality and gender, lifestyle, family planning and the effects of child-rearing on identity (*Taboos*, 2006).

This line of argumentation is problematic on two grounds: first, questions about the moral consequences or the effects of biotechnologies on family life and

---

23   See Eva-Sabine Zehelein, "Carl Djerassi's Seed", *Critical Survey* 20:1 (2008), pp. 56-68, pp. 56-7. Subsequently abbreviated as "CDS". Zehelein refers to Djerassi's "Contemporary 'Science-in-Theater': A Rare Genre" and to his book *This Man's Pill* (Oxford: OUP, 2001), Chapter 11: "Science on Stage", pp. 244-79.

24   Zehelein, "CDS", p. 57. See also Vanden Heuvel, who criticises Djerassi's treatment of literature as "a transparent window or medium of clear communication" and to "the helpmeet's role of making science more palatable and pellucid" (p. 210).

social relationships *are* speculative, hence shared with science fiction. Second, they are not just 'additional' but intimately connected with scientific practices (such as assisted reproductive technologies).

In her discussion of the two plays *An Immaculate Misconception* (2000) and *Taboos* (2008) Zehelein, almost despite herself, undermines both Djerassi's and her own standpoint by arguing that the former "focus[es] more on the practical side of ICSI (the play also includes a video of an ICSI procedure) and on describing the technique in didactic detail", whereas the latter "highlights much more the *sociocultural* and *legal ramifications* of ART in a very special setting" (Zehelein, "CDS", p. 64, emphasis ours). Focusing on such 'ramifications' makes it apparent that neither 'science-in-theatre' (Djerassi) nor 'science plays' (Shepherd-Barr, Zehelein) can be as neatly separated from speculative literature as these commentators would have it – science fiction being a major speculative genre, as recent criticism has stressed.[25] No doubt, *An Immaculate Misconception* may place more

---

25 See e.g. Brian W. Aldiss and David Wingrove, *Trillion Year Spree: The History of Science Fiction* (Thirsk: House of Stratus, 2001); Robert W. Bly, *The Science in Science Fiction: Eighty-Three SF Predictions That Became Scientific Reality* (Dallas: BenBella, 2005); Marvin Keith Booker, *Contemporary Speculative Fiction* (Hackensack: Salem Press, 2013); Mark Bould, et al., ed., *The Routledge Companion to Science Fiction* (London: Routledge, 2009); Mark L. Brake and Neil Hook, *Different Engines: How Science Drives Fiction and Fiction Drives Science* (London: Macmillan, 2008); Istvan Csicsery-Ronay, Jr., *The Seven Beauties of Science Fiction* (Middletown, CT: Wesleyan UP, 2008); Thomas M. Disch, *The Dreams Our Stuff Is Made Of: How Science Fiction Conquered the World* (New York: Simon & Schuster, 1998); Carl Freedman, *Science Fiction and Critical Theory* (Hanover, NH: UP New England for Wesleyan UP, 2000); David G. Hartwell, ed., *The Science Fiction Century* (New York: Tor, 1997); Gilbert Hottois, ed., *Philosophie et science-fiction* (Paris: Vrin, 2000); Sandra Jackson, ed., *The Black Imagination: Science Fiction, Futurism and the Speculative* (New York: Lang, 2011); Edward James and Farah Mendlesohn, ed., *The Cambridge Companion to Science Fiction* (Cambridge: CUP, 2005); Frederic Jameson, *Archaeologies of the Future: The Desire Called Utopia and Other Science Fictions* (New York: Verso, 2005); Roger Luckhurst, *Science Fiction* (Cambridge: CUP, 2005); Thomas Macho, ed., *Science & Fiction: Über Gedankenexperimente in Wissenschaft, Philosophie und Literatur* (Frankfurt a.M.: Fischer, 2004); Graham Dunstan Martin, *An Inquiry into the Purposes of Speculative Fiction: Fantasy and Truth* (Lewiston, NY: Edwin Mellen Press, 2003); Gerald Alva Miller, *Exploring the Limits of the Human through Science Fiction* (New York: Palgrave Macmillan, 2012); Robert M. Philmus, *Visions and Revisions: (Re)Constructing Science Fiction* (Liverpool: Liverpool UP, 2005); Eric S. Rabkin and George E. Slusser, ed., *Intersections: Fantasy and Science Fiction* (Carbondale and Edwardsville: Southern Illinois UP, 1985); William Shatner and Chip Walter, *I'm Working on That: A Trek from Science Fiction to Science Fact*

emphasis on scientific knowledge and procedures, but its plot nonetheless hinges on socio-political considerations (politics in the Near East, gender inequality in the professional world, the effects of child rearing and ART on human identity). Zehelein's summary of *Taboos* makes apparent that even Djerassi's own 'science-in-theatre' plays depend less on techno-scientific detail than on the dramatic tension between characters:

> The plot is about a lesbian couple, Harriet and Sally, who want to start a nuclear family, a family consisting of two mothers and a biological child of one of the two partners. [...] we end up with two couples and three children, with two biological fathers and three biological mothers. *In addition*, the play asks: what will happen to the other excess embryos created through ICSI? Should they be implanted, destroyed or given away for adoption, as some radical evangelists in the U.S. promote and practice? *The Evans-Johnston case has recently brought the legal and social status of frozen embryos to the public's awareness.*[26]

Reference to the Evans-Johnston case further points to the importance of the socio-political 'ramifications' of science in Djerassi's plays.

While Zehelein connects scientific content with socio-cultural issues ("in addition"), her synopsis makes one immediately think of Mark Ravenhill's *Handbag* (1998), a play with a similar character constellation raising similar ethical questions and, without ever mentioning any scientific details, achieving a similar effect. Indeed, neither Djerassi nor Zehelein specify the nature of the relationship between the broader ethical or social concerns and the kind of actual 'science communication', 'authentic' representation and scientific accuracy they call for.

What follows from all this is that, irrespective of the *degree* of science explication in drama (whether stressed, as in Djerassi's *An Immaculate Misconception*, or left out completely, as in Ravenhill's *Handbag*), science never constitutes what Zehelein calls "the narrative heart and bone"[27] of these plays, but first and

---

(New York: Pocket, 2002); David Seed, ed., *A Companion to Science Fiction* (Malden, MA: Blackwell Publishing, 2005); Brian Stableford, *Science Fact and Science Fiction: An Encyclopedia* (New York and London: Routledge, 2006); Peter Stockwell, *The Poetics of Science Fiction* (Harlow: Longman, 2000); Paul L. Thomas, *Science Fiction and Speculative Fiction: Challenging Genres* (Rotterdam: SensePublishers, 2013); Gary Westfahl, et al., ed., *The Greenwood Encyclopedia of Science Fiction and Fantasy: Themes, Works, and Wonders* (3 vols.) (Westport, CT: Greenwood Press, 2005); Gary K. Wolfe, *Critical Terms for Science Fiction and Fantasy: A Glossary and Guide to Scholarship* (New York: Greenwood Press, 1986).

26 Zehelein, "CDS", p. 64, emphasis ours.
27 Ibid., p. 57.

foremost a means of instigating plot. What makes the play *a play* are the dramatic tensions between characters, between parental figures and artificially created children. Besides, the underlying questions concerning humanity in a science-dominated society remain the same, whether science is presented 'authentically' or whether it is treated in an 'estranged' form. In these respects, Djerassi's own plays – necessarily – fail to comply with his definition of science-in-theatre, central aspects of his plays being different from the ones he sets up as key genre exemplars.

By reducing the stage to a site of knowledge transfer, both Djerassi and Ze-helein fail to understand science drama as drama. In order to shift the focus, we need to take into consideration the metaphorical mechanisms of science drama and its connections with speculative (science) fiction. Darko Suvin's concept of the 'novum', established in science fiction studies in 1979, provides a pertinent starting point in this respect.[28]

3. Science as metaphor: the novum

According to Suvin, science fiction is marked by estrangement and cognition (p. 3), which demarcate it against literary realism, on the one hand, and myth and fantasy, on the other.[29] Both estrangement and cognition negotiate the real at the level of literature (p. 8) by creating "*an imaginative framework alternative to the author's empirical environment*" (p. 8, emphases in original). Hence, the central momentum in science fiction is "*the narrative dominance or hegemony of a fictional 'novum' (novelty, innovation) validated by cognitive logic*" (p. 63, emphases in original), which Suvin defines as "a totalizing phenomenon or relationship deviating from the author's and implied reader's norm of reality" (p. 64). The novum does not primarily constitute "scientific facts or [...] hypotheses" but refers to "the presence of scientific cognition as the sign or correlative of a method (way, approach, atmosphere, sensibility) identical to that of a modern philosophy of science" (p. 65). The hallmark of Suvin's theory is his idea that realism and mimetic imitation (science content and authenticity) do not hold as distinctive features for defining *science fiction*. This idea may

---

28 Darko Suvin, *Metamorphoses of Science Fiction: On the Poetics and History of a Literary Genre* (New Haven: Yale UP, 1979).

29 Suvin writes that "a very useful distinction between 'naturalistic' fiction, fantasy, and science fiction, drawn by Robert M. Philmus, is that naturalistic fiction does not require scientific explanation, fantasy does not allow it, and SF both requires and allows it." (p. 65)

equally be applied to *science plays* as it highlights precisely the metaphorical strategies by which science works in science plays, even in plays where it is absent, as our exemplary reading of Caryl Churchill's *A Number* and Elfriede Jelinek's *Kein Licht* will demonstrate.

3.1. Caryl Churchill's *A Number*

Set in an alternative near future, *A Number* is categorised both by Shepherd-Barr and Zehelein as a 'science play' according to their criteria. The grading of science in terms of its level of authenticity or reality, as proposed by them, is, however, irrelevant to both the dynamics of the play and the audience's response. Its logic corresponds to the logic of the novum in science fiction.

A *Number* deals with Salter, a sixty-year-old man who abandons his four-year-old son Bernard after his wife's suicide (the boy's mother) and after abusing him grossly, in order to have a new version of Bernard – B2 – cloned from the latter's genetic material. What Salter does not know is that "some mad scientist [...] illegally"[30] and secretly cloned 'a number' of several further versions of Bernard, one of whom appears towards the end of the play. The themes of identity and origin are astutely reflected structurally in form of telling names and character configuration. While the dramatis personae only distinguish between B1, the original, and B2, his clone, the third clone to appear is given a full name: Michael Black. (Initially, one might assume that B2 is denied a name owing to his being a clone, but soon one realises that the original, B1, has equally been dispossessed of a full identity. This use of 'telling names', reducing both Bernards to the status of a number, neither reflects their 'natural' nor 'artificial' genesis, but their troubled relationship with their father. Interestingly, though, the 'B' in Michael's surname, Black, subtly connects him with the others. Churchill uses similar strategies throughout the play to undermine reductive notions of identity.) The play consists of five scenes, with the first four alternating between B1's and B2's separate appearances, the first scene, titled "1", beginning with a conversation between Salter and B2. The play opens when B2 as an adult learns that he is a clone. The action culminates in a fatal confrontation between Salter and B1, who murders B2 and subsequently commits suicide. Whereas B1 and B2 voice a similarly negative view on cloning, emphasising their loss of identity, the last scene ends with a conversation between Salter and Michael Black, who whole-heartedly embraces his artificial origin.

---

30 Churchill, p. 11.

How does this plot compare with science fiction plots? Contrary to Zehelein's argument, the primary orientation in science fiction is *not* extrapolation.[31] Whatever assumptions about the future there may be, their relevance is secondary in the aesthetics of science fiction.[32] What constitutes the novum is not the anticipatory quality of a text but its "unalienable historicity" (p. 64), its way of negotiating between 'fictive' and 'empirical' reality. According to Suvin, science fiction "estranges the empirical norm of the implied reader" (p. 64) by introducing the unknown or Other into the *"author's empirical environment"* (p. 8; emphasis in original).

---

31 According to Zehelein, it is "vital" to "separate 'real' science and future scenarios, namely science fiction" (*SD*, p. 88), and "The Science Plays focus on 'real' science in order to be clearly set apart from science fiction" (*SD*, p. 84); see also pp. 6, 13, 99, 102, 105, 131-2, 320. Shepherd-Barr takes a similar stance by emphasizing that her book focuses "on real science" (*Science on Stage*, p. 8), which she strictly distinguishes from science fiction (pp. 7-8). Without ever considering the generic specifics of science fiction, Zehelein's and Shepherd-Barr's distinctions are unconvincing; apart from this, it is problematic to differentiate a dramatic from a prosaic genre simply on grounds of thematic representations.

32 See Suvin: "any futurological function [...] SF might have [...] [is] strictly secondary, and [...] stressing it [...] [is] dangerous since it tend[s] to press upon SF the role of a popularizer of the reigning ideology of the day (technocratic, psionic, utopian, dystopian, hip, or whatever). Thus, although extrapolation was historically a convention of much SF [...], pure extrapolation is flat, and the pretense at it masks in all significant cases the employment of other methods. Theoretical defining of any SF as extrapolation should therefore be decently and deeply buried. It seems clear that SF is material for futurology (if at all) only in the very restricted sense of reflecting on the author's own historical period and the possibilities inherent in it: Bellamy's and Morris's different socialist twenty-first centuries use the anticipation device so effectively because they are about incipient collective human relationships in the 1880s as they (differently) saw them, while *1984* or *2001* are about incipient collective human relationships in 1948 or 1967 as certain aspects of or elements within Orwell's or Kubrick's mind saw them. [...] Any significant SF text is thus always to be read as an analogy, somewhere between a vague symbol and a precisely aimed parable, while extrapolative SF in any futurological sense was (and is) only a delusion of technocratic ideology [...]. For extrapolation itself as a scientific procedure (and not pure arithmetic formalization) is predicated upon a strict (or, if you wish, crude) analogy between the points from and to which the extrapolating is carried out: *extrapolation is a one-dimensional, scientific limit-case of analogy*" (p. 76). Suvin also distinguishes between *extrapolation* and *anticipation*: "[...] the valid SF form or subgenre of *anticipation* – tales located in the historical future of the author's society – should be strictly differentiated from the technocratic ideology of extrapolation on the one hand and the literary device of extrapolation on the other" (p. 78).

Hence, the estranging effect of the novum rests on the tension it creates between the recipient's historical vantage point, "the author's 'zero world' and the new reality". As it points back to the "human relationships it implies", its major role is that of a "reality displacement" (p. 71).

In *A Number* the Other is represented by clones that, in an alternative near future, become a site of warning of the potential dangers of cloning humans. Hence they fulfil a function in the play that aligns them with the alleged "future scenarios" (*SD*, p. 88) that Zehelein ascribes to science fiction. Both Churchill's *A Number* and science fiction texts (such as the clone fiction Zehelein criticises to be 'un-scientific')[33] share scientific extrapolation or speculation and, what is more important, both explore alternative scenarios to address fundamental social and ethical questions. Hence extrapolation, as Suvin states, proves secondary, because the clones in both 'clone fiction' and in *A Number* are "used as signifiers, they can only signify human relationships, given that we cannot – at least so far – imagine other ones" (p. 71). Zehelein criticises science fiction on three counts: (a) that these novels use "science as a metaphor without elucidating the science as such" ("CDS", p. 57); (b) that "the scientific facts of human cloning are never explained; in all three cases, the plot is based on future scientific advances – in stark contrast to the realism of 'science-in-fiction'"; and (c) that "the portrayal of the human element is prioritised", particularly "the social and human implications of such research" (p. 58). This is, however, equally the case in *A Number*, categorised as a science play by both her and Shepherd-Barr.

Despite its admittedly futurological impression, Churchill's play is firmly an-chored in contemporary western culture. Her clone-figures are embedded in fa-miliar social structures and, within these, entertain human relationships, such as filial and sibling relations, relations between individuals and groups, whilst acting out the life-giving and life-destroying forces of humans. Their rivalries and tensions, hatred and distrust reflect prevalent western power ideologies, no-tably consumerism, capitalism, and neo-liberalism. Similar concerns are voiced in anarcho-capitalist and libertarian science fiction as well as social science fiction,[34]

---

33 The examples given include: Kazuo Ishiguro's *Never Let Me Go* (2005), Kevin Guilfoile's *Cast of Shadows* (2005), or Eva Hoffman's *The Secret* (2001).

34 We are here referring to recent science fiction studies stressing the political and socio-logical dimensions of the genre: Mark Bould, *The Routledge Concise History of Science Fiction* (London: Routledge, 2011); Tony Burns, *Political Theory, Science Fiction, and Utopian Literature: Ursula K. Le Guin and The Dispossessed* (Lanham, MD: Lexington Books, 2010); Philip John Davies, ed., *Science Fiction, Social Conflict and War* (Manchester: Manchester UP, 1990); Jan A. Fuhse, ed., *Technik und Gesellschaft*

such as Robert A. Heinlein's *The Moon is a Harsh Mistress* (1966), Ira Levin's *This Perfect Day* (1970), Ursula K. LeGuin's *The Dispossessed: An Ambiguous Utopia* (1974), Ken MacLeod's four-part *Fall Revolution* (1995, 1996, 1998, 1999), or Neil Stephenson's *The System of the World* (2004), to give only a few examples.[35]

References to science and the representation of science and scientists in Churchill's play are of little importance in the sense of 'communicating science' or 'transferring knowledge'. The scientific background of cloning, which triggers Churchill's drama of malevolent and mutually destructive instincts, fulfils none of the functions Zehelein proposes as constituents of science plays: authenticity, communication of knowledge, explaining and teaching science. It equally falls short of Shepherd-Barr's categories.[36] On the contrary, the clones raise awareness

---

in der Science-Fiction (Berlin: Lit, 2008); Donald M. Hassler and Clyde Wilcox, ed., *New Boundaries in Political Science Fiction* (Columbia: U of South Carolina P, 2008) and *Political Science Fiction* (Columbia: U of South Carolina P, 1997); Andrew Milner, *Locating Science Fiction* (Liverpool: Liverpool UP, 2012); John Rieder, *Colonialism and the Emergence of Science Fiction* (Middletown, CT: Wesleyan UP, 2008); Torben Schröder, *Science-Fiction als Social Fiction: Das gesellschaftliche Potential eines Unterhaltungsgenres* (Münster: Lit, 1998); Brian M. Stableford, *Historical Dictionary of Science Fiction Literature* (Lanham, MD: Scarecrow Press, 2004); Darko Suvin, *Defined by a Hollow: Essays on Utopia, Science Fiction and Political Epistemology* (Berne: Lang, 2010); Jutta Weldes, ed., *To Seek Out New Worlds: Exploring Links Between Science Fiction and World Politics* (New York: Palgrave Macmillan, 2003).

35 Other examples include: Any Rand's *Atlas Shrugged* (1957), Cecelia Holland's *Floating Worlds* (1976), J. Neil Schulman's *Alongside Night* (1979), L. Neil Smith's *The Probability Broach* (1980), Vernor Vinge's *Marooned in Real Time* (1986), Larry Niven, Jerry Pournelle, and Michael Flynn's *Fallen Angels* (1991), Neal Stephenson's *Snow Crash* (1992) and *The Diamond Age* (1996), S. Andrew Swann's *Hostile Takeover Trilogy* (1995, 1996), Victoria Koman's *Kings of the High Frontier* (1996), Max Barry's *Jennifer Government* (2003), and John C. Wright's trilogy *The Golden Age, The Golden Transcendence* and *The Phoenix Exultant* (2002, 2003, 2003).

36 Cloning in *A Number* is neither explained nor dramatically focused. Considering that in the "*author's empirical environment*" of 2002, when the play was first staged and published, cloning was not applied to humans at all. Hence, calling for the 'real', "[i]mpeccable accuracy of the science described", or "high probability of its existence" (Zehelein, "CDS", p. 57) in respect of *human* cloning, seems doubtful. Science is neither at the core of the text nor is it communicated (Zehelein's first category of '*docere et delectare*', Djerassi's third constitutive element); there is no didactic element (Djerassi's fourth constitutive defining element); scientists never appear in the play (Zehelein's 'tribal culture' and Djerassi's second constitutive defining element), and there are no scientific spaces staged. Zehelein's first two categories ('*docere et delectare*' and 'tribal culture'), which largely cover Djerassi's demands for science-in-theatre, are not met in

of some of contemporary humanity's most pressing concerns and, like most of science fiction, the play's thrust is dystopian.

Suvin's concept of the 'novum' proves more apt to approach *A Number* as a science play. The human clones' 'inalienable historicity' is obvious. At the time of its first performance in 2002, there were no human clones, and as this paper is being published, there are not any yet.[37] A society that practices human cloning invariably relates to a society without human clones (the author's 'zero-world'). According to Samuel Delany's theory of the conjunctivity of literary genres, *A*

A Number. Zehelein's third category does not apply to the play either, as "no historical event figures prominently" (Zehelein, *SD*, p. 285). In Zehelein's taxonomy, *A Number* could only be subsumed as a border case. But this category seems to be self-defeating since she admits that "[a] significant number of Science Plays belong to this borderline category" and that "it is of course only a matter of degree and emphasis whether a play is pigeonholed here or even excluded from Science Plays altogether" (ibid.). If such a "significant number" (ibid.) of her corpus of Science Plays fall under a category that *could* be excluded, there seem to be few texts left to validate her taxonomy. Shepherd-Barr does not provide convincing reasons either, *why* science plays like *A Number* are different from science fiction texts *thematically*. She even concedes that the play "contains hardly any scientific detail about cloning, nor does it use an extended scientific metaphor. [...] Rather than provide lengthy explanations of cloning and genetics, *A Number* draws on our own understanding of these issues to fill in the blanks, as it were. There is an implicit assumption that we have at least some common base of knowledge about the science of cloning through news stories and general discourse. The success of the play confirms Churchill's assumption" (*Science on Stage*, p. 125). It is not that the play's success would confirm Churchill's alleged assumption, but rather that its inclusion in the corpus of science plays proves Shepherd-Barr's arguments to be flawed. Rather than convincingly arguing for a distinction between science plays and science fiction, Shepherd-Barr unintentionally explains the play with the same logics inherent in Suvin's novum: "[...] *A Number* [...] takes cloning as a means to explore the problem of identity. [...] It is a modern twist on the story of Cain and Abel [...]" (ibid.).

37 The first human embryos were 'accidentally' cloned and subsequently destroyed by Shoukhrat Mitalipov and his team at the Oregon Health & Science University in 2013; still, cloning has so far not been used to reproduce humans; see: Ulrich Bahnsen and Martin Spiewak, "Kopie aus dem Labor", *Zeit Online* (15 May 2013), <http://www.zeit.de /2013/21/klonen-mensch-durchbruch> (1 August 2013); and Francie Diep, "Scientists Create First Cloned Human Embryo", *PopSci: The Future Now* (15 May 2013), <http:// www.popsci.com/science/article/2013-05/scientists-create-human-clone-embryo-stem-cell-harvesting> (1 August 2013).

Number complies with the mode of 'has not yet happened', which he characterises as the mode of science fiction.[38]

Like the strange characters in science fiction, the clones hold up "a mirror to" humanity, to use Suvin's image, albeit a cracked one that distorts it rather than reflecting it (Suvin, p. 5). The clones are human in the way they act and interact, but alien due to their origin. As in science fiction, the purpose of their estranged status is to probe into the relation between self and other. The clones embody the fundamental human need to comprehend reality in anthropomorphic patterns of thought.[39] Scientific content (DNA, genome) and practice (cloning) become meaningful as they are humanised in the dramatis personae. Such 'meaningfulness' is by no means identical with scientific 'disambiguation', and its effect is not 'density of information', but a 'diluted'[40] form of science. *A Number*, commonly labelled a 'science play', actually corresponds to the epistemological mechanisms of science fiction.

These require a particular reception strategy by which the reader must assess how the play's diegesis "engages with contemporary epistemologies [...] and how [...] [it] innovates with respect to such epistemologies."[41] We may therefore hold against Shepherd-Barr's argument that science has moved from a *metaphorical, marginal* position to centre-stage in science plays, Lakoff and Johnson's notion that "*human thought processes are largely metaphorical*".[42] Metaphor, according to them, "is not just a matter of language, that is, of mere words" (p. 6), but of structuring our experiential reality (p. 5). This is exactly how we may see the operation of science in drama, both cognitively and dramatically (even in Djerassi's science-in-theatre).

Metaphor establishes a relation between two things different in kind, where, usually, imagery from the phenomenological world is used to illustrate abstract ideas. With regard to science plays, metaphorical structuring refers to all levels commonly understood in modern drama theory as composite elements of

---

38 See Carl D. Malmgren, *Worlds Apart: Narratology of Science Fiction* (Bloomington: Indiana UP, 1991), p. 8.

39 See ibid., p. 43.

40 See Storm, p. 248: "[T]he science that is talked about is, of necessity, diluted. In accord with the tendency of science-oriented plays, the subject matter must be kept within reach for a non-scientific audience. In this particular connection, the nature of the theater itself, with its varied audiences, dramaturgical structures, and time limitations, can be delimiting in the communication of science or even of scientific characters, especially if these are of a typed or stock variety."

41 See Brett M. Rogers and Benjamin Stevens, "Classical Receptions in Science Fiction", *Classical Receptions Journal* 4:1 (2012), pp. 127-47, p. 132.

42 George Lakoff and Mark Johnson, *Metaphors We Live By* (Chicago: U of Chicago P, 1980), p. 6.

drama.[43] In *A Number*, the abstract domain of science is metaphorically structured by dramatic figures, language, and space in order to make the implications
of a scientific practice like cloning understandable to an audience. Metaphorical
structuring thus involves a dilution of scientific information.

The primary role of *dramatic figures* in this diluting process derives from their
status as ontological metaphors, which reconfigure an abstract notion into a concrete object. Given the relationship of our bodies with other concrete physical
entities, humans tend to divide phenomenological reality into concrete items
in order to make sense of it (see Lakoff/Johnson, pp. 25-6). The characters in *A
Number* answer this human need for translating everything we encounter into a
familiar human context and form.[44] The figures involved in science are, strangely
enough, not scientists. In fact, scientists never enter the stage, but are only referred to in terms of popular, stereotypical 'Faustian overreachers':[45] "some mad
scientist" (p. 11); "the mad old professor" (p. 61). As such they are particularly
unsuited for conveying knowledge or representing science. It is the clones and
their father that serve as metaphors of an abstract science.[46] Being a play *"for two
actors"*, one *"play*[ing] *Salter, the other his sons"*,[47] *A Number* focuses on the private
encounter between father and son, thus individualising the clones' life stories and
highlighting the alarming and irrational dimension of scientific practices as they
affect the individual in society.[48] Stylistically, the figures express vague and sweep-
ing speculations on cloning and speak in jumbled, anacoluthic and fragmented
sentences. Far from giving the audience any closure, the play refuses to inform or
educate. Churchill's specific choice of dramatis personae, character constellation,
and language functions solely to root scientific conceptions of cloning in the lived,
everyday world of the individual and thereby put pressing social and existential
concerns into new relief.

---

43 For a precise overview of these constituents, see Manfred Pfister, *The Theory and
    Analysis of Drama*, trans. John Halliday (Cambridge: CUP, 1993).
44 See Stolberg, p. 428.
45 Shepherd-Barr considers these characters to be constitutive of older science plays like
    Doctor Faustus (see *Science on Stage*, pp. 15-16).
46 See Churchill, pp. 11, 15, 16, 19, 29, and 34 for examples. Cf. Storm, pp. 246-7, for a
    discussion of the problematic status of characters representing science in drama ow-
    ing to their occupying a "borderline between fictive representation and actuality" (p.
    247). Again, Storm points the way to a crucial aspect of science plays, which needs to
    be pursued in more depth and which we are attempting in this essay.
47 Ibid.
48 See Malmgren, pp. 50, 167.

Dramatic space is equally vital for linking the abstract and the concrete meta-phorically, whilst again subverting the level of knowledge and rational science communication.[49] On the surface, *A Number* has a plain spatial structure, with Salter's living room being the only physical setting: "[t]*he scene is the same through-out, it's where Salter lives*."[50] The reader/viewer, however, has to construct a number of implied settings, so-called *subterranean spaces*,[51] which are discursively evoked and prove highly charged metaphors. Related to isolation, confinement, suffering, fear, night and death, they indirectly connect the characters B1, B2, and Michael Black. Significantly, all scenes take place in an enclosed space. B1's traumatic childhood furnishes a prime example of how this metaphorical layering works. His memories are charged with claustrophobic images of space:

> You know you asked me when you used to shout in the night. [...] That was just a short period you used to shout, you grew out of that, you got so you'd rather not see me, you wanted to be left alone in the night, you wouldn't want me [Salter] to come any more. You'd nearly stopped speaking do you remember that? not speaking not eating I tried to make you, I'd put you in the cupboard do you remember? or I'd look for you everywhere and I'd think you'd got away and I'd find you under the bed.[52]

"It was one long night out", is how Salter describes the two years he was alone with B1 after the mother's suicide. Conversely, Salter represents "a dark dark power" (p. 24) for B1. B1's murder of B2 ("Just a small room, rather dark, one window and the shutters" in a hotel "in a street just a side", p. 49) and the mother's suicide ("She did it under a train under a tube train, she was one of those people when they say there has been a person under a train and the trains are delayed she was a person under a train", p. 40) take place in subterranean spaces. Interestingly, B1 follows B2 on a train (p. 52) when pursuing him to death, and Michael Black paints a range of uneasy subterranean spaces in words, almost suggesting a collective unconscious of the clones:[53]

---

49 See in this context John Shanahan's two papers on Renaissance science drama, in which he equally concentrates on the importance of dramatic space: "Theatrical Space and Scientific Space in Thomas Shadwell's *Virtuoso*", *SEL: Studies in English Literature 1500-1900* 49:3 (Summer 2009), pp. 549-71; and "Ben Jonson's *Alchemist* and Early Modern Laboratory Space", *Journal for Early Modern Cultural Studies* 8:1 (Spring/Summer 2008), pp. 35-66.

50 Churchill, no pagination; italics in original.

51 See Henri Lefebvre, *The Production of Space* (1974/1984), trans. Donald Nicholson-Smith (Oxford: Blackwell, 1991), p. 236.

52 Churchill, pp. 51-2.

53 See ibid., pp. 30-3; 48-9; 51-2; 56-7.

Well here's something I find fascinating, there are these people who used to live in holes in the ground, with all tunnels and underground chambers and sometimes you'd have a chamber you'd get to it through a labyrinth of passages and the ceiling got lower and lower so you had to go on your hands and knees and then wriggle on your stomach and you'd get through to this chamber deep deep down that had a hole like a chimney like a well a hole all the way up to the sky so you could sit in this chamber this room this cave whatever and look up at a little circle of sky going past overhead. And when somebody died they'd hollow out more little rooms so they weren't buried underneath you they were buried in the walls beside you. And maybe sometimes they walled people up alive in there, it's possible because of how the remains were contorted but either way of course they're dead by now and very soon after they went in of course.[54]

These subterranean spaces are ingeniously connected to scientific spaces ("there was this batch and we were all in it", p. 17; "in the test tubes the dishes", p. 26), which are in turn connected with family spaces: "in a cradle" (p. 27). In this way, the alien scientific is constantly fused with the everyday familial. This is equally achieved by spatial opposites, such as public space (the laboratory) versus private space (Salter's home). Being excluded from on-stage space, the laboratory remains as mysterious as the scientists.

Setting and dramatic space are particularly important in science plays because our metaphorical concepts partly evolve from senso-motorical experience of space. In *A Number*, many such 'orientational metaphors'[55] are used to structure conceptually the science of cloning and its social effects. While the absent, off-stage space of the scientific becomes an all powerful force, the family space, a life-giving force traditionally understood in terms of "HEALTH AND LIFE ARE UP", is here turned into a subterranean space dominated by "SICKNESS AND DEATH ARE DOWN" (Lakoff/Johnson, p. 15). Since B1 and B2 are exchangeable numbers in Salter's eyes, and since the figures in *A Number* anthropomorphise the scientific application of cloning, science is also metaphorically structured in terms of capitalism and moral depravity: Salter is confronted by his off-spring in his claustrophobic home, the spatial equivalent of his egotism and solipsism. If this home becomes a

---

54 Ibid., pp. 56-7.

55 According to Lakoff/Johnson, an orientational metaphor is a "metaphorical concept [...] that [...] organizes a whole system of concepts with respect to one another. [...] [M]ost of them have to do with spatial orientation: up-down, in-out, front-back, on-off, deep-shallow, central-peripheral. These spatial orientations arise from the fact that we have bodies of the sort we have and that they function as they do in our physical environment. Orientational metaphors give a concept spatial orientation; for example, HAPPY IS UP." (p. 14); see also pp. 56-7.

terrible, *un-homely* place of dehumanising confrontations, it casts a dark shadow on cloning and, in a wider sense, on the audience's perception of science.

Drama does not enact science. It dilutes it. This is why we need to understand these orientational metaphors when reading or watching science plays rather than naively look out for science in theatre. Revealing many similarities with Churchill's play, Elfriede Jelinek's *Kein Licht* constitutes an extreme example of how metaphors go to dilute science, even to the point of obliterating it.

3.2. *Kein Licht* [No Light]

Jelinek's play *Kein Licht* was for the first time produced in Austria in 2012 at the Salzburg Schauspielhaus, together with the world première of the play's *Epilog* [Epilogue], actually written after the play in the manner of Jelinek's ongoing writing process – a tremendous challenge for both the actors and the audience. Many of Jelinek's texts are quick responses to disruptions of contemporary society through disasters, crimes or other hazards. *Kein Licht* responds to the nuclear catastrophe of Fukushima in 2011. It is an intricate, multi-layered text with metaphorically interlinking levels of meaning, divided into two voices that actually refer to musical instruments, whilst constantly stating their inefficiency and insignificance. While Churchill still allocates text to her voices, her various efforts to de-humanise B1 and B2 in *A Number* are radically completed in Jelinek's textual spaces – dialogically, chorally or contrapuntally delivered on stage and no longer attributable to any particular figure. Fukushima is never mentioned explicitly, nor is science communication or pop-science any of Jelinek's concerns. Far more radically, *Kein Licht* verbalises the very failure of communication, the lack of information and the impossibility to know reality, given the complexity and the scale of the issues addressed. For there is no less at stake in her 'play' than human life on earth. Global extinction is beyond the compass of the theatre, in fact beyond the compass of any art or mode of human expression.

The technical jargon in Jelinek's play, which the theatre-goer easily associates with nuclear energy, represents the common knowledge about nuclear power available to the average citizen through the media. Reading the vague utterances of Churchill's clones, Jelinek's wordplay and associative word-chains completely distort the epistemic, suggesting the arbitrariness of the signifier drained of the signified. Science is not just the absent space on stage relegated to subterranean settings, as in Churchill, it becomes the all-absorbing hollow of the apocalypse, metaphorically eroding all rational mechanisms of constructing meaning. Here are some examples: "Schatzhaus" ('treasury') – "Schutzhaus" ('shelter'), "Strahler" ('radiator') – "Reaktoren" ('reactors') – "Reagierende" ('people reacting'), "Abkühlbecken" ('cooling pool') – "Abklingbecken" ('fuel cooling installation'), "Leptiden" ('leptides') – "Leptonen" ('leptons'), "Betonköpfe" ('concrete heads'), "Halbwertszeit" ('half-life'). The audience 'learns' nothing about nuclear power except the little they already know.

In fact, the play's alarming effect lies in its sounds and rhythms, in the absurd ways in which the voices engage or fail to engage with one another, in the very lightness of puns and jokes so terribly incommensurate with the topic, and in vague associations and allusions, obviously devoid of authority. What is particularly haunting, is a perpetual undertow of words and phrases, many times repeated and modified throughout the play, which indicate suffering, end-time and violent death: rift, crack, flood, a cavity, rottenness, milliseconds, menace, violence, 'eating enemy', squeeze, ill, poison, mud, screams, crying, groaning, weeping. As in Churchill, this semantic ground-pattern provides the ideational context in which scientific cognition has become impossible. The play resonates with disaster rather than stating or showing it. Its effect is metaphorical chaos rather than discursive clarity, and the impression of something violent being imminent rather than certain. The sheer and purely verbal force of the suggested nuclear failure in the dramatic space – a phenomenological vacuum – is suggestive of the collapse of communication in contemporary knowledge culture and, more disturbingly, of the very limits of knowledge.

For almost two hours textual avalanches inundate the audience, provoke and accuse it, up to the final 'scene' when a single voice speaks the epilogue: defeated, hysterical, crushed by utter failure – a voice truly speaking from the perspective of Nagel's 'nowhere',[56] which in theatre amounts to the obliteration of dramatic space. Hers are the last words of humankind (in the Salzburg performance the epilogue was spoken by an actress) – both of the guilty ones and the victims, who have become indistinguishable and who, in white masks and protective gear, form the amorphous chorus of the 'undead'. Overlapping registers of technology and bureaucracy, of family and music create what has been referred to as Jelinek's *Sprachflächen* ('language spaces'), ultimately voicing what is beyond saying, beyond seeing and beyond hearing – all that is not, and is the very opposite of, knowledge. As the voices constantly address their own failure to hear and to be heard, they pinpoint the individual's paradoxical solipsism in modern communication societies and the failure of language to communicate knowledge, because knowledge in terms of a shared understanding itself proves flawed, and human communities founded upon it appear bound to go down.

Denying its voices distinct bodies to circumscribe their identity, a distinct text to speak and a distinct physical space to act, Jelinek's *Kein Licht* fully subverts

---

56 See Thomas Nagel, *The View from Nowhere* (Oxford: OUP, 1986).

the features of science plays posited in current theories of science plays and discussed at the outset of this paper: scientific content, knowledge transfer and science teaching. Yet, deriving its momentum from technologies whose meaning is
metaphorically transformed into an apocalyptic void, Jelinek's aesthetic illustrates
how dramatic properties reconfigure science. The radicality of *Kein Licht* lies in
its self-begetting critique of scientific cognition.

4. Conclusion

Both Churchill and Jelinek's literary answer to a functional, science-oriented
society is not – as Djerassi claims for science-in-theatre – a functional theatre
opening its stage to the teaching of science, but the literariness and theatricality
of the theatre, its affective strength and appeal, and its existential authenticity, not
in the sense of a mimetic representation of science, but in the sense of creating
a metaphorical text- or stage-world that provokes, shocks, entertains, touches,
concerns or disturbs its audiences, in short: a theatre that draws on the reality of
experience and confronts us with ourselves and our environment – in a way no
form of science communication does.

Science plays cannot represent scientific practices in the sense of Djerassi's
criteria of accuracy and realistic representation, simply because man is never fully
in control of technologies and their implications, as *Kein Licht* shows, and because
every attempt at 'realistic representation' only offers a furtive glimpse of a tiny
segment of rapidly widening horizons of knowledge. What science plays *can* do,
however, is express real needs, anxieties and shortcomings of modern life, given
the close interconnection between everyday life and science, especially the life
sciences and information technologies. In this respect, science plays appear less
as a sub-genre aiming to describe (Zehelein's category of 'what') or even prescribe
(Djerassi's category of 'how') scientific themes and intentions, as they renegotiate
genuinely theatrical and aesthetic strategies (dramatic language, figures and space)
in particular socio-historical, existential and ethical contexts. The intentional or
modal spectrum – from didactic, expository, popularising, propagandist to warning, ironic, humorous, biting and satirical – proves equally inadequate as a generic
criterion, given the tendency to "create ambiguity"[57] in art as distinct from science.

We therefore understand science plays neither as a didactic forum for teaching
'real' science, as Djerassi and Zehelein claim; nor as distinct from genres featuring
futurological scenarios, as Zehelein argues; nor as communicating science via

---

57 Stewart, p. 306.

performance, as Shepherd-Barr holds; but in terms of their effect on audiences and with regard to productive and receptive strategies of metaphorically encoding and decoding the epistemic into the anthropomorphic and vice versa.

Knowledge in Jelinek's play is the preserve of the dead, and only in theatre can a dead voice express itself – too late, as she suggests. Such are the closing words of the mourning voice in *Kein Licht*, for 'she is free to do what she likes' ("Eine Trauernde, sie kann machen, was sie will"):

> Dieses Stück ist hiermit beendet. Endlich ganz beendet. Denn schlimmer als etwas, das schlimmer ist als schlimm, das geht nicht. Das kann man nicht sprechen. Davon schon, vielleicht. Aber man kann es nicht sprechen. Man kann es vielleicht sagen, aber nicht sprechen.
> [This play is ended thus. At last ended completely. For there can be nothing worse than what is worse than bad. One cannot speak this. One may speak about it. But one cannot speak it. One can say it, but one cannot speak it. [our translation]]

To apply Jelinek's distinction to science plays, which are less indebted to scientific discourse than to theatre's affectivity, experiential appeal and aesthetic ambiguation: science 'says', whereas the theatre 'speaks'.

Dorothea Flothow

Evil Encountered? – Childhood, Violence and Innocence in British Crime Fiction

1. Introduction

When we think of the classic crime novel, as it was written in the 'Golden Age of Crime Fiction' by authors such as Agatha Christie and Dorothy Sayers, child characters hardly spring to mind. Sayers's and Christie's novels are peopled mainly by adults; children, if they are present at all, are usually merely assigned minor roles: in Christie's *The Secret of Chimney's* (1925), which hinges on the death of a well-known politician and on the theft of famous crown jewels, the two young children are only of importance because their governess turns out to be the culprit. She is the former queen of a small (fictitious) Balkan state and disguises as a governess to find the jewels.[1] To this end, she murders those who stand in her way. When her true identity is revealed, everybody is surprised, yet no one seems to consider that her two protégées might have been in considerable danger under her care. In *The Hollow* (1946), Hercule Poirot solves the murder of Dr. John Christow. Christow has been killed by his devoted yet jealous wife Gerda, who finally dies of poison herself.[2] The couple's two children, however, are carefully shielded from the crime: they are not present at the murder, which takes place at an all-adult weekend party; and at the end of the novel, Poirot decides to conceal the murderer's identity and to protect not least the orphaned children. As these examples illustrate, in Christie's novels, children are usually unconnected with the crimes, both as victims and suspects.

In contrast to the 'Golden Age Whodunit', for the last 30 years child characters have featured more frequently and far more prominently in British crime fiction. In the narratives of Barbara Vine (alias Ruth Rendell), Kate Atkinson, Val McDermid and Reginald Hill children take on a variety of different roles: they are present as victims, witnesses or the crimes' causes; moreover, they feature more actively – as conspirators and criminals. Children are thus much more central to the crimes than they were in earlier novels. The image of childhood emerging from these recent novels is therefore very different from that of the Golden Age Whodunit.

---

1   See Agatha Christie, *The Secret of Chimney's* (London: Bodley Head, 1925).
2   Agatha Christie, *The Hollow* (New York: Berkley Books, 1984 [1946]).

Against the background of childhood studies, which see childhood as a construct that is historically and culturally variable and shaped through discourse,[3] this paper proposes to analyse the images of childhood[4] emerging in recent British crime fiction and to place these within the developments of the genre and within changes in British culture. We will argue that the constructs of childhood as emerging from recent crime fiction are part of a wider debate about the status of childhood in modern British society. Here, the prevailing attitude towards children can perhaps best be described as one of unease, and it is particularly the frequent presence of crime in discourses about children that has called into question traditional concepts of childhood 'naturalness' and 'innocence'. By extension, the threat that crime seems to pose to childhood is also seen as a threat to British society as a whole.

As crime is their chief business, crime novels have joined the debate surrounding children and crime and have contributed to construct childhood as precarious and problematic. And yet, as this paper hopes to show, in many cases the novels contain intriguing twists that not only serve to baffle the reader and to keep him or her guessing as to the crime's solution but that also reveal the prejudices and preconceptions involved in recent debates about childhood. Crime fiction is thus frequently a more thoughtful place of debate of contemporary issues than its status as a popular genre would lead one to assume.

2. Childhood and crime fiction

The comparative absence of child characters from Golden Age crime fiction is mainly due to the development of the genre: the dominant form after Word War

---

3   As Allison James and Chris Jenks point out: "The biological facts of infancy are but the raw material upon which cultures work to fashion a particular version of 'being a child'." ("Perceptions of Childhood Criminality", *The British Journal of Sociology* 47:2 (June 1996), pp. 315-31, p. 317). Childhood studies were initiated by Philippe Ariès's *Centuries of Childhood* (Harmondsworth: Penguin, 1986 [1960]); for more recent studies see Chris Jenks, *Childhood* (London: Routledge, 1996); Allison James and Alan Prout, ed., *Constructing and Reconstructing Childhood: Contemporary Issues in the Sociological Study of Childhood* (London: Palmer, 1997); Colin Heywood, *A History of Childhood: Children and Childhood in the West from Medieval to Modern Times* (Cambridge: Polity, 2003); Harry Hendrick, *Children, Childhood and English Society, 1880-1990* (Cambridge: CUP, 1997).

4   This paper will concentrate on images of 'children' up to the age of about twelve. However, many of the issues apply also to teenagers, as 'children' often refers more broadly to those under age.

One was the "clue-puzzle".[5] In this formulaic genre, a murder with multiple suspects is solved by a detective-figure. The crime is presented as premeditated and rational; its chief victim is an unpleasant character. To the reader, the victim's death therefore comes as no surprise and provokes little compassion: "The emotionless treatment of death is a constant in Christie [...]."[6] The multiple suspects are all given good motives for wishing the victim dead. On the whole, the novels concentrate on a selective cast of victims, suspects and detectives. The clue-puzzle thus presents a restricted view of crime and its social context, and it concentrates on the crime's solution as rational pleasure. The novels are usually set within the realms of the British upper or upper-middle classes, and many of its authors also came from this section of society. Unsurprisingly, the clue-puzzle encompasses the conservative attitudes and values of this class,[7] such as a disdain for the lower classes or the belief in British supremacy. Though the established order is briefly threatened by the crime, it is restored and confirmed through its solution[8] – the clue-puzzle tends not to question the dominant discourses, it enhances them. Consequently, as a genre, it has often been called escapist in its depiction of reality.[9]

From what has been said so far, it seems logical that child characters are of little importance in classic crime fiction, for here, too, the genre reflected the idealised assumptions of the British establishment: especially for the better-off, childhood had become increasingly removed from the every-day adult world. As children were confined to schools for increasingly longer periods, childhood was created as a separate and protected realm.[10] Children became economically worthless, as they were gradually shut out from the work process. Instead, the child became invested with emotional value. This ideal childhood (as it first emerged in the upper classes) was universalised – it held that children "should all display innocence,

---

5   See Stephen Knight, *Crime Fiction, 1800-2000* (London: Macmillan, 2004), Ch. 4.

6   Stephen Knight, *Form and Ideology in Crime Fiction* (Bloomington: Indiana UP, 1980), p. 115.

7   See ibid., p. 107; Martin Priestman, *Crime Fiction: From Poe to the Present* (Plymouth: Northcote House, 1998), p. 21.

8   See Julian Symons, *Bloody Murder: From the Detective Story to the Crime Novel: A History* (London: Faber & Faber, 1972), p. 18.

9   See Lee Horsley, "From Sherlock Holmes to the Present", in Charles J. Rzepka and Lee Horsley, ed., *A Companion to Crime Fiction* (Malden, MA: Wiley-Blackwell, 2010), pp. 28-42.

10 On the creation of modern childhood, see Hendrick, *Children*; Ann Higonnet, *Pictures of Innocence: The History and Crisis of Ideal Childhood* (London: Thames & Hudson, 1998); and Heywood, *History*.

vulnerability, ignorance and asexuality."[11] Of course reality has always been different from this "traditional" and "romantic"[12] notion of childhood, especially for the lower classes, and there have always been crimes involving children – both as victims and culprits.[13] Yet the ruling classes' ideal child as dominant in these escapist crime novels largely excludes children from the more brutal aspects of reality. Instead, it establishes childhood as confined to nurseries and schools and protected from bad news and violence. As Chris Jenks points out:

> The view of children as being in possession of a special and distinctive nature, which is both innocent and vulnerably dependent, is what makes any link between children and violent crime particularly problematic, for the imagery of childhood and that of violent criminality are iconographically irreconcilable.[14]

It would be difficult for a child to fit the requirements of a murderer as someone rational and cunning; equally, a child victim would presumably make it difficult to describe the detecting process as a rational game. The 'traditional', 'romantic' image of childhood thus largely excluded children from the Golden Age Whodunit.

The seeming incompatibility of children and crime is perhaps best demonstrated in what Christie considered her best novel: *Crooked House* (1949). Here, she was able to play on her readers' idealised image of childhood by using a child as the 'least-likely suspect', a popular device in her novels. Eleven-year-old Josephine kills her Nanny and her grandfather because he "wouldn't let [her] do bally dancing."[15] Though she fits the picture of the murderer perfectly, the detective-narrator does not consider her a suspect because she seems outside the realm of potential criminality:

> I was to wonder afterwards that I could have been so blind. The truth had stuck out so clearly all along. Josephine and only Josephine fitted in with all the necessary qualifications. Her vanity, her persistent self-importance, her delight in talking, her reiteration on how clever *she* was, and how stupid the police were.
> I had never considered her because she was a child. (p. 183)

---

11 Hendrick, *Children*, p. 12. Of course, the ideal of childhood innocence owes much to the writings of Jean-Jacques Rousseau; see in particular James/Jenks, "Perceptions", pp. 319-22.

12 See Shirley R. Steinberg and Joe L. Kincheloe, ed., *Kinder-Culture: The Corporate Construction of Childhood* (Boulder: Westview, 1998), and Higonnet, *Pictures*, respectively.

13 In the Victorian era, crimes of working-class children were a much-debated issue. See Hendrick, *Children*, pp. 42-3.

14 Jenks, *Childhood*, p. 125.

15 Agatha Christie, *Crooked House* (London: Fontana/Collins, 1990 [1949]), p. 185.

While all the adults are suspects, Josephine, the child, succeeds in baffling the detective to the end.[16]

In the period after the Second World War, the limitations of the clue-puzzle form have become increasingly obvious. Thus, the formula lost its dominance, and it has been largely abandoned by British crime writers today. Crime fiction has become diverse, tackling many different forms of crime and developing into a variety of subgenres. Moreover, it has also adapted to the changes of the outside world. Today, crime novels deal with racism, drugs, organised crime and sexual violence and reflect common fears of youthful delinquents and dysfunctional families.[17] They are usually set in towns and ordinary homes and show social problems and domestic violence; they have turned "attention [...] towards a more 'realistic' notion of crime as something that happens every day, arising from the pressures of a common life."[18] According to John G. Cawelti, "the detective story has become a genre in which writers explore new social values and definitions and push against the traditional boundaries of human relations."[19] Thus, crime fiction may be considered a good indicator of contemporary concerns and a form of discourse by which these are discussed.

3. Recent discourses on childhood in Britain

Contemporary discussions of childhood often perceive it in a state of crisis and transition, as is evident from phrases such as "the disappearance of childhood", "the knowing child", or "children grown up too fast".[20] As children become more knowledgeable about sexuality, as they mature increasingly early, traditional, romantic notions of childhood innocence are indeed changing. Neil Postman

---

16 Though the novel thus seems to connect children and crime, childhood innocence is still protected as it is pointed out from the beginning that Josephine is not a 'normal' child. She is described as "ghoulish" (p. 69), a "goblin" (p. 68) and a "malicious gnome" (p. 96). At the end, Josephine is removed from adult justice as her aunt causes a fatal car accident.

17 See Ernest Mandel, *Ein schöner Mord: Sozialgeschichte des Kriminalromans* (Frankfurt a.M.: Athenäum, 1987) on this trend.

18 Priestman, *Crime Fiction*, p. 27.

19 John G. Cawelti, "Canonization, Modern Literature, and the Detective Story", in Jerome H. Delamater and Ruth Prigozy, ed., *Theory and Practice of Classic Detective Fiction* (Contributions to the Study of Popular Culture 62, Westport, CT: Greenwood P, 1997), pp. 5-15, p. 8.

20 See Neil Postman, *The Disappearance of Childhood* (London: Comet, 1982); Higonnet, *Pictures*; and Steinberg/Kincheloe, *Kinder-Culture*, respectively.

blames the media for 'adultifying'[21] and destroying childhood in order to create a uniform category of consumers: "Everywhere one looks, it can be seen that the behaviour, language, attitudes, and desires – even the physical appearance – of adults and children are becoming increasingly indistinguishable."[22] Other writers have been equally critical of the changes affecting traditional childhood, which they claim becomes ever shorter.[23]

On the other hand, as Chris Jenks points out, traditional notions of childhood are still treasured. For "contemporary childhood remains an essentially protectionist experience."[24] Though postmodernism has eroded even the seeming 'naturalness' of the innocent child, childhood is often seen as "dependable and permanent, in a manner to which no other person or persons can possibly aspire."[25] It seems to offer one of the last remaining certainties in a constantly changing society. Children are by necessity imagined as innocent in a world that is not. Therefore, attacks on children are perceived as crucial to the welfare of society as a whole. It is this conflict between an ideal and a seemingly radically different reality that characterises many discussions of contemporary childhood.

Crimes involving children have therefore become a recurring theme in debates on childhood. "Images of mothers drowning children, baby-sitters torturing infants, kids pushing kids out of fourteenth-floor windows […] saturate the contemporary conversation about children."[26] Of course, spectacular cases of child criminals have been of prime importance here, particularly perhaps in Great Britain.[27] Thus, Jenks considers the murder of James Bulger by two ten-year-olds central to British discourses on childhood in the 1990s. Though "[w]e must assume and acknowledge that some children have always killed other children",[28] he sees this case as symbolising the "death of 'childhood'", as it so utterly contradicted the ideal of childhood as innocent and dependent. James Bulger's murder came to be a symbol for where Britain as a society had gone wrong, a symbol of "a nation

---

21 See Postman, *Disappearance*, p. 124.
22 Ibid., p. 4.
23 See a summary in Hendrick, *Childhood*, pp. 94-6. On the other hand, some adults also seem to (try to) stay 'forever young'.
24 James/Jenks, "Perceptions", p. 318.
25 Jenks, *Childhood*, p. 107.
26 Steinberg/Kincheloe, *Kinder-Culture*, p. 3.
27 See the articles in Phil Scraton, ed., *'Childhood' in 'Crisis'?* (London: UCL P, 1997); and Bill Osgerby, *Youth in Britain Since 1945* (Oxford: Blackwell, 1998), Ch. 13.
28 Jenks, *Childhood*, p. 126.

in a state of moral decline".[29] Urged on by the media,[30] politicians repeatedly called for a tougher reaction against young offenders. John Major, then Prime Minster, asked that society should "condemn a little more and understand a little less"[31] – a feeling that was echoed by Labour MPs. In subsequent years, the reaction towards youth crime was enhanced.[32] The media now frequently depicted young offenders and their crimes – profiting from the shock impact of such stories and starting what has frequently been called a "moral panic"[33] about the development of British society.[34] Rising divorce rates, single parents, incompetent failing teachers, working mothers and a growing yob culture were important key words of subsequent debates.[35] Child criminals were essentially presented as "childhood's failures",[36] and it was suggested that they possess inherent evil, from which society needed to be saved.[37]

In recent years, debates concerning the status of British childhood have continued to stress the criminal potential of British youth – thus, the London riots of 2011 have been blamed on youth gangs, though most of the offenders were over eighteen, and only a minority of them were gang members.[38] The general feeling of unease about the nature of childhood in today's society seems to be epitomised by discussions centring on children and crime. This unease is perhaps best illustrated

---

29 Ibid., p. 119.
30 On the media reaction, see Jenks/James, "Perceptions"; and Howard Davis and Marc Bourhill, "'Crisis': The Demonization of Children and Young People", in Scraton, 'Childhood', pp. 28-57.
31 Quoted in Osgerby, Youth, p. 212.
32 See ibid., p. 213.
33 See James/Jenks, "Perceptions", p. 327.
34 As Barry Goldson ("'Childhood': An Introduction to Historical and Theoretical Analyses", in Scraton, 'Childhood', pp. 1-27, p. 5) points out, similar reactions occur periodically. Nevertheless, it is an element of these crises that they hark back to a "previous 'golden age' of childhood" (Davis/Bourhill, "'Crisis'", p. 28).
35 Thus, as Goldson ("'Childhood'") points out, these debates also contain a strong element of social control on the basis of class, gender, ethnicity and age.
36 See Jenks, Childhood, p. 122.
37 The concept of the 'evil child' is not new, but harks back to early-modern concepts of the child. See Heywood, History, pp. 22-3.
38 Mark Easton, Britain, etc.: The Way We Live and How We Got There (London: Simon & Schuster, 2012), p. 273.

by the fact that England and Wales have the lowest age of crime responsibility in Europe – with children as young as ten being tried in adult courts.[39]

While discussions on youth crime are of course to be found in other countries as well, it has been remarked that the British have a particularly troubled relationship with their young. This was for instance pointed out by *Time Magazine*, which in April 2008 ran the headline "Unhappy, Unloved, and Out of Control: An Epidemic of Violence, Crime and Drunkenness Has Made Britain Scared of Its Young" on its front page.[40] Similarly, a sensational editorial in the same magazine made much of the British "propensity to recoil in horror from their children"[41] – as a result of the problem of youth crime. Yet the article also points to other issues which affect the situation of British youth negatively: thus, the author refers to the findings of a 2007 UNICEF study, which discovered that in Britain there exists a considerable gap between parents and their children, who spend far less time together than in other European countries. Because of this "many British adults seem to view children as an entirely separate species".[42] Amongst the other issues that affect the situation and the perception of youth in the United Kingdom are the high rate of teenage pregnancies, binge-drinking and the significant inequality between state and independent schools. As this last issue shows, the British class system is thus an important factor in the problems affecting British children.[43] In recent years, debates on British childhood have continued along similar lines.[44]

4. Childhood in recent crime novels

Due to their natural interest in crime, crime novels take up and discuss the issues described. Thus, amongst the much more extensive casts of many contemporary crime novels, children feature frequently. Unlike earlier novels, these modern narratives rarely present ordinary, happy and carefree children – childhood in contemporary crime fiction is usually troubled. Children feature as victims,

---

39 See Barry Goldson, "Children in Trouble: State Responses to Juvenile Crime", in Scraton, *'Childhood'*, pp. 124-45.

40 See *Time Magazine* (7 Apr. 2008), <http://www.time.com/time/covers/europe/0,16641, 20080407,00.html> (access 27 Mar. 2013).

41 Catherine Mayer, "Britain's Mean Streets", *Time Magazine* (26 Mar. 2008), <http://www. time.com/time/magazine/article/0,9171,1725547,00.html> (access 27 Mar. 2013).

42 See ibid.

43 Class prejudice and the assumption that most child criminals are from the lower classes play an important role in discussions on children and criminality; see the articles in Scraton, *'Childhood'*.

44 See Easton, *Britain*.

witnesses, conspirators and culprits – and childhood is shown to be threatened and threatening at the same time.

4.1. Child victims and child innocence

Unlike the novels of the Golden Age, then, which normally show adult victims who deserve their death, contemporary texts frequently depict children as the victims of capital crimes, including murder. Reginald Hill's *Under World* (1989) has as its back-story the killing of a little girl, a crime which triggers off much violence and further deaths; in Kate Atkinson's *When Will There Be Good News* (2008), a little girl and her brother are unexpectedly butchered by a passing stranger.[45] From the way the affected adults react, it becomes clear that child murder is considered the worst possible crime. Thus, a policeman in Kate Atkinson's *Started Early, Took My Dog* (2010) exclaims: "'Yea. They're [dead kiddies] the worst.' Arkwright agreed. Dead children were trumps. Every time."[46] The novels thus also use the victims' youth to stress the evil nature of criminals and to enhance the interest of the readers by presenting them with particularly shocking crimes.

The emotional impact of having a child victim becomes perhaps most obvious in Reginald Hill's *On Beulah Height* (1997), a novel in the Dalziel and Pascoe series. Here, a little girl disappears on a morning walk from a village community which had lost three other girls under similar circumstances fifteen years before. The novel repeatedly stresses how even for the police, cases involving children are a particular "nightmare".[47] Even Andi Dalziel, a detective infamous for his bull-like appearance and insensitivity, appears uncharacteristically affected by the crime:

> … he looked absolutely drained, which was as shocking as visiting Loch Lomond and finding it empty. He talked about […] the missing child, talked about the Dendale children, in an uncharacteristically disconnected way, till it was difficult to separate one from the other. What was clear was that he seemed to feel responsible in some way for all of them, and the pain of their parents weighed so heavily that even those broad shoulders were close to bending. (p. 273)

Dalziel's feelings are mirrored by Chief Inspector Pascoe, whose daughter contracts meningitis and nearly dies. Fearing for her life, Pascoe can feel the parents' pain; and by letting the reader into Pascoe's feelings (a character of course well known to the readers of the Dalziel and Pascoe series), *On Beulah Height* is able

---

45 Reginald Hill, *Under World* (London: HarperCollins, 2003 [1989]); Kate Atkinson, *When Will There Be Good News? A Novel* (New York: Little, Brown, 2008).

46 Atkinson, *Started Early, Took My Dog* (London: Doubleday, 2010), p. 20.

47 Hill, *On Beulah Height* (London: HarperCollins, 1997), p. 52.

to highlight the special situation of a parent (almost) losing a child (see p. 329). While child death is thus frequent in contemporary crime fiction, it is still portrayed as an extraordinary, abnormal kind of crime. Moreover, it is always a highly emotional crime even to the police, who had, after all, no previous relationship with the child as a person. This reaction confirms the special, if no longer safe nature of childhood which the policemen and -women would still like to believe in. Childhood, then, is shown as an ideal that needs to be protected from crime and violence but is increasingly threatened by them.

Yet Hill's *On Beulah Height* also shows some of the problems in the assumed relationship between children and crime. For it transpires at the end of the novel, that Betsy, who was a close friend of the three little girls that disappeared in the past, is not quite the innocent, ignorant victim that she pretended to be. For not only did she know all along who the killer of her friends was (i.e. her own father); the "'only one to get away'" (p. 283) from the killer (as she was called by the police and the press) was also never in any danger herself and merely fabricated a story of being attacked – thus implicating an innocent young man, who was then left to drown by the father of one of the missing girls. Though it is clear that Betsy was too young to have been fully aware of, and responsible for, her actions (and thus will not be prosecuted), and though she herself suffered serious psychological damage from the past crimes,[48] she herself has also benefited considerably from them, as she was adopted by a rich family who had lost their daughter. Unlike her biological parents they were able to further her talent as a singer: "'Except, of course, if what happened hadn't have happened, I'd likely never have had the chance to use it. Singing down the pub. Karaoke. That would likely have been the limit'" (p. 367). By keeping silent for fifteen years, she also prolonged her adopted parents' suffering and led to further deaths,[49] as Pascoe tells her, accusingly: "'Think of the pain your silence has caused. Ok, a mixed-up child can't be blamed for keeping quiet, but you did more than keep quiet, didn't you? Think of the consequences. Think of that poor man drowning in a cellar. Think of little Lorraine'" (p. 435). In a twist of appearances versus reality that is typical of crime fiction, good and evil, innocence and guilt are therefore not as clear-cut as they

---

48 As a teenager, she suffered from severe anorexia and needed psychological help (see p. 283).

49 As Betsy did not tell the truth, her adopted father killed an innocent boy, whom he considered the murderer.

initially seem,[50] and the adult assumption that an innocent child would tell the truth is severely called into question.

Contemporary crime novels such as Ian Rankin's *Black Book* (1993), *The Complaints* (2010), and *Dead Souls* (1999), as well as Kate Atkinson's *Case Studies* (2004) frequently feature child abuse as a crime which, in the last decades, has come to epitomise the precarious nature of contemporary childhood.[51] While many studies point out that abuse is not a new phenomenon and it is just the awareness of this issue which has increased,[52] there have been attempts to explain its perceived growth as the result of increasingly fragmented families.[53] What makes the issue of abuse perhaps most frightening is the fact that abuse usually takes place within the family, which is really the place where it is felt that childhood should be at its safest.

More than any other crime, child abuse is therefore used in the novels to stress the evil character of the adult criminals involved. This is shown by the police reaction, which also mirrors the readership's disgust at this crime. This is obvious in Val McDermid's *A Place of Execution* (1999), which starts with the disappearance of thirteen-year-old Alison from a small village. For Inspector Bennett, the ensuing search is an emotional task and becomes even more so when he hears that he, too, is to be a father soon:

> A child. His child. All he had to do now was to figure out how to manage what had been beyond every parent since Adam and Eve: how to keep it safe. Up to that point Alison Carter had been an important case to Detective Inspector George Bennett. Now it had symbolic importance. Now it was a crusade.[54]

Bennett is convinced that Alison has been killed rather than abducted and the evidence seems to bear this out. Moreover, the police discover that Alison had

---

50 This is strengthened by that fact that the adult Betsy is actually a rather unprepossessing, unfeeling character, who states: "'Kids die, all the time'" (p. 258). This probably also influences the readers' attitude towards her past suffering.

51 Ian Rankin, *Black Book* (London: Orion, 1993); *The Complaints* (London: Orion, 2010); *Dead Souls* (London: Orion, 1999); Atkinson, *Case Studies* (London: Black Swan, 2004).

52 See Jenks, *Childhood*, p. 87. See also Jenny Kitzinger, "Who Are You Kidding? Children, Power, and the Struggle Against Sexual Abuse", in James/Prout, *Constructing and Reconstructing Childhood*, pp. 165-89.

53 Thus, this discussion also contains a criticism of today's more mobile world. As such, these explanations have also come under criticism. For details see Jenks, *Childhood*, Ch. 4.

54 Val McDermid, *A Place of Execution* (New York: St Martin's, 1999), p. 90.

been sexually abused by her stepfather, Philip Hawkin. The attitude taken to this crime becomes clear in a conversation between Bennett and a colleague:

> "If I knew [...] that some pervert had molested a kid belonging to a friend of mine, I couldn't let him walk away. I'd have to find a way of making him pay. Either through the law or ..."
> "I thought you didn't believe in the dark alleyways of justice?" [...]
> "It's different with kids, though, isn't it?" (p. 258)

As in other novels,[55] even the police are not averse to using force where child abuse is concerned. Unsurprisingly, Philip Hawkin is found guilty of murder and is executed – though no body had ever been found.

Yet thirty-five years later, it transpires that the reality hidden from the police was very different, for in fact, Alison had never been murdered. Her disappearance and death had been fabricated by the village community, who had discovered that Hawkin had been abusing the children from the village. The parents wanted to get Hawkin punished and to spare the children the ordeal of a public trial. The villagers had thus deliberately played with the policemen's feelings and preconceptions concerning childhood innocence by fabricating Alison's murder. And yet, the prevailing feeling at the end of the novel is that Hawkin deserved his punishment for destroying childhood innocence. Thus, all those involved in the punishment of Hawkin – an act, which, after all, led to his execution – in the end go free with full police consent. In McDermid's novel, then, the violation of childhood innocence is a crime to be punished at all costs.

While *A Place of Execution* thus presents a fairly conventional view of childhood innocence and child abuse, other novels use the genre of crime fiction to question dominant preconceptions: public discourses on child abuse tend to be saturated by class prejudice. For while the evidence seems to suggest that child abuse is more common in lower-income families, where the parents are less educated, this is by no means exclusively so.[56] In fact, child abuse is far more complex, a fact that is reflected in a number of crime novels. While Ruth Rendell's *Harm Done* (1999) starts conventionally in a council estate which erupts in violence as a former inhabitant, a well-known paedophile, is released from prison,[57] the novel

---

55 See similar remarks in Ian Rankin's *Knot and Crosses* (London: Orion House, 1998 [1987]).

56 See the statistics in Janet Curry and Erdal Tekin, "Understanding the Cycle: Childhood Maltreatment and Future Crime", *Journal of Human Resources* 47:2 (Spring 2012), pp. 509-49.

57 The parents in the estate set up a movement in an attempt to rid the paedophile's neighbourhood. This soon becomes very violent indeed.

soon begins to thwart expectations – not by downplaying the issue,[58] but by laying bare the prejudices involved.

Thus, the novel questions, for instance, the bleak view of children and single mothers living on council estates so common in the media by pointing out:

> In one class in Kingsmarkham St Peter's Primary School it was tactless to ask after some-one's father because most of the children were unsure about who their fathers were. Raised on crisps and chips and chocolate and take-away, they were nevertheless the healthiest generation of children the country had ever known. If one of them had been smacked he or she would have taken the perpetrator to the European Court of Human Rights.[59]

And indeed, at first, the novel seems to confirm the worst prejudices: the police fear abuse of the children from the estate; a little girl is made a culprit of theft, and the parents are violent. Yet in the end, nothing happens to the children from the estate[60] – and indeed, their parents' attention soon turns away from their children towards their own business. The way this is presented in the novel is almost comical, for the parents are so preoccupied with organising a society to protest against the paedophile and to make sure that their actions appear in the media that they completely forget about their children – who are left unsupervised in spite of the danger and who are only discovered again – unharmed – several hours later:

> Those children [...] were not discovered for some hours. By the time Debbie and Colin and Lizzie got home, they had left, having consumed everything edible in the house, helped themselves to the 500 duty-free cigarettes Colin had brought back from a day trip to France and gone down to Kingsbrook weir for a swim. (p. 107)

Though the novel repeatedly stresses the danger the paedophile represents, the parents' behaviour calls into question adult reactions, especially those edged on by the desire for media fame.

The novel finally turns to the much more sinister case of a millionaire husband abusing his wife. His violent behaviour has severe implications for his children – his two boys are seriously disturbed and on the brink of becoming violent, and the little girl is so frightened that she refuses to talk. His desperate wife then stages the little girl's kidnapping in order to protect her from her father. Because this is a

---

58 Indeed, the horrific nature of this crime is repeatedly emphasised as it is presented through the feelings of Chief Inspector Wexford, a character known to readers of the series as sympathetic and empathetic.

59 Ruth Rendell, *Harm Done* (London: Quality Paperbacks Direct, 1999), p. 2.

60 As indeed, the novel announces on page 1: "Not one of them was physically injured, not one of them suffered bodily pain or was even made to cry beyond the common lot of people of their age."

well-off family, no one suspects this violence even though the novel abounds with obvious hints, which Wexford and his colleagues, however, miss – something they clearly would not have done, had the people involved lived on a council estate. Chief Inspector Wexford's wife voices the incredulity that all involved probably feel:

> "What amazes me", said Dora Wexford, "is that these are middle-class people – well upper-middle-class if you go in for all these gradations. They're well-off, he must be earning a couple of hundred thousand a year. [...] If they got divorced, she'd still get a huge allowance. [...] I don't understand it." (p. 291)

Abuse and violence, this novel shows, may happen anywhere; middle-class children and women are just as likely to be victims as people from estates.

Curiously, Rendell's *Harm Done* never lets the readers into the feelings and thoughts of the children involved – neither in those from the estate nor those from the millionaire's house. Yet much is made of their parents' fury when the paedophile moves into the neighbourhood: "'How would you feel like if a child murderer and rapist came and lived next door to your kids? Is that right? Is that fair?'" (p. 198), as well as of the police and their fear for the children. If at all, the children's feelings are only evident indirectly, through what adults think they feel: "But in the eyes of these two was something more than that, something they shared but he had seen in few others, a look of bitter bewilderment" (p. 254). This concentration of the adults' reaction towards the children's (probable) suffering is frequent in the novels discussed here.[61] While this lack might suggest that the authors want to spare their readers the unpleasant experience of encountering child suffering to such an extent (an assumption that would strengthen the ideal of the special and vulnerable nature of children), Rendell's novel suggests a different interpretation. At the very beginning, the novel asks: "Who knows what impression certain sights leave on children? And who can tell what actions those impressions will precipitate?" (p. 1). Indeed, throughout the novel, it is the police, parents and social workers who react against violence and suffering. The result of this, however, is that though children are present as victims, they are also curiously absent and only defined from the outside.[62] Childhood is thus created as a symbol, a reflection of adult fears, desires and uncertainties, rather than as a real

---

61 This observation can also be made in other novels, see Rankin, *Knot and Crosses*, pp. 141 vs. 225.

62 Kitzinger ("Kidding") has made similar observations on the discourse on child abuse in general.

presence and as an active agent in its own right, even though most of the adults are undoubtedly well-meaning towards the children.

4.2. Children as culprits

Surprisingly, though childhood criminals are very important in media discourses on contemporary childhood, they play only a small role in contemporary crime fiction.[63] The novels thus avoid the moral panic that these cases usually trigger, as, for example, in the case of Atkinson's *Case Studies* (2004), where crime is presented in such a way that the reader is bound to feel compassion for the child killer's motive. In *Case Studies*, a book which teems with lost and murdered girls of different ages, one of several sub-plots involves the disappearance of three-year-old Olivia back in the 1970s. On the surface, her family looks like an untypical one for a crime to occur in. It is a traditional family: her father is a respected Cambridge don; her mother stays at home to look after the children, and Olivia has three elder sisters.

Yet in the course of the novel, the problems in the family are increasingly revealed: the mother, who is substantially younger than the father, hates her family. The father takes no interest in his children. Olivia's sisters grow up to be seriously disturbed: thirty years later, Sylvia, who at the time of Olivia's disappearance was a twelve-year-old girl prone to fainting and religious hallucinations, has escaped her family by becoming a nun. Her sister Amalia attempts to commit suicide. Gradually, through many hints, it emerges that their father had been sexually abusing his elder daughters in his study. At the very end of the novel, in one of the unexpected revelations that are so typical of crime fiction, it is revealed that Sylvia killed Olivia as a sacrifice, in order to protect her from their father:

> Suffer the little children to come unto me. A sacrifice. Sylvia had thought that she was going to be the sacrifice, martyred because God had chosen her. But it turned out that it was Olivia who was meant to be given up to God. [...] Olivia was sacred now. [...] She couldn't be touched. She would never have to go into Daddy's study [...].[64]

Unlike the child murderers represented in the media, Sylvia is not an evil child from the estates but a seriously disturbed little girl from what looks like an ordinary home. Indeed, her guilt is never revealed by the private-eye who was asked to look for Olivia many years later, as he, too, seems to feel that she and

---

63 Though, as in Rendell's *Harm Done*, the involvement in petty crime, such as shoplifting, is frequent. See Atkinson's *One Good Turn* (New York: Little, Brown, 2006), where the inspector's teenage son is involved in this as a past-time.

64 Atkinson, *Case Studies*, p. 407.

her family have suffered enough. Sylvia is thus not prosecuted (though it transpires in a later novel that she commits suicide). Though the novel questions
the ideal that children are merely innocent sufferers, it does so unsensationally
and thoughtfully.

Considering the conventions of crime fiction, the novel's balanced way of explaining Sylvia's deed is perhaps not surprising, for, after all, presenting mysteries
and their surprising solutions, offering explanations and motives for a criminal's
deeds, presenting the dark secrets of those involved are standard themes of crime
novels.[65] As a result of this, however, *Case Studies* offers important insights into
the preconditions for childhood criminals rather than the blunt condemnation
so common in more sensationalist discourses on child criminals.

4.3. Wanting a child

In a number of crime novels, children also feature as the causes of crimes as adults
desperately want a child. In Rendell's *End in Tears* (2006), two dishonest teenagers
earn money by pretending to act as surrogate mothers for couples incapable of
conceiving children. In *The Dark-Adapted Eye* (1986), a Barbara Vine novel, two
sisters, Vera and Eden, fight for a little boy, and Vera finally kills Eden.[66] Children,
here, are literally perceived as something to kill for and to die for.

With these stories, crime novels again enter a debate of great topicality: as con-
traceptives have turned having children into a matter of choice, children also become a rare good. As reproductive methods such as IVF (In Vitro Fertilization)
have become widely available, children are theoretically achievable for everyone.
And yet, most discourses surrounding children and reproductive techniques are
characterised by feelings of unease: "Making possible the making of children that
otherwise could not be born through the use of medical intervention and technologies has alternatively been seen as a Frankensteinian corruption of science, an
appropriation of the role of god [...]."[67] Apart from ethical questions involved as to
whether the prospective parents should be able to determine the generic make-up
of their child, however, Karén Lesnik-Oberstein has pointed out that discourses

---

65 See Peter Hühn, "The Politics of Secrecy and Publicity: The Functions of Hidden
     Stories in Some Recent British Mystery Fiction", in Delamater/Prigozy, *Classic Detective
     Fiction*, pp. 39-50.
66 Rendell, *End in Tears* (London: Arrow, 2006); Barbara Vine [alias Ruth Rendell], *The
     Dark-Adapted Eye* (Harmondsworth: Penguin, 1986).
67 Karén Lesnik-Oberstein, *On Having an Own Child: Reproductive Technologies and the
     Cultural Construction of Childhood* (London: Karnac, 2008), p. xi.

on reproductive techniques and genetic engineering are characterised by another issue, as far as childhood is concerned. For in these discourses, the child itself is again curiously absent. It becomes a mere symbol of its parents' desires, a commodity that can be valued in cash. "When the child is involved in considerations around reproduction, it is largely in relation to two issues: disability or the search for the 'perfect' child (or 'designer baby'), and, closely related to this, ideas of the child as 'commodity.'"[68] Thus, the child becomes a mere article, something to be desired and acquired.

This problem is also discussed in Vine's *The Blood Doctor* (2002), which establishes a contrast between Martin Nanther and his great-grandfather Henry, an eminent Victorian physician. In the course of the novel, which shows Martin reconstructing the story of his great-grandfather's life, Martin's wife has a series of miscarriages. These are the result of a genetic incompatibility between the prospective parents. Owing to the progress of modern science, they are able to have two healthy 'super babies' from specially selected, fertilised eggs. Martin's enthusiasm about the babies is somewhat mixed, especially when he discovers that his great-grandfather, whose special field in medicine was haemophilia, married a woman, Edith, whom he knew to be a carrier of the defective gene that causes this illness. He did this so that he could experiment on those of his sons who inherited the illness. Indeed, Henry's 'experiments' were 'successful' as his son George was a 'bleeder' and died a slow and painful death. The contrast between the two men's designs is evident, yet Martin seems to feel that, in both cases, the children are somehow turned into mere objects of their parents' designs:

> I feel the twins move, what was at first the merest tiny flutter increasing now to kicks and thrusts. [...] A hundred years later, Edith's embryos would have been removed and the hemophilia-free ones selected and George would never have been born.
> It can't have been anything like this that Henry hoped to attain by his study of his son's disease. Designer babies would have been beyond his imagination. Did he intend experimenting with the child? Trying out various methods of stopping the bleeding?[69]

Though Martin and his wife have no evil designs on their children (unlike his great-grandfather), the parallel shows the problematic nature of parental desire. In *The Blood Doctor*, then, childhood is no longer an unproblematic natural gift.

---

68 Ibid., p. 89.
69 Vine, *The Blood Doctor: A Novel* (New York: Vintage, 2002), p. 89.

The problematic nature of adult desires is also discussed in Atkinson's *Started Early, Took My Dog* (2010), in which the retired, lonely Detective Superintendent Tracy Waterhouse solves her problems by buying a child off a notorious prostitute.

> Something gave inside Tracy. A small floodgate letting out a race of despair and frustration as she contemplated the blank but already soiled canvas of the kid's future. Tracy didn't know how it happened. One moment she was standing at a bus stop on Woodhouse Lane, contemplating the human wreckage that was Kelly Cross, the next she was saying to her, "How Much?" (p. 39)

Tracy, however, is of course aware that she breaks the law in doing so; indeed, she is on the run with the little girl for the rest of the novel. Though Tracy constantly tries to soothe her own bad conscience – especially by imagining the kind of life the girl would have had without her (see pp. 92, 96, etc.), the novel questions this repeatedly. Firstly, because it is not clear whether the prostitute was really the girl's mother; secondly, comically, because the novel's detective, Jackson Brodie, also acquires a new friend, a dog, who had also been maltreated by the previous owner. Like Tracy, Jackson now feels less alone, yet by paralleling the fates of the dog and the girl,[70] the novel undermines the idea that Tracy merely acted in the child's best interests. Like the dog, the child represents a companion for a lonely adult, not a person in her own right.

This feeling is strengthened by the fact that Tracy repeatedly reveals very strong prejudices about the girl's upbringing, most of which, however, are not corroborated as the girl speaks very little and reveals nothing about her past life: "she had probably been around drunks all her short life, so instead Tracy made a sober cup of Typhoo" (p. 118). Nevertheless, as the novel also shows Tracy's growing affection for the child,[71] the novel's control of sympathy contradicts this, as the reader also feels with Tracy and wants the two to be happy together. By contrasting these different interpretations, however, the novel shows the problematic issues involved in the longing for a child as well as in adults' preconceptions of a child's best interests. As Tracy's story is recounted alongside other story lines, many of them dealing with crimes involving children, in the hands of Kate Atkinson, the crime novel, with its secrets, twists and villains, becomes a particularly apt genre with which to discuss these issues.

---

70 Their feelings are mirrored and they go through similar stages in their respective relationships.
71 Thus, the reader is told for instance: "Courtney smiled. […] Tracy beamed back, a bubble-burst of mixed emotion – ecstasy and agony in equal, confusing measure inside her – rising in her chest." (p. 124).

5. Conclusion

By probing into what happens to children when they come into contact with crime, violence and conflict, British crime fiction offers a variety of images of childhood in today's society. Children feature in a number of different roles in the crimes presented in the novels, as innocent and knowing victims, as conspirators and even as killers. Perhaps surprisingly for a genre that has traditionally been pre-occupied with the re-establishment of order and the ethics of right and wrong,[72] and unlike many other discourses on childhood, most crime novels avoid simple explanations and condemnations and instead use the genre's inherent quest for knowledge to probe into prejudices and preconceptions surrounding this important aspect of British society.

---

72 See Hühn, "Politics".

MATTHIAS MÖSCH

Failure, Farce, and Futile Rage: Cultural Criticism and the Crisis of 'High Art' in Thomas Bernhard and William Gaddis

> Indignation is no longer possible. It is at this point, then, that the critique of culture necessarily becomes repetitive.
> – Antonio Negri[1]

> ... the rage is there at the heart of it, the sheer energy, the sheer tension.
> – William Gaddis[2]

1. Introduction

In this paper I examine the performance of contact and conflict between 'high' culture and 'mass' culture in two of the most scathing cultural critiques in modern fiction. Thomas Bernhard's *Concrete* (*Beton*, 1982) and William Gaddis' *Agapē Agape* (2002) feature two self-proclaimed defenders of art, tracing where culture allegedly took a wrong turn towards indifferent mass consumption. These satirical novelettes, however, are by no means belated endorsements of elitism to be taken at face value. Writing with ghoulish humour against the malcontents of their times, Bernhard and Gaddis depict in a tongue-in-cheek manner how the stock-taking of high cultural ideals becomes an exercise in the self-defeat of subjects in sole affinity with the "dead white guys" on the shelf (*AA*, p. 38). Putting their dramatised crises of cultures in a dialogue with contiguous cultural criticism, I show how the two authors subversively analyse the socio-political preconditions for the rift between the ivory tower and an allegedly mindless mass of entertainment consumers. Focussing in particular on Gaddis' narrative exploration of contemporary American society, I finally trace how the American author utilises the model provided by Bernhard's failing elitists in order to dismantle exclusivist cultural agendas and proposes a communal model of art production and reception beyond this rift.

---

1 Antonio Negri, "Art and Culture in the Age of Empire and the Time of the Multitudes", *SubStance* 36:1 (2007), pp. 48-55, p. 48.
2 William Gaddis, *Agapē Agape and Other Writings* (London: Atlantic Books, 2002), p. 57. Subsequently abbreviated to *AA*.

2. Failed culture, failed criticism

The story of Gaddis and Bernhard is one of an American and an Austrian author writing against the perceived folly of their countrymen. What connects them is the harsh criticism of state institutions, religion and commerce, but most of all a particular focus on the sphere of culture and its role in a society determined by administered order, false piety and greed. Despite these and a plethora of further parallels, there was no direct contact between the two, and Bernhard's influence on Gaddis only became more widely known through correspondence of the latter with critic Gregory Comnes, the American author citing a section from *The Lime Works* (*Das Kalkwerk*, 1970) and commenting on it with the words "you may see where I have found my Cicero for all future engagements".[3] This admiration becomes most tangible in Gaddis' last engagement, the posthumously published novella *Agapē Agape*, which takes Bernhard's *Concrete* as its narrative model.[4] Like the latter, it is a skilfully repellent rant delivered by an ill man who embarks on finishing his magnum opus. Gathering some last steam, Gaddis' unnamed narrator sets himself the task of finally organising his notes on what he intends to be an authoritative piece of criticism on

> … what America was all about, what mechanization was all about, what democracy was all about and deification of democracy a hundred years ago and this technology at the service of entertaining [the] stupefied pleasure seeking trash out there. (*AA*, p. 5)

The main object of his apparently snobbish observations is the player piano – a mechanical instrument based on the same principles as Jacquard's loom, Babbage's difference engine, and the computer – an instrument he considers emblematic of the split between *ars* and *technē* in Western modernity. The juxtaposition of the words *agapē agape* throughout the text most clearly indicates this rift: *agapē* referring to a communal celebration of spiritual love appearing to be lost in a

---

3   See Gregory Comnes, "Unswerving Punctualities of Chance: The Aporetics of Dialogue in William Gaddis", repr. in http://www.williamgaddis.org/critinterpessays/comnesaporetics.shtml (accessed 10 February 2013).

4   The narrator of *Agapē Agape* also copiously alludes to *Beton* (and occasionally to *Der Untergeher*). He even quotes Bernhard only to exclaim: "He's plagiarized my work right here in front of me before I've even written it!" (*AA*, p. 10). A further irony involved in this is that another author paid plagiaristic homage to Bernhard briefly before, namely Elfriede Jelinek, in her dramatic monologue *Das Schweigen* (2000). For a brief discussion of Gaddis' use of Bernhard in *Agapē Agape*, see Joseph Tabbi, "Afterword", in William Gaddis, *Agapē Agape and Other Writings* (London: Atlantic Books, 2002), pp. 71-2.

society of dumbed-down entertainment consumers with their mouths hanging *agape* (*AA*, p. 38).

At first glance the old critic's inquiry into the case of *lyre versus loom* belongs to what Andreas Huyssen designated the "Great Divide", a "discourse which insists on the categorical distinction between high art and mass culture",[5] which is why the novella only partly relates to an American tradition of critical fiction as represented by Kurt Vonnegut's dystopian *Player Piano* (1952), Thomas Pynchon's novels, or E. L. Doctorow's *Ragtime* (1975). By presenting mass culture as an abhorrent Other, *Agapē Agape* appears even more so to be a belated addition to the Culture-and-Civilisation debate and the Frankfurt-School criticism of the culture industry.[6] In fact, Gaddis had initially intended to turn his research on the player piano into a critical cultural history, a "satirical celebration of the conquest of technology and of the place of art and the artist" that pursues the growth of "both the patterned structure of modern technology and the successful democratization of the arts in America".[7] These two trends, according to Gaddis, converged to technicism, "the application of systems designed to accomplish tangible and predetermined ends, to such intangible goals as those of the arts".[8] Not incidentally, the popularity of the player piano coincides with the first heyday of American computation: it embodies, as Gaddis wrote in a sketch of his research project, more than any other instrument, "a distillation of the goals that had surrounded its gestation in an orgy of fragmented talents seeking after the useful",[9] the aim of this search being the elimination of contingency through analysis, measurement, and prediction in every domain of life. As the narrator of *Agapē Agape* states: "whole point of it to order and organize to eliminate chance, to eliminate failure because we've always hated failure in America like some great character flaw" (*AA*, p. 11). Art as communal praxis is marginalised in such an environment of total administration and the artist either reduced to interchangeable raw material for the culture industry or tempted to withdraw to the ivory tower.

---

5   Andreas Huyssen, *After the Great Divide: Modernism, Mass Culture, Postmodernism* (Bloomington: Indiana UP, 1987), p. viii.

6   Gaddis draws from, and is in many instances contiguous with, a bulk of critical material that ranges from Matthew Arnold's *Culture and Anarchy* (1869), Freud's writings and Johan Huizinga's work, to Max Weber, Adorno and Horkheimer's work on the culture industry and Walter Benjamin's "Work of Art in the Age of Mechanical Reproduction" (1936).

7   Gaddis, "Appendix: Summary Notes on the Work in Progress" (*AA*, p. 243).

8   Ibid.

9   Gaddis, "Agapē Agape: The Secret History of the Player Piano" (*AA*, p. 113).

As much as Gaddis' project was in line with the writings of the Frankfurt School, however, it could have hardly added much to the existing body of criticism, as Joseph Tabbi notes.[10] Thus, Gaddis came to regard his endeavours as a "dim pursuit of scholarship headed for the same trash heap I'm upset about in the first place".[11] A second reason for growing concerns about the feasibility of such criticism was that he suspected naivety in the notion "that through calling attention to inequities [...] these will be promptly corrected by a grateful public", in other words, he did not invest belief in the transformative power of gestures of unmasking.[12] Gaddis laid the project aside yet frequently included parts of it in his novels, most notably in J R (1975), in which one of the characters, Jack Gibbs, is labouring on a book entitled *Agapē Agape*. In an equal measure, as Steven Moore notes, the "failure to achieve something that was perhaps not worth doing in the first place became a signature theme" in Gaddis' novels.[13] Eventually, however, he turned his criticism into an independent work of fiction and by doing so circumnavigated the 'trash heap'. As Niklas Luhmann notes in *Art as a Social System*: "Failed works of art are still works of art, if unsuccessful ones."[14] However, by fictionalising his criticism Gaddis not only saved what could not have been utilised otherwise. Measured against the background of a social system aimed at commerce, calculability, and the elimination of chance, I think, the inclusion of failure suggests a model of art independent of utility,[15] while achieving a subversive

10 Tabbi, "Afterword", p. 96.
11 Cited ibid., p. 69.
12 Gaddis, "How Does the State Imagine? The Willing Suspension of Disbelief" (*AA*, p. 223).
13 Steven Moore, "William Gaddis: The Nobility of Failure", *Critique* 51 (2010), pp. 118-20, p. 119.
14 Niklas Luhmann, *Art as a Social System*, trans. Eva M. Knot (Stanford: Stanford UP, 2000), p. 194. Writing in such spirit, Gaddis frequently utilised a principle that equally bracketed the dichotomy of success and failure, playing *aporia* the Greek "parlour game proposing questions there was no clear answer to so winning wasn't the point" (*AA*, p. 6). As he explains in a letter to Comnes: "NEW (for me) WORD: APORIA (from a Gertrude Himmelfarb review)/'difference, discontinuity, disparity, contradiction, discord, ambiguity, irony, paradox, perversity, opacity, obscurity, anarchy, chaos'/LONG LIVE!" (cited in Tabbi, "Introduction to the Other Writings", *AA*, p. 89).
15 Cf. Luhmann, *Art as a Social System*, p. 137: "What happens to art if other social domains, such as economy, politics, or science, establish themselves as functional systems? What happens when they focus more narrowly on a special problem, begin to see everything from this perspective, and eventually close themselves off with an eye toward this problem? [...] What happens to art if the functionally oriented differentiation

analysis of the processes that caused art's reification in the first place. Eventually, such inclusion is all the more fitting for a last piece by Gaddis, who had been criticised throughout his writing career (most infamously by Jonathan Franzen) for writing novels too difficult to be digested with pleasure.[16]

3. In dialogue with Bernhard

Ironically, Bernhard's work assumes a crucial role here. Not only had he described in *Concrete* the failure Gaddis experienced as a critic. Bernhard's work is also strongly concerned with the perceived corruption of culture, and his characters respond to this, just like Gaddis' narrator, with a discourse that almost exclusively oscillates between what critic William H. Gass describes as "The Kvetch, the Rant, and the Bitch".[17] While for Konrad in Bernhard's *The Lime Works*, for instance, society in general "remains inimical to all creative endeavours",[18] especially Reger in *Old Masters* (*Alte Meister*, 1985) and Rudolf in *Concrete* show contempt for the masses and mass culture. Reger, who despises institutionalised religion, tourism, and popular literature, holds that the music industry is the real mass murderer of humanity.[19] In Rudolf's case the scapegoat is entrepreneurship and an anti-intellectual state, where the minister for agriculture is also minister for culture, and the capital of which is identified as the core of farcical art, stale music, and nightmarish literature. Yet, Bernhard equally questions the function of the critic as much as that of art, and his work features a plethora of intellectuals (*Geistesmenschen*) embarking on projects they are unable to complete. Konrad in *The Lime Works* will never finish his study on hearing – for which he has worked through several hundred studies – claiming that although it is complete in his mind he

---

of other systems pushes society as a whole toward functional differentiation? Will art become the slave of other functional systems, which dominate from now on? Or does [...] the increasing automatization of functional systems challenge art to discover its own function and to focus exclusively on this function?"

16 See Rone Shavers, "The End of Agape: On the Debate around Gaddis", in Joseph Tabbi and Rone Shavers, ed., *Paper Empire: William Gaddis and the World System* (Tuscaloosa: U of Alabama P, 2007), pp. 161-81.

17 See William H. Gass, "The Kvetch, the Rant and the Bitch", in Crystal Alberts, Christopher Leise, and Birger Vanwesenbeeck, ed., *William Gaddis, 'The Last of Something': Critical Essays* (Jefferson, NC: McFarland, 2010), pp. 27-34.

18 David W. Price, "Thoughts of Destruction and Annihilation in Thomas Bernhard", *Journal of English and Germanic Philology* 102:2 (2003), pp. 188-210, p. 192.

19 Thomas Bernhard, *Old Masters* (London: Penguin, 2010), p. 223; *Alte Meister*, ed. Martin Huber and Wendelin Schmidt-Dengler (Frankfurt: Suhrkamp, 2008), p. 279.

constantly misses the point of writing it down, then asserting that he wants to transform it into a piece of art, wondering whether the piece must first fall to pieces again in order to be eventually reassembled.[20] Finally, Konrad considers the act of writing itself flawed:

> Words ruin one's thoughts, paper makes them ridiculous, and even while one is still glad to get something ruined and something ridiculous down on paper, one's memory manages to lose hold of even this ruined and ridiculous something.[21]

In the end, however, it is suggested that the only thing he lacked for the completion of his study was the fearlessness of realisation, of finishing his work. Similarly, Rudolf, the narrator of *Concrete*, is about to write a major scholarly work on Mendelssohn Bartholdy, which he has been postponing for the past ten years. His work is clearly a case of overresearch and obsessive perfectionism. Yet again, external causes are blamed for this state of affairs, in this case his sister, an entrepreneur who enjoys life to the full and is, according to Rudolf, driven by two aims: persecuting intellect and making money. His bouts of indignation, however, cannot conceal the fact that rant is hardly an agent of cultural or social change in Bernhard's novelistic universe and that his critics often cling to art because they have nothing else. As Reger holds:

> Art is the most sublime and the most revolting thing simultaneously, he said. But we must make ourselves believe that there is high art and the highest art, [...] otherwise we should despair. Even though we know that all art ends in gaucherie and ludicrousness

---

20 In the latter respect Konrad resembles Gaddis' art forger Wyatt, who struggles with such "fragile situations": "Why, all this around us is for people who can keep their balance only in the light, where they move as though nothing were fragile, nothing tempered by possibility, and all of a sudden bang! something breaks. Then you have to stop and put the pieces together again. But you never can put them back together quite the same way. You stop when you can and expose things, and leave them within reach, and others come on by themselves, and they break, and even then you may put the pieces aside just out of reach until you can bring them back and show them, put together slightly different, maybe a little more enduring, until you've broken it and picked up the pieces enough times, and you have the whole thing in all its dimensions." William Gaddis, *The Recognitions* (London: Atlantic Books, 2003), pp. 113-14. Subsequently abbreviated to *TR*.

21 Thomas Bernhard, *The Lime Works* (New York: Vintage, 2010), p. 128; *Das Kalkwerk*, ed. Renate Langer (Frankfurt: Suhrkamp, 2004), p. 126: "Die Wörter ruinieren, was man denkt, das Papier macht lächerlich, was man denkt, und während man aber noch froh ist, etwas Ruiniertes und etwas Lächerliches auf das Papier bringen zu können, verliert das Gedächtnis auch noch dieses Ruinierte und Lächerliche." Gaddis was very fond of this quotation; see Comnes, "Unswerving Punctualities of Chance".

and in the refuse of history, like everything else, we must, with *downright self-assurance*, believe in high and in the highest art …[22]

The reason for believing in art, he states, is because otherwise one perishes. Art, being a manifestation of high culture, grants us an existence as thinking and feeling beings. Rudolf in *Concrete* represents the utmost extreme of this position. His object of scrutiny and admiration has long become the sole purpose of his life. Yet, rather than celebrating the merging of lifeworlds, a participation in the composer's music and thoughts, Rudolf has, as it transpires, sacrificed, twisted and deadened Mendelssohn Bartholdy for the sake of parasitic speculation.[23] His hoarding of facts, however, merely contributes to his social isolation.[24] Rudolf's sister, a voraciously vital entrepreneur, rightly says: "[y]ou associate only with the dead […] You sit there in your house, which is nothing but a morgue, and cultivate the society of the dead", and he concedes that the only friends he has are the great minds of bygone times who left him their writings.[25]

4. *Agapē Agape* and the Great Divide

Gaddis' critic in *Agapē Agape* follows the same trajectory, attempting to grasp "what America is about" but failing, alone amongst stacks of paper. Yet, unlike Bernhard, Gaddis eventually exceeds the discursive divide between isolationist elitism and its mass cultural Other by proposing a radically open model of art production and reception.

In an Adornian fashion, Gaddis sees his version of the culture industry as a result of superstructural changes in Western civilisation. For him, the technologisation and democratisation of culture between the 1870s and the 1930s engendered two types of losses: firstly, of authentic creativity lost in the course of an imposed democratisation of culture along utilitarian principles, and, secondly,

---

22 Bernhard, *Old Masters*, p. 59; *Alte Meister*, p. 79.
23 According to Rudolf, "[t]he so-called man of the intellect constantly walks all over others, killing them and making corpses of them for his intellectual purposes." Thomas Bernhard, *Concrete* (New York: Vintage, 2010), p. 25; cf. *Beton*, ed. Martin Huber and Wendelin Schmidt-Dengler (Frankfurt: Suhrkamp, 2006), p. 25. [Verbatim original]
24 Reger, in *Old Masters*, describes this experience as follows: "A person hoards things all his life, in all fields, and in the end he stands there empty […] Suddenly you realize what emptiness is when you stand there amidst thousands and thousands of books and writings which have left you totally alone, which suddenly mean nothing to you except that terrible emptiness" (Bernhard, *Old Masters*, pp. 229-30; *Alte Meister*, p. 288).
25 Bernhard, *Concrete*, p. 17; *Beton*, p. 18.

of the possibility of deriving meaning from culture by experiencing the difference between actuality (one's self) and potentiality (what Gaddis' narrator calls
a "self who can do more", AA, p. 64). What remains is enforced homogeneity and
eventual meaninglessness, "the collapse of everything, of meaning, of language, of
values, of art, disorder and dislocation wherever you look, entropy drowning everything" (AA, p. 3). Discontent with the status quo, he then embarks on tracing
the historical roots of these processes. Knowing that machines are social before
they are technical, and rather than blaming mythically autogenetic machines for
transforming its users into a mindless herd of sorts, he examines social practices
that gave rise to the success of mechanised entertainment in the first place and
identifies the Platonic polis as their cradle. According to him, it is the principle
of pleasure and pain, devised in Plato's Nomoi and Politeia and furthered in pragmatic exegeses that culminate in Jeremy Bentham's infamous formula, "Pushpin
is as good as poetry if the quantity of pleasure given is the same" (cited in AA,
p. 5), which relocates art from its position of purposive purposelessness to that
of a social lubricant. Thus, autonomous art is pressed into the service of social
control, and the Dionysian becomes equally part and parcel of the system as a
domesticated spectacle. What remains, then, is "entertainment and technology
and every four year old with a computer" (AA, p. 4). The artist, "real artist Plato
warned us about" (ibid.), is expelled from the modern polis America,[26] while the
audience – the "ultimate collective, the herd numbed and silenced agape" (AA,
p. 38) – is provided with prefabricated and neat pleasure packages that evoke a

> ... romantic illusion of participating, playing Beethoven yourself that was being destroyed
> by the technology that had made it possible in the first place, the mechanization exploding
> everywhere and the phantom hands the, Kannst du mich mit Genuss betrügen yes that,
> If I ever say to the moment don't go! Verweile doch! Du bist so schön! No match for the
> march of science that made it possible. (AA, pp. 13-14) ·

Under the aegis of technicism, the democratisation of culture, according to Gaddis' critic, is no longer a matter of organically grown communities but of social
administration motivated by an obsession for order. This thought mirrors Herbert

---

26 Gaddis saw clear relations between increasing organisation and the devaluation of
    art: "When we note that a chief element in dealing with information programming in
    modern communications and control systems is that of entropy, the measurement of
    chaos and disorder which constantly threatens flawless functioning of the system, the
    analogy of the artist's threat to the social fabric becomes obvious, and the 'scientific'
    case for order demanding his elimination is made clear" ("Summary Notes", p. 244).
    The narrator of Agapē Agape relates this to the actual death of artists: "1890 van Gogh
    shoots himself [...], Rimbaud's gone next year, and so is Melville" (AA, p. 57).

Marcuse's argument against the democratisation of culture as a "historically premature" assimilation into the culture industry that established "equality while preserving domination".[27] As culture is subordinated to the dominant system of utilitarianism,[28] the cultural product itself becomes a commodity, which is what Paul Mann in *Theory-Death of the Avant-Garde* describes as "a dense encystation of needs, desires, fantasies; it is the matrix of all forms of social regulation, the ground of an elaborate seduction and the dominant means by which the citizen is woven into the fabric of society".[29] Such processes constitute for Gaddis' narrator a moment of loss:

> That's the heart of it, where the individual is lost, the unique is lost, where authenticity is lost not just authenticity but the whole concept of authenticity, that love for the beautiful creation before it's created. (*AA*, p. 26)

Determined to cope with the loss of such creative love and elevating experience of reception, Gaddis' narrator then enquires what kind of community art creates.[30] He does so again by citing the critics, and again he follows binary strands of opinion. One position, represented by Leo Tolstoy, foregrounds the artist's obligation *to* the people.[31] Gustave Flaubert's notion of art for "a small group of minds, ever the same, which pass on the torch" (*AA*, p. 35), forms the complementary elitist approach, which is then promptly seconded by a full score of thinkers, most notably represented by Sigmund Freud: "my golden Sigi [...] talking about his own high ethical standards. 'I subscribe to a high ideal,' he tells Reverend Oscar Pfister 'from which most of the human beings I have come across depart most lamentably. [...] In my experience most of them are trash'" (*AA*, p. 5).

This elitist perspective appears to dominate, especially since the narrator's vocal contempt for the so-called masses is complemented by the insinuation that they are merely capable of appreciating the inauthentic:

> Everything becomes an item of commerce and the market names the price. And the price becomes the criterion for everything. Absolutely Mr. Huizinga! Authenticity's wiped out when the uniqueness of every reality is overcome by the acceptance of its reproduction,

---

27 Herbert Marcuse, *One-Dimensional Man*, cited in John Storey, *Cultural Theory and Popular Culture: An Introduction* (3rd edn.) (Harlow: Prentice Hall, 2001), p. 90.

28 See Niklas Luhmann, *Art as a Social System*, p. 137.

29 Paul Mann, *Theory-Death of the Avant-Garde* (Bloomington: Indiana UP, 1991), pp. 20-1.

30 Birger Vanwesenbeeck, "*Agapē Agape*: The Last Christian Novel(s)", in Alberts, Leise, and Vanwesenbeeck, ed., *William Gaddis*, pp. 86-100, p. 94.

31 Ibid.

so art is designed for its reproducibility. Give them the choice, Mr. Benjamin, and the mass will always choose the fake. Choose the fake, Mr. Huinziga! Authenticity's wiped out, it's wiped out Mr. Benjamin. Wiped out, Mr. Huinziga. Choose the fake, Mr. Benjamin. Absolutely, Mr. Huinziga! Positively Mr. Benjamowww! Good God! (*AA*, p. 25)

The case for elitism seems closed. However, one should be careful in taking these voices at face value.[32] As indicated, *Agapē Agape* addresses the high-modernist insistence on the autonomy of the work of art, the artist's hostility to mass culture, and the radical separation from the culture of everyday life.[33] Yet, these strategies are clearly dismissed as blind alleys.

Firstly, autonomous art cannot be found in Gaddis' novelistic universe, despite his continual indictment of art in the service of commerce, and those of his characters posing as cultural missionaries are frequently exposed as the most sanctimonious and self-contradictory ones. In *The Recognitions* (1955), for instance, a satirical exploration of New York post-war culture, which in many respects it presented along the formula "Art today is spelled with an *f*" (*TR*, p. 34), the forger Wyatt Gwyon dedicates his existence to creating masterpieces in the manner of the Flemish Primitives. Repelled by the phony self-adulation of his Greenwich Village surroundings, Wyatt immerses himself into the lifeworld of painters such as Van Eyck or Van der Goes to a degree of self-denial, imitating not only their techniques but also their personal beliefs and character traits. His rhetoric of authenticity, necessary suffering, and artistic truth, however, cannot belie that his mimetic practice is part of a self-aggrandising agenda (his own paintings were commercial failures) that eventually serves commodity fetishism. As much as he considers his works some sort of a philosopher's stone capable of transforming all perceived evils of modern society, they are, to draw on Adorno and Horkheimer, "wares all the same".[34] On trying to defend this oversight, his partner in crime, the art critic Basil Valentine, accuses him as follows:

---

32 Gaddis' writings may easily evoke the impression of an idealisation of art. Yet, as Joseph Conway, for instance, notes, "readers do Gaddis disservice when they [...] make Gaddis himself into a figure martyred for the eternal sanctity of art" ("Failing Criticism: *The Recognitions*", in Alberts, Leise, and Vanwesenbeeck, ed., *William Gaddis*, pp. 69-85, p. 85). Vanwesenbeeck similarly argues in this context that Gaddis' own attitude should "not be mistaken for the late remnants of a Romantic or modernist elitism à la Shelley, T. S. Eliot, or Ezra Pound" ("Art and Community in William Gaddis' *The Recognitions*", *Mosaic* 42:3 (2009), pp.141-56, p. 144).

33 Cf. Andreas Huyssen, *After the Great Divide*, p. vii.

34 Theodor W. Adorno and Max Horkheimer, *Dialectic of Enlightenment*, trans. John Cumming (London: Verso, 1997), p. 157.

... and you think it was different then? [...] In a world where everything was done for the same reasons everything's done now? for vanity and avarice and lust? [...] Do you know what it was? What it really was? that everything was so afraid, so uncertain God saw it, that it insisted its vanity on His eyes? Fear, fear, pessimism and fear and depression everywhere, the way it is today, that's why your pictures are so cluttered with detail, this terror of emptiness, this absolute terror of space. [...] And your precious van Eyck, do you think he didn't live up to his neck in a loud vulgar court? [...] Do you think a van Eyck didn't curse having to whore away his genius [...]?[35]

This tirade, derived from Johan Huizinga's *The Waning of the Middle Ages* (1919, 1924), could equally have been uttered by Bernhard's art critic Reger in *Old Masters*, who denies that there ever have been any truly autonomous artists outside the reach of either church or state.[36]

Secondly, Gaddis complicates notions of authenticity. The narrator of *Agapē Agape* indeed employs this term several times in order to describe what is lost in this "democracy of every man his own artist where we are today" (*AA*, p. 32), apparently blaming techniques of mass production and communication for this loss.[37] However, I am reluctant to see a direct correlation between the inauthentic and mass-reproduced cultural products fully at work here.[38] The first reproducing pianos, as the critic states, were invented to "make the transient permanent, given the fleeting nature of music of great performances of great music a permanence that's the heart of authenticity, that preserved the whole concept of authenticity" (*AA*, p. 28), that is, as he states, the "love for creation" (*AA*, p. 26). This is not a question of mechanical reproduction or mass distribution per se. Even though he attributes to art, especially music, an aura, if not transformative powers, such

---

35 Gaddis, *The Recognitions*, pp. 689-90.

36 See Thomas Bernhard, *Old Masters*, pp. 46, 49; *Alte Meister*, pp. 62, 66. Gaddis, as Shavers has observed, leaves no doubt that the "myth of the artist in isolation", the Romantic vision of the one chosen by the muses, "is equally destructive as the myth of the artist as the true agent of social change" (Shavers, "The End of Agape", p. 179).

37 Christopher J. Knight, "William Gaddis' Parthian Shot: Social Criticism in the Posthumous *Agapē Agape* and *The Rush for Second Place*", *Critique* 49:2 (2008), pp. 205-20, p. 211.

38 In *Dialectic of Enlightenment*, Adorno and Horkheimer correlate the opposition between mass culture and modernist art with a distinction between inauthentic and authentic art, an observation that has been called arrogant by Luhmann (*Art as a Social System*, p. 141), for instance. Equally, Walter Benjamin's argument that the authenticity of a work of art is endangered by reproduction techniques has been discredited as too simplistic; see Theodor W. Adorno, *Aesthetic Theory* (London: Continuum, 2004), p. 72.

experience is not bound to original artistic performance.[39] What is foregrounded in such notion of authenticity is the "love for creation", the pleasure of being engulfed by the artwork, of being "the music while the music lasts" (*AA*, p. 61), as Gaddis' critic quotes T. S. Eliot. Such authenticity is not endangered by the masses' alleged inability to discriminate but lost where creation is replaced by production and the artwork reduced to an exchangeable commodity.

Eventually, Gaddis' novella leaves no doubt either that the (modernist) "strategy of exclusion" ends in isolation.[40] Basil Valentine in *The Recognitions*, a character for whom "sophistication becomes an end in itself" far away from the plebs, may count as one of the most pitiful examples of loveless isolation.[41] Equally, the narrator of *Agapē Agape*, like Bernhard's Rudolf, realises that he dwells alone "with the dead white guys" on the shelf (*AA*, p. 38) and wonders whether he has wasted his life among paper stacks. Whatever the redemptive qualities of culture may be, they do not lie in accumulating cultural capital, for the latter at best leads to what Jonathan Flatley designates as "learned helplessness".[42] As Gaddis' narrator states: "That was Youth [...] pursued by Age where we are now, looking back at what we destroyed, what we tore away from that self who could do more" (*AA*, p. 64).

For these reasons it is difficult to consider his perspective as "a look from the heights down on the mass of men who aren't worth anything in the first place" (*AA*, p. 38), difficult to assume that he advocates an exclusivist model of culture in which only Kantian 'men of taste' are able to identify what is valuable and appropriately derive sweetness and light from it. Thus, between the indefinite suspensions of double negatives – "can't say Tolstoy wasn't serious can you? That our literary language isn't suited to his common herd" (*AA*, p. 41) – lurks the suspicion that it is not technology that creates this "ultimate collective" of pleasure seekers, but the discourse of the proponents of high culture, which conjures up its deprived Other by associating the mechanical and reproducible with the culturally invaluable. This trick becomes ever more apparent when one observes that despite the narrator's aim to write a piece of "impeccable" (*AA*, p. 10) scholarship, he admittedly "can't read music and can't play anything but a comb" and uses "only second hand material" (*AA*, p. 60).

---

39 For a critical discussion of transcendence as the "historically dominant Western mode of aesthetic experience", see Jonathan Flatley, *Affective Mapping: Melancholia and the Politics of Modernism* (Cambridge, MA: Harvard UP, 2008), p. 5.

40 Huyssen, *After the Great Divide*, p. vii.

41 John Johnston, *Carnival of Repetition: Gaddis' 'The Recognitions' and Postmodern Theory* (Philadelphia: U of Pennsylvania P, 1990), p. 50.

42 Flatley, *Affective Mapping*, p. 31.

5. Conflict and recognition

Failure has come full circle, and, indeed, there could not be greater discrepancy between the object of the critic's study and his own capacities. The problem is not so much that the moribund, bleeding, and numbed narrator is physically unable to coordinate his meticulously documented research material. It is rather that his basic premise – the intangible experience of art can be "all sorted and organized" (*AA*, p. 20) – is flawed from the start. His inclination towards binary modes and his reliance on two paper stacks – one for the absolutely necessary material and one for that which can be expelled from his miniature polis – render him an ill-equipped recognition machine. And, of course, the stacks tumble into each other and with that his thoughts: he finds analogies where there are none, takes the metaphorical literally and short-circuits the incommensurable, while his compulsively expository assaults and his excessive redundancies, circumlocutions, repetitions, and revisions merely reproduce the "swamp of paradox, perversity, ambiguity, aporia" (*AA*, p. 6) he intended to keep at bay in the first place. As a consequence, he is also "unable to avoid identification with the [...] abject, material 'Other'" his imagination has created.[43] At the peak of his indecision between the two kinds of community in relation to art, elitist isolation and collective entertainment, Gaddis' narrator thus experiences a personal crisis:

> Got to stop it's got to end right here can't breathe the other can't speak can't cross the room can't breathe can't, can't go on and I'm, I am the other. I am the other. Not the two of us living side by side like the, like some Goldyadkin he invented in a bad moment no, no not those Zwei Seelen wohnen, ach! in meiner Brust one wants to leave its brother, one clings to the earth the other in derber Leibeslust no, no, no can't breathe can't walk, can't stand I am the other. (*AA*, p. 15)

This traumatic experience directly relates to the (modernist) high cultural "anxiety of contamination by its other".[44] Bernhard's Rudolf is similarly confronted by otherness, as much as by failure, yet shies away from any conflict, first by leaving for Palma de Mallorca, then medication,[45] but Gaddis' critic directly steers into confrontation with his Other. Yet, in this confrontation, this enforced identification and fusion, lies exactly what grants him a perspective on what culture could actually achieve, that is to overcome the split between the Faustian "two souls" as representatives of higher and baser cultural aspirations respectively (*AA*, p. 14).

---

43 Tabbi, "Afterword", p. 76.
44 Huyssen, *After the Great Divide*, p. vii.
45 Bernhard, *Concrete*, p. 155; *Beton*, p. 131.

The mythological overtones are not incidental, for just as Faust (at least in Goethe's version) is redeemed by love, so *agapē*, a form of love, is suggested by Gaddis as a way out of the Great Divide. Appropriating the Christian concept of selfless communal love, he translates *agapē* as "that natural merging of created life in this creation in love that transcends it, a celebration of the love that created it" (*AA*, p. 26). Art as *agapē* then is an inherently social form of culture, a form of merging. It does neither signify a study of perfection in Arnold's terms, nor a mode of elitist self-sustainment, but the "capacity for imaginative projection into the lifeworld, thought, and language of another person".[46] This engagement with multiplicity does not only enable creative agency but, as Gaddis' narrator asserts, "transfigures you yourself into the self who can do more" (*AA*, p. 64).[47] It is, as he claims, able to carry you "off into another state of being that's not your own, of feeling things you don't really feel, of understanding things you don't really understand, of being able to do things you aren't really able to do" (ibid.). Such "self", as Vanwesenbeeck argues, can be best imagined as "an enlarged subjectivity that […] engages with its artistic others".[48] Gaddis' narrator eventually acknowledges an inspirational Other, and the engagement with it points to a multitude beyond the divide between technological solipsism and the ivory tower secluded from the culture of everyday life.

6. *Agapē* as praxis: beyond the Divide

Conflict thus leads to recognition. The contact between 'high' culture and 'mass' culture in *Agapē Agape* appears to end in crisis, and, like Bernhard's characters, Gaddis' critic spells an irreversible cultural decline. Yet, this conflict is first of all presented as a self-made crisis of an elitist subject desperately trying to abject his material Other. Even more scathingly than in Bernhard's *Concrete* the elitist subject is not merely presented as indecisive, trying to retain potential greatness

---

46 Tabbi, "Afterword", p. 77.

47 The phrase is derived from Michelangelo but also resonates with Matthew Arnold's distinction between the "ordinary self" and "best self" of a person; see Matthew Arnold, *Culture and Anarchy*, ed. J. Dover Wilson (Cambridge: CUP, 1960), p. 109. Gaddis' notion of perfection is not entirely unrelated to Matthew Arnold's. While the latter argues that culture is a study of perfection with the aim of self-perfection, "which consists in becoming something rather than having something" (ibid., p. 48), Gaddis continuously makes a case in his work, especially in *The Recognitions*, for the things "worth being" rather than those "worth having"; see Elaine B. Safer, "Ironic Allusiveness and Satire in William Gaddis' *The Recognitions*", in Harold Bloom, ed., *William Gaddis* (Philadelphia: Chelsea House, 2004), pp. 71-100, pp. 71, 74.

48 Vanwesenbeeck, "*Agapē Agape*", p. 99.

and erudition at the cost of abstraction and incompletion, but as a hypocritical figure who admittedly did not care for an Arnoldian agenda of (self-)perfection in the first place. *Agapē Agape* undoubtedly ends on a nostalgic note, its narrator mourning the lost possibilities of a "[y]outh who could do anything" (*AA*, p. 64), but at the same time Gaddis' mourning critic still "can't read music" or master his plethora of notes. Thus, despite his chaotic attempts of gaining the upper hand on what modern "America was all about", one cannot fail to gain the impression that the problem addressed is not the case of Beethoven versus player piano, nor the question of art for a select group or for the masses, but that art of any kind remains a commodity and tool for social administration in a system dominated by instrumental reason and economic interests. I think through this implication *Agapē Agape* takes the same course as this thought by Adorno, expressed in a letter to Benjamin, that "[b]oth [modernist art and mass culture] bear the scars of capitalism, both contain elements of change. Both are torn halves of freedom".[49]

The position of the 'dead guys' on art for a select few and art for the masses both lead Gaddis' critic to dead ends, and it is only through an enforced contact between elitism and its material Other, the player piano, that the narrator ceases to maintain irreconcilable perspectives on the 'torn halves', thereby gaining a new perspective. Identifying with his Other, he arrives at an aesthetic that suggests an alternative to both commodification and elitist withdrawal, encapsulated in the concept of *agapē*. His notion of *agapē* is the celebration of an enlarged subjectivity, of a communal, inclusive realisation of artistic and human potential. The creation and reception of art, according to such an aesthetic, is neither a matter of individuals measuring their work against tradition nor of 'high' (modernist) practices of including only those deemed capable of appreciating what bears the stamp of distinction. It is a radically inclusive praxis that establishes a dialogue with a multiplicity of voices from each area of culture, inspiring, expanding, if not transforming the subject. The fruitfulness of such praxis could not be more manifest than in Gaddis' own mode of writing. As Tabbi notes, Gaddis' orchestration of a vast network of texts first of all needs to be understood as a communal act, as a "refusal of the novelist's own separate existence as a speaking presence within novelistic discourse".[50] In this respect, he is again very close to Bernhard,

---

49 Cited in Huyssen, *After the Great Divide*, p. 58.

50 Tabbi, "William Gaddis and the Autopoiesis of American Literature", in Tabbi and Shavers, ed., *Paper Empire*, pp. 90-117, p. 99. Vanwesenbeeck goes even further in considering the (pre-)text incorporated as an inspirational other ("*Agapē Agape*", p. 20).

who claimed not to invent stories but merely to arrange found material,[51] and, like Bernhard, he is a master of exaggeration, of rant and deliberate convolutedness. Gaddis' texts, more than Bernhard's, are chaotic, overburdened with quotations and allusions, not all of which are treated entirely seriously. Yet his radical incorporation of culture, be it the 'dead white guys', contemporaries, or popular or mass-produced 'wares',[52] as much as his refusal to have his narrator provide explicit and definitive answers to the question of what art under capitalism and administered democracy is 'all about', suggest what art as an inclusive practice and embracement of contact with what is Other can be under such circumstances – without following calls for either social utility or exclusivity.

---

51 Bernhard cited in Martin Huber and Wendelin Schmidt-Dengler's commentary on *Concrete* (*Beton*, pp. 138, 140).
52 Much of the working material of *Agapē Agape* "was cut out from popular magazines and newspapers" (Tabbi, "Afterword", p. 68).

Notes on Contributors

JULIA AVERILL is a doctoral student of the Ohio State University while engaged in coursework at the University of Innsbruck, Austria. She has conducted her doctoral research in Innsbruck, where she studied the attributes accompanying hip hop discourses of high school students there. She earned a Bachelor of Fine Arts from Otterbein University and a Master of Arts in Teaching from Brown University in the United States.

SABINE COELSCH-FOISNER is Professor of English Literature and Cultural Theory at the University of Salzburg. She is the author of award-winning *Revolution in Poetic Consciousness: An Existential Reading of Mid-Twentieth-Century British Women's Poetry* (2001) and has edited over twenty books, recent ones including: *Life-Course Models in Literary Narratives* (2011), *The Museal Turn* (2012), *New Directions of the European Fantastic* (2012) and *Memorialisation* (2015). She has lectured widely in Europe and the USA and is Head of the Department of English and American Studies. She is the leader of the transdisciplinary research group "Cultural Dynamics" at the Austrian Research Association (ÖFG), and she directs the public programme "Atelier Gespräche", in which she collaborates with prestigious cultural institutions both in Salzburg and abroad. Her research areas include aesthetics, fantastic literature, Shakespeare, Romantic, Victorian, and Twentieth-Century Literature, theatre studies, cultural infrastructures, opera, literature and the creative arts.

NORA DORN is a lecturer at the Department of English at the University of Vienna. She studied English and Italian at the Universities of Bologna and Vienna, where she received her MA in 2010. Her research interests include English as a Lingua Franca, multilingualism, and foreign language teaching.

EVA DURAN EPPLER is Reader in Linguistics at Roehampton University, London. She graduated from Vienna University in 1993 and completed her PhD in syntax at University College London in 2005 (cf. *Emigranto* (Vienna: Braumüller, 2010)). Her main research interest currently lies in structural and processing aspects of impaired and non-impaired speech of early and late bilinguals. She recently published *English Words and Sentences* (with Gabriel Ozon, CUP 2013).

DOROTHEA FLOTHOW is Assistant Professor at the Department of English and American Studies, University of Salzburg (Austria). She studied English Literature and Modern History at the University of Tuebingen (Germany), where she also wrote her PhD on children's literature and the First World War. She is currently working on a study of the Restoration period in popular historiography. Her research interests include literature and history, historical drama, children's literature and nineteenth-century popular culture.

DAVID FULLER is Emeritus Professor of English at the University of Durham, where he was also the University's Public Orator. He is the author of *Blake's Heroic Argument* (1988), *James Joyce's 'Ulysses'* (1992), *Signs of Grace* (1995, with David Brown, on literary treatments of the sacraments), *The Life in the Sonnets*, with a complete recording of the poems (Shakespeare Now!, Bloomsbury, 2011), and essays on a range of poetry, drama, and novels from Medieval to Modern. He is the editor of *Tamburlaine the Great* (1998), for the Clarendon Press complete works of Marlowe, of *William Blake: Selected Poetry and Prose* (Longman Annotated Texts, 2000), co-editor (with Patricia Waugh) of *The Arts and Sciences of Criticism* (1999), and co-editor (with Corinne Saunders) of *Pearl*, modernized by Victor Watts (Enitharmon, 2005). He is currently working on a book on Shakespeare and the Romantics for the series 'Oxford Shakespeare Topics'. He trained as a Musicologist, and has written on opera and ballet.

CHRISTOPHER HERZOG is a PhD student at the Department of English and American Studies at the University of Salzburg, where he is currently working on his thesis on concepts of consciousness and (dis-)embodiment in contemporary (neuro)science plays. He graduated from the University of Salzburg with a Master's thesis on the political and the ideological in contemporary science fiction. During a study-abroad year at the University of Glasgow he specialised in Scottish literature. His main research interests centre on speculative literatures with a specific focus on interdisciplinary connections, critical and cultural theory, and contemporary drama.

GABRIELLA MAZZON is full professor of English Linguistics at the University of Innsbruck. Her main research interests are connected to the fields of English as a second language and of historical linguistics, especially in relation to historical sociolinguistics and pragmatics (forms of address, dialogic sequences), but also to changes in forms (lexical change, history of negative forms). She has published extensively in both strands of research, and her recent publications concentrate particularly on Middle English dialogue and on Post-Colonial English.

MATTHIAS MÖSCH is a Senior Lecturer in British and American Cultural Studies and Literature at the University of Innsbruck. After receiving a teacher's degree in English and German at the University of Heidelberg, he wrote a PhD thesis on the Faust myth in American postmodern literature at Durham University, where he also taught literature, literary theory, and the history of the English language. He has published various essays on paremiology, German grammar, and the works of Thomas Pynchon.

ALEXANDER ONYSKO is currently an adjunct lecturer at the Department of English and American Studies at the University of Klagenfurt (Austria) and Senior Researcher at EURAC, Bolzano (Italy). He holds a doctorate in English linguistics from the University of Innsbruck (Austria), and his interests and publications are in the areas of language contact, bi/multilingualism, and cognitive linguistics. A main part of his present research focuses on bilingualism in Māori and English and the variety of Māori English following research stays at the School of Māori and Pacific Development, University of Waikato.

ANITA SANTNER-WOLFARTSBERGER is a sociolinguist currently on leave from her research position at the Department of English, University of Vienna. Following her undergraduate education at the University of Vienna, at University College London, and the NYU in London, she worked for several years at the Vienna University of Economics and Business before she joined the English Department at the University of Vienna in October 2009. Her main research interest lies in interactional pragmatics in English as a Lingua Franca workplace communication.

CLAUDIO SCHEKULIN is a researcher and lecturer at the Department of English, University of Vienna. He studied at the Universities of Toronto and Vienna, where – in 2009 – he received his MA in English and American Studies. His research interests are the many manifestations of sociolinguistics, with a particular focus on variationist methodology. His current work addresses the question of how this approach can be applied and adapted in order to elucidate ELF (English as a Lingua Franca) data.

HERBERT SCHENDL is retired Professor in English linguistics at the University of Vienna. He has published extensively on historical phonology and morphology, Old English language, and historical sociolinguistics. His recent research interests have focused on historical multilingualism and code-switching. His book publications include *Historical Linguistics* (OUP 2001), *Rethinking Middle English* (with N. Ritt, Lang 2005) and *Code-Switching in Early English* (with L. Wright, De Gruyter 2011).

BARBARA SEIDLHOFER is Professor of English and Applied Linguistics at the University of Vienna. Her research and teaching focus on English as an international language, intercultural communication and multilingualism and their implications for teacher education. She is the founding director of the Vienna-Oxford International Corpus of English (VOICE) and author of *Understanding English as a Lingua Franca* (OUP). Her other books include *Controversies in Applied Linguistics, Foreign Language Communication and Learning* (with K. Knapp) and *From International to Local English – and Back Again* (with R. Facchinetti & D. Crystal). She was editor of the *International Journal of Applied Linguistics* and is founding editor of the *Journal of English as a Lingua Franca*.

Austrian Studies in English

Edited by Sabine Coelsch-Foisner, Gabriella Mazzon and Herbert Schendl

Volume 1-102 published by W. Braumüller.

Vol.　103　Eva Flicker/Monika Seidl (eds.): Fashionable Queens. Body–Power–Gender. 2014.

Vol.　104　Sabine Coelsch-Foisner/Herbert Schendl (eds.): Contact and Conflict in English Studies. Assistant editors: Christian Grösslinger/Christopher Herzog. 2015.

www.peterlang.com